# THE IBOGA EXPERIENCE

*Stories from the Sacred & Secret Plant that Saves, Heals, & Transforms Lives.*

LEO VAN VEENENDAAL

# DISCLAIMER AND COPYRIGHT

The information provided in this book, "The Iboga Experience", is based on the personal experiences of the interviewees, subject experts, and the Author. It is intended for informational, educational and entertainment purposes only. The author and most of the interviewees are not medical professionals. This book does not constitute medical advice. The author and the interviewees are not responsible for any actions taken based on the information presented in this book.



**Warning**

The improper use of Iboga can have serious health consequences, including death. The information provided in this book is not medical advice and should not be used as a substitute for professional medical advice, diagnosis, or treatment. The author is not responsible for any harm or injury that may result from the use of the information presented in this book. Readers should consult with a medical professional before using Iboga or any other plant medicine or practice mentioned in this book.

## TABLE OF CONTENTS

# INTRODUCTION

## WHERE DOES THIS BOOK FIND YOU NOW?

Iboga is a hell of a plant. A mind-bending, soul-healing, psyche-splitting, titan of a plant. The experience is likened to more than 100 Ayahuasca ceremonies in one journey. It has the power to drag someone through their own underworld physically, mentally, and spiritually. It can help someone alchemize their regular reality to become more closely aligned to their own personal dream. It is a plant used for "those who need to be saved," whether that be from their own traumas, their mind, or addictions. Iboga is best seen as a technology: a plant with the capacity to enable someone to confront their own hell, which they might be inadvertently living in, and assist them to claw their way out of it. **Iboga is not a plant anyone should consider taking by themselves. It requires facilitation by a trained professional. The outcome for someone inexperienced working with Iboga alone is likely to be extremely negative, potentially horrible, and possibly fatal.**

My Iboga experience radically transformed my life. It taught me to be less judgmental of myself, others, and the world around me. I learned to no longer see anything as good or bad, but rather on a spectrum of either fostering chaos or facilitating order. We are all free to choose how much order and chaos we want in our life. Our notion of "good and bad" is just a perspective built by our desires and cultural conditioning. The bedrock of the universe is love, made up of chaos and order, constantly, and brutally, making love to one another. This was one of the many lessons Iboga shared with me. My own encounter with Iboga was more impactful than can be adequately described here. I would also like to be mindful of preconditioning readers with my personal story before exploring this collection of interviews. If you are interested, my personal experience can be found at the very end of this book.

This book is intended to be a guide and essential resource for people considering working with Iboga, Ibogaine, or other analogs and formulations of Iboga. Further, it can serve as a blueprint for working with most psychedelic plant medicines, which will likely be less intense than an initiation level dose of Iboga. Even if you only aspire to get into local mountaineering, learning from those who climbed Mt Everest (Iboga), can be a great resource. Hopefully, through reading this book, you will acquire beneficial information and advice to ensure that your own experiences are as safe and healing as possible.

This book aims to dispel the myths and misconceptions that circulate around Iboga. There are countless experiences shared online, around campfires, and in everyday conversations, that present Iboga without context or are sensationally misleading. This collection of first-hand accounts aims to dispel these misrepresentations so that people who work with Iboga in the future are not predisposed or preconditioned to any particular outcome. Once the myths have been dispelled, a highly unique and undiluted personal experience can be facilitated.

It is crucial to note that Iboga is an extremely powerful tool. Alongside deep work, it can radically change the trajectory of one's life. With that said, it can also be deadly. A common folklore statistic is that 1/100 people who work with Iboga, die. This is a prime example of the sensational myths that engulf Iboga.

Although there are deaths that occur while working with Iboga, and deaths occur probably more frequently than any other mainstream psychedelic medicine, this statistic has been muddied by internet forums, lack of context, pioneering (western) practitioners who did not have adequate training, and the early clientele who were drawn to Iboga. Iboga's first major entrance into the western collective consciousness was through New York doctor Howard Lotsof as his "miracle cure for addiction." Naturally, the majority of souls who followed were people with serious drug addictions. Who else would consider an extremely powerful, unheard-of African medicine, that tastes like condensed battery acid (in the author's personal and cultivated culinary opinion)? The truth of the statistic is hard to obtain, but it is likely much safer than 1/100. Many facilitators interviewed have served medicine to over one thousand people and never had a death.

For people of ill health (especially if dealing with chronic substance misuse), taking Iboga at home, without preparation, medical screening, or a trained facilitator, the 1/100 death toll is probably an understatement. For people in good health, with no health complications due to addiction, who have been adequately prepared (and medically screened), Iboga can be very physically safe. This book will demonstrate the very present dangers of working with Iboga and also highlight the practices and protocols to make it a safer experience.

Psychonauts and psychedelic aficionados, people with a fondness and predilection for the psychedelic adventure, may also enjoy reading this book. Iboga can be thought of as a postgraduate degree, or a Ph.D., in terms of the potency of the psychedelic experience, when compared to other psychedelic experiences. This is due to its intensity, duration, depth, and transformative effect it can facilitate. It is not for the faint-hearted.

Please note, this book is not medical advice. It is a collection of expert advice and personal experiences from many different souls. Please consult with your doctor or health care practitioner, at length, before considering working with Iboga or engaging in any of the practices shared throughout the personal experiences in this book.

## WHAT CAN THIS BOOK OFFER FOR PEOPLE WITHOUT PHYSICALLY WORKING WITH IBOGA?

Many people reading this book may never have an intention to work with Iboga. However, there is still a lot to be gained from openly engaging with the stories and lessons of Iboga. Many of the lessons can be shared and applied easily to all readers. Although a lot of the lessons are best learned through physically working with the medicine, many of the lessons, themes, and experiences Iboga illuminates can still be gleaned through the veil of others' experiences. The easiest way to explore this, without taking Iboga, is through the broader discussion of the themes that emerged through the writing of this book.

The content in this book can act as a master class on both preparation and integration for people engaging in any kind of plant medicine or psychedelic medicine ceremony. Additionally, the content can aid anyone walking along their spiritual path. The juice squeezed from Iboga's lessons can be drunk by anyone. Iboga can best be seen as a key, a powerful technology, with the capacity to unlock our minds, hearts, and souls. With this, many challenging emotions, memories, and experiences can resurface. Contained in this book are the tools, methods, regrets, mistakes, and protocols people undertook during their Iboga experience. Iboga is one of the most intense and grueling ceremonial experiences someone can undertake, and the lessons learned from it can be applied to other experiences. Broadly speaking, all of the preparation, integration, and 'during ceremony' advice can be applied to any psychedelic or altered state of consciousness experience.

## COMMON THREADS AND THEMES.

In compiling this collection of accounts, several notable patterns stood out in the characteristics of Iboga "graduates," as well as commonalities in their experiences. A predominant theme to emerge from these interviews was the loss of control and surrender to the experience that Iboga demanded. For many people interviewed, being in control or having very controlling tendencies was something Iboga addressed immediately and vehemently.

Sometimes, being totally out of control, whilst held in a safe container can be the best medicine for someone with controlling tendencies. In a safe container, pure chaos can be explored and the monsters of our mind can emerge with limited judgment. Here we can explore them, befriend them and ultimately let them go. Are we out of control because we are deliberately suppressing, avoiding, and trying to manage a deeper trauma, story, or belief? Are we letting our hidden monsters control our lives, manipulating us from the shadows of our subconscious? If this is the case, any period of time, where someone sets aside time to connect with the monsters lurking in their subconscious, can be profoundly positive. Common alternative ways of doing this include meditation, journaling, art therapy, traditional talk therapy, and hypnosis. A "bad psychedelic trip" often refers to being confronted with the repeated resurfacing of a very unpleasant emotion or memory, in an altered, "out of control" state of consciousness. Often these are actually the best trips where life-changing transformations and liberation can occur.

Another theme that emerged was "Living through and facing nightmares leads to our dreams." For many of the people interviewed, their experience with Iboga made them realize that they were previously living a nightmare as if they were drowning at sea. Through working with Iboga and facing the nightmare, over time they were guided to an idyllic, dream-like life on the other side. In this context, Iboga can be seen as a wonderful and powerful tool, like a lighthouse, guiding people adrift at sea back to shore. Iboga is not crucial to this process. People find their way back home, to their dream life, without Iboga frequently. While Iboga encourages learning about prayer, ceremony, trust, surrender, and intention, all these tools can be used without Iboga to guide someone back home, to the safety of shore.

It is almost as if Iboga can pick up someone drowning at sea and put them in a speedboat directed towards shore. Prayer, intention, surrender, community, reflection, repackaging our stories, time, gratitude, love, and trust are ultimately what heal someone of the ailments of the mind, spirit, and even body. Swimming or getting in a row boat (alternative options to Iboga) may be a better option for some, rather than getting seasick and being shell-shocked from the wild ride of Iboga's speedboat.

Notably, all the contributors expressed a tone of palpable respect and gratitude to Iboga in the conversation. A humility and deep reverence for the medicine shone through, not dissimilar to how someone might speak about sharing a home with a *benevolent* silverback gorilla. Almost as if they knew that at any moment the gorilla (a higher consciousness) could crush them if they were unkind or disrespectful. I personally like the notion of treating all deep conversations, medicine work, and people with the respect that a mature and benevolent silverback gorilla (the medicine/God/life) is in the room.

Although contributors represented a variety of backgrounds, they all reflected a shared essence of kindness, vulnerability, and generosity of spirit. It was a breath of fresh jungle air to engage and interview people who appeared to be so kind to themselves and even kinder to others. Their kindness and passion for work on projects that were personally important to them were nourishing and inspiring to me as an author. A good lesson from this was when we engage ourselves with less judgment and foster acceptance and love, it is much easier to extend this to other people. By treating ourselves with love, it is much easier to treat others with love. Many interviewees seemed to engage both with others and themselves without judgment, but rather with deep acceptance of where they are in life. This seems to make the ride of life much softer; knocks, crashes, and all.

The final, broader theme was the open-mindedness and curiosity to appreciate how distinctive is each person's own healing and life journey. Interviewees were generally very happy to share their *integrated* stories with deliberate attention. There was no projectile word vomit of "look how crazy my experience was!" Rather, contributors were people who accepted an invitation to share what was appropriate. Many people in plant medicine and healing circles are quick to verbally "projectile vomit" their experiences and current lessons onto others. It was heartwarming and useful to experience people sharing lessons with a suitable audience, after they had understood and integrated them.

We can damage others when we inconsiderately share things we have not fully comprehended, or share without being asked. There was a softness and curiosity in sharing and listening to each other's stories, which is a good practice for people engaged in the world of alternative healing. Broadly speaking, there was an open-mindedness to the magic, mystery, and sheer insanity of the mind-blowing nature of each person's healing journey.

## AUTHOR'S INTENTIONS.

As the author, I am writing this book to give back to the plant, community, and culture that radically transformed my life. My experience was particularly brutal and took a VERY long time to recover from. My arrogant, headstrong, and critical mind required a particular flavor of ego-crushing medicine. I often wonder if I am still on an Iboga trip, many years later, as my life has become so wonderful, strange, and foreign to my life before Iboga. In a sense, sitting with Iboga opens a ceremony that never ends. It was a beautiful and perfect experience for me, but there are many things I could have done to improve my preparation and integration.

My personal intention for this book is to be of service to the broader Iboga and psychedelic medicine community. If I can help one person have a slightly less brutal Iboga experience, but still receive the transformative magic of Iboga, then my time writing this book will have been well spent. With that said, a very challenging experience might be required for someone's healing journey, and the compiled advice in this book seeks to assist readers through recovery from and integration of challenging experiences. If someone is meant to have a tough experience, there is no way around that. A monster that lurks in someone's subconscious mind puppeteers them from behind their conscious awareness. It can take them through hell until confronted. But, there are many things one can do to return from a hellish place faster, and with a little more grace. Finally, there are many charlatans, cowboys, predators, well meaning but undertrained idealists, and lost souls facilitating Iboga. I hope reading this book will prepare you to steer clear of them.

A primary motivation for sharing this book is to directly support the health of the plant and cultures of Iboga. This is targeted by way of spreading information in alignment with the sustainability of Iboga and through direct contribution from sales. More than 50% of the royalties from this book are donated to "Blessings of the Forest," a Gabonese-owned and operated charity that is leading the charge on Iboga conservation and protecting the rich heritage and culture that enshrouds the plant. Rampant overharvesting of wild Iboga, coupled with the psychedelic revolution, necessitates that the world of Iboga is conserved. If Iboga is not protected, it may become critically endangered or extinct in the wild in coming years. Furthermore, the cultural foundation and tradition surrounding Iboga, the backbone that supports the magic, is facing extreme stress as well. Blessings of the Forest (BOTF) does an excellent job at both ensuring the physical survival of Iboga through Gabonese plantations and protecting the traditional, cultural, and spiritual heritage surrounding Iboga.

Many well-meaning people may buy Iboga from online places like Instagram, not realizing the downstream effects of further engorging desperate poachers. The work of Yann Guignon conclusively demonstrates that Iboga poaching is also accompanied by many other forms of trafficking. In effect, engaging with "Instagram traffickers" supports the trade of many other nefarious enterprises and strains, if not destroys the local Gabonese culture that revolves around Iboga.

Personally, it was delightful to talk to so many different people on interesting paths who have worked with Iboga for many reasons. I found it extremely beneficial to my own continued integration and understanding of Iboga. I learnt a lot about preparation, choosing facilitators, how to make the most of a ceremony, and how to integrate the experience. I was blown away by all of the interviewee's kindness, generosity, and vulnerability. If there is one common thread of the people interviewed, it would be their kindness, respect for Iboga, and generosity of spirit. That, in itself, may be the greatest compelling factor for someone to work with Iboga.

This book is my own way of saying thank you to the plant, community, culture, and spirituality that saved me from my own mind. Before working with Iboga, my mind was a complete mess, like a drug-addled hamster, ruminating and exhausting itself in its own misery. Iboga gave me the opportunity to reset my life and mind. Hopefully, the stories and experiences shared in this book can help others to work with Iboga, in the perfect time, manner, and approach for each.

## A Reader's Checklist

After reading this book you should have:

1. An informed perspective of how varied and personal the Iboga experience is for each person who works with it
2. Clarity regarding the many now dispelled myths and misconceptions about Iboga
3. A useful introductory resource on how to find a trustworthy facilitator, center, or community to work with Iboga
4. A list of essential safety precautions to take
5. A basic guide on how to prepare for an Iboga experience
6. Some broad tips on how to integrate Iboga and the benefits of working with a counselor, therapist, or coach
7. Reflections on what others wish they had known before their experiences
8. A well-rounded exploration of 23 people's unique Iboga experiences

## SERVICE & CHARITY OF THIS BOOK.

This book is priced at a higher-than-normal Amazon rate in order to support Iboga. $4 USD per kindle book and $8 of the hard copy format, which is more than 50% of the royalties, goes directly to Blessings of the Forest (BOFT), an NGO owned and based out of Gabon. BOTF supports the sustainable planting, growing, protection, and harvesting of Iboga. In addition, BOTF is committed to preserving the cultural and societal heritage intertwined with Iboga. This means that for every 3-6 books sold, one Iboga tree can be planted and grown to maturity.

Iboga is currently facing tremendous pressure in the wild and is critically endangered. It is unlikely to become extinct, due to extensive private plantations, but it is of the utmost importance to protect it for future generations and preserve the wild Iboga for Gabonese communities. Additionally, it's a nice thought that everyone reading this book will be directly supporting Iboga in a small way.

Finally, the higher price of the book is also motivated to serve as a defense mechanism for Iboga. Only those who are seriously motivated to learn and work with Iboga will be motivated to pay the higher price. This way, Iboga remains somewhat under the radar and protected against mass consumption.

## BLESSINGS OF THE FOREST.

Blessings of the Forest is the premier Iboga charity in the world. It was chosen as the charity to partner with, due to its incredible track record, efficiency, and dedication to the health of Iboga. The author has no financial benefits or ties to Blessings of the Forest, beyond donating a percentage of profits from this book to them.

The following is a statement provided by one of the founders, David Nassim:

"Blessings of the Forest is a Community Interest Company – C.I.C. (Company n°: 9816364), based in the UK linked to an NGO in Gabon of the same name. This is a social-enterprise or not-for-profit company based currently on donation. It was started in October 2015 by Yann Guignon and David Nassim. The company was founded on over a decade of previous research and study of the intricacy of the issues around the massive international demands placed on Tabernanthe Iboga by Yann Guignon. Yann lived in Gabon working closely with Jean Noël Gassita, Doctor of Pharmacy and the world authority on Iboga research. Yann also studied traditional rites and became an integral part of the national community around Iboga awareness in Gabon which culminated in an official paper he wrote for the Gabonese Presidency. This informed and asserted the Gabonese government to sign the Nagoya Protocol on 21st of November 2011. The Gabonese became the first country in the world to sign this treaty that officially enforces reciprocity in any international access to inherited resources (in this case Iboga) and a fair and equal share of the profits they bring. It also requires that traditional people's rights are prioritized.

Since that time BOTF has, with very little resources, funded and supported a network of 7 villages in Gabon who are now self-sustaining and legal entities which have grown over 8,000 Iboga trees. BOTF helps reassure villagers to follow their traditional-permaculture principles, to grow Iboga naturally rather than using modern methods of monoculture. BOTF supplies them with what they need to set up their own program of planting and help them to connect to government and local NGOs to support day-to-day running issues. Also, we try to indicate the value of their traditional knowledge and expertise from a western perspective, that in fact, they have vital resources that greatly reveal the poverty of the seemingly "rich" modern western world.

The main goal of BOTF today is a continuation of our projects and a gradual expansion to other villages throughout Gabon. We now focus on the implementation of the Nagoya Protocol and advise Gabonese authorities on these matters. We aim to aid the international export of fair-trade Iboga and other wildcrafted/artisan products from the forest and traditional communities which are, in themselves, alternatives to poaching and the logging industry for Gabonese villagers. This completes the united human-environment conservation picture and balance/benefit on all fronts which is BOTF's main objective."

## WHAT IS IBOGA?

Tabernanthe Iboga, commonly called Iboga, is a perennial rainforest shrub, native to Central-West Africa: primarily Gabon, Cameroon, and the Congo basin. Folklore and myth envelop the origin of the plant. Some believe that it was the tree created by God to ensure more Africans made it to heaven or the true tree of knowledge in the garden of Eden. Synchronistically, its orange fruits are generally not eaten but do contain seeds that look identical to a human brain, neocortex, and all.

*A selection of Tabernanthe Iboga Seeds*

*A handful of Iboga seeds - complete with Neocortex!*

*A mature Iboga tree. Photo by Yann Guignon*

In the realm of plant medicine and the traditional practitioners, Iboga is referred to as "the one who heals" or "the one who saves someone who needs to be saved." In fact, the name "Iboga" originates from the Tsogo language, meaning "to care for." It's not the plant someone takes to accelerate the healing of a burn or a seasonal cold. An initiation into Iboga is reserved for the most serious, life-threatening conditions, psychological maladies, intense initiations, and rites of passage.

The most common response from interviewees and experts as to how Iboga helps heal the psyche is through showing us where we are wrong, where our blindsides are. It helps us examine the issues we are afraid of, or keeping in the dark. It is believed that through these blind spots, mental oversights, and unconscious habits, disease, and misery can enter our lives. Iboga brings a light (and sometimes a raging fire) to our own unconscious patterns and blind spots, helping to liberate us from a captor hidden in the dark.

For a more detailed exploration of what Iboga is and the rich culture that surrounds it, please read the excellent book *Iboga, the Root of All Healing* by Daniel Brett.

**FORMS OF IBOGA.**

This book is primarily focused on the treatment method of a prepared medicine, herein referred to simply as "Iboga", harvested directly from the Tabernanthe Iboga tree. It is traditionally prepared and served as semi-pulverized shavings from the mature roots of the Tabernanthe Iboga tree. It takes 5-7 years for the tree to reach maturity and for its roots to have adequate concentrations of Ibogaine, the primary active compound in the Iboga tree's medicine, as well as other alkaloids, to be served as medicine. Many practitioners talk about the increasing potency with age. Iboga trees that are 30-50 years old are commonly reserved for special initiatory ceremonies. The majority of people interviewed worked with Iboga in the form of shaved Iboga root bark from a tree which was 5-10 years old.

*Shaved Iboga root bark being prepared for ceremony*

A modern and popular preparation of Iboga known as TA (Total Alkaloid extraction) is also featured in this book. Dr. Chris Jenks, believed to be the inventor of both TA extraction and Ibogaine extraction from Voacanga Africana (another method described in the following paragraphs), states that TA is exactly what is found in the original Iboga wood minus the wood pulp from the plant. TA is frequently used in modern Iboga treatment centers, as it is easy to administer, store, and easier to ingest than regular Iboga (a few capsules vs many spoons worth of pulverized wood shavings). Many people interviewed had worked with Iboga in this form (TA).

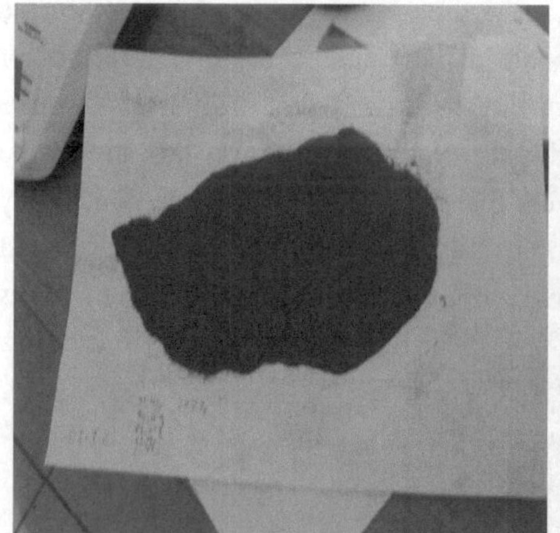

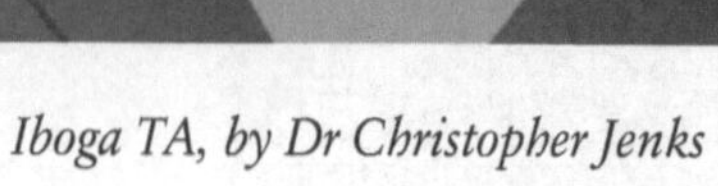

*Iboga TA, by Dr Christopher Jenks*

*Pulverized Iboga root bark, ready for ceremony*

Ibogaine is the most famous and commonly used singular alkaloid extracted from Tabernanthe Iboga and is often served in isolation as another treatment method. While there are believed to be over 20 alkaloids in the Iboga root bark, Ibogaine is the most widely known and used. Ibogaine is sometimes called Ibogaine HCL, HCL, and Ibogaine chloride. This is because the extraction method often entails using hydrochloride to extract the Ibogaine from either Tabernanthe Iboga or Voacanga Africana. By the number of people working with some form of Iboga, “Ibogaine” is most likely the most common treatment modality. This is due to its shorter duration, and fewer and lessened contraindications compared to Iboga root bark and TA, as well as its ease of administration and reduced intensity. Several people interviewed worked with Ibogaine.

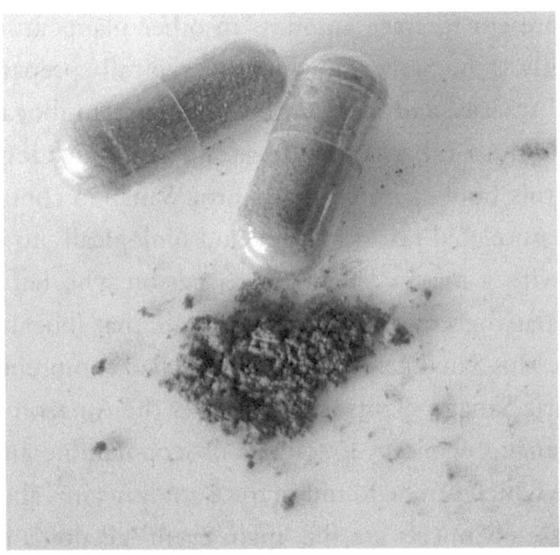

Iboga TA – prepared in capsules for ceremony. Extra Iboga TA outside the capsule for education. Photo by Levi Barker

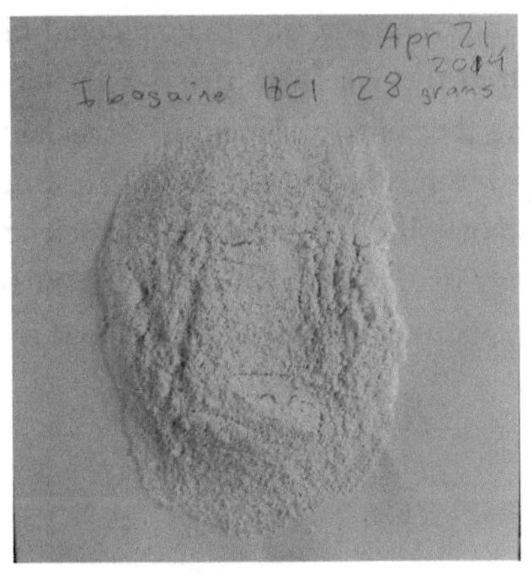


*Ibogaine hydrochloride made from Voacanga Africana. Photo by Dr. Christopher Jenks.*

*Crystals of Ibogaine base made from the voacangine of Voacanga Africana. Photo by Dr. Christopher Jenks.*

Ibogaine can also be extracted from the Voacanga Africana tree, a relative of Tabernanthe Iboga prevalent throughout Central-West Africa. The alkaloid,

Ibogaine, is also present in trace amounts in other plants around the world. Sananga (specifically Uchu Sananga, which is a typically prepared in drops for the eyes) in South America and Star Jasmine both contain Ibogaine and similar Ibogaine like alkaloids to Tabernanthe Iboga, albeit at much lower levels. In an earlier edition of this book, I stated that Chiric Sanango contained Ibogaine. Chiric Sanango is unrelated taxonomically and biologically to Uchu Sanagno. After consulting with a master Sanangero (a person who has apprenticed to work with Chiric Sanango medicinally), I can state that Ibogaine is not found in Chiric Sanango. This Sanangero, Roman Hanis, had comprehensive chemical biopsies from Chiric Sanago plants found all over the Amazon basin area. The leaves of Chiric Sanango contain low levels of scopolamine and scopoletin, a potent dissociative which can be found in trace amounts in Tabernanthe Iboga. But neither of these chemicals are the 'main event' alkaloids found in either plant, or traditionally consumed for medical reasons. Since writing the first edition of this book, I have worked with Chiric Sanango in Peru. Chiric Sanango looks very similar to Iboga, and in my personal opinion seems like a long lost South American brother to Iboga.

The alternative source of Ibogaine, Voacanga Africana is not endangered like Tabernanthe Iboga. Ibogaine extracted from the Voacanga tree is a far more sustainable option. For people considering Ibogaine treatment, it is crucial to ask the provider if the Ibogaine was sourced from Voacanga or Iboga. Voacanga Ibogaine is highly preferred, due to its sustainability, prevalence, and efficiency. When Ibogaine is extracted from the Iboga tree, many alkaloids of Iboga are lost, and one less person will have the opportunity to work with the Iboga root shavings in its full experience.

*An Iboga Tabernanthe (left) and a Voacanga Africana (right) tree that had been planted at the same time. Photo by Dr. Christopher Jenks.*

Other forms of Iboga are also used in treatments such as Purified Total Alkaloid or Precipitated Total Alkaloid (PTA). Only a few people interviewed had worked with these. They are much rarer than Ibogaine, Iboga, or TA.

## METHODS OF WORKING WITH IBOGA

The four most common routes that people take to work with Iboga are as follows:

1. A traditional initiation, which normally occurs in Gabon, Cameroon, or the greater Congo Basin area. It normally entails the consumption of a large amount of Iboga root bark shavings, anywhere from 1-40+ heaped teaspoons. An initiation process typically takes a minimum of one week, and sometimes months, for the entire preparation and ceremonial process. Most who do this will only consume an initiatory dose of Iboga one time in their life.

2. A modern (western) initiation, using a mixture of Iboga root bark shavings, Total Alkaloid extract (TA), and other Iboga-based extractions facilitated at many modern retreat centers in Mexico, Costa Rica, Portugal, and underground in the USA. This type of treatment may contain one or two initiatory level doses over an 8-day period. The doses are generally smaller than those served in Gabon and frequently the majority of the dose is comprised of TA extract in capsule form. One or two teaspoons of Iboga root bark shavings may be offered at the start, but large doses of Iboga root bark are uncommon due to the logistics and safety of working with large amounts of root bark.

3. Working with a facilitator who comes to a private space and holds the treatment at a non-permanent location, such as a hotel room, house, or rented property. Often these facilitators use TA or Ibogaine HCL in their treatments. This is a riskier option, as it is unregulated, commonly underground, and reviews and accountability are sparse. Additionally, the lack of a stable "home base" may arouse fear of safety for some participants. There are also concerns about the legality and safety of this option.

4. The least desirable option is to work with Iboga by yourself. The author and most of the interviewees would plead with you not to choose this method. It is the most dangerous and it likely supports the overconsumption and illegal trafficking of poached Iboga. Furthermore, once you account for the

risks of complications and the ensuing medical bills that might follow, it is probably not a cheaper option and definitely a dangerous one!

## IMPORTANT DISCLAIMER FOR ADDICTION

Although some people can have profound, even miraculous, healing from working with Iboga in Gabon, on the sum of things many people recommended that it's likely a better move to seek a specialized detox or addiction facilitator. Many communities in Gabon do not have experience helping people detox from methamphetamine, fentanyl, or other modern pharmaceutical medications. This is not to disparage them, the best healers and medicine carriers are in Gabon. It's a matter of how frequently they deal with and how deeply they understand the particularities of western ailments and conditions. Additionally, there is not the same culture of thorough pre-screenings, or facilities supporting an EKG or other emergency medical support, as are common in the western world. Doctors or nurses are rarely onsite or readily available to deal with complications.

Additionally, going to Gabon can be a daunting and insurmountable task, the cultural differences are stark. Difficulty compounds with the added challenge of detoxing and dealing with a substance addiction. It can be unnecessarily challenging for someone struggling with drug or alcohol dependency. Finally, the rigorous and physically demanding initiations may place undue stress on someone in already compromised health. For these reasons, the author and many participants believe that for people working with addiction, travel to Gabon would not be the best option. That said, if you have a great recommendation and connection to a particular provider in Gabon that has specialized in your condition, it may be appropriate and beneficial.

## ACCESS AND SUSTAINABILITY OF IBOGA.

Iboga is critically endangered in the wild. It is native only to the Congo Basin area (Gabon, Cameroon, and DRC), where it faces enormous pressure from illegal poachers and overconsumption. The tsunami of westerners, earnestly seeking treatment also places enormous stress on the culture and traditions surrounding Iboga. Many Gabonese communities accept foreigners into their traditions to work with Iboga. But this places the communities in a tricky position. Although they have a rich tradition of working with Iboga, there isn't the multi-generation tradition of initiating westerners. People based outside of Gabon and the wider Congo basin area must be mindful of how they are impacting the wider world of Iboga both physically through consuming Iboga, and culturally by visiting the communities working with Iboga. With any deep work, there is a transference of culture, conditioning, and even the ailments that affect each group of people. The globalized nature of the world entails that western culture is seeping into the traditional culture around Iboga.

Blessings of the Forest does an excellent job with limited financial resources to ensure that Gabonese communities can sustain, build, and enrichen their work with Iboga.

Further, the work of Dr. Christopher Jenks has been revolutionary in the sustainability of Iboga. Without the work of Dr. Jenks to find a sustainable alternative to Ibogaine sourced from the Tabernanthe Iboga tree, it is possible that Tabernanthe Iboga may have already become extinct in the wild.

People seeking to work with Iboga should ask themselves a few questions:

- Where is this Iboga coming from? A sustainable plantation or is it poached from the wild?
- Am I in true reciprocity with the plant and the community that is helping me? What am I giving and taking from them?
- What impact will my treatment have on the community or people helping me? What will I leave behind?
- Have the people helping me dealt with people like me before? Do they have adequate experience to address my intention (eg: drug addiction or misuse of modern pharmaceuticals)?
- Is there an option closer to home where what I leave behind will have less of an impact?

# METHODOLOGY.

## ETHICS OF INTERVIEWS

Many communities in Gabon and facilitators in the West were firm in their request for participants not to share their experiences or visions with people too early, or indeed at all. This is done to prevent people from sharing before they have understood their visions for the safety of everyone, to maintain a sacred confidentiality for the tradition, and to avoid preconditioning future participants. With this in mind, the author sought explicit permission from his facilitator, elders, and the Ebando community, to share the stories of Iboga. The agreed intention was that every precaution would be taken not to precondition people or portray Iboga in a sensationalized light. It is important not to focus too narrowly on any one vision or story. When viewed as a collection of works, they paint a much better picture than any one vision. Iboga presents itself in many different forms, perfectly composed for each person. Focusing on any one vision or experience breaks the magic and complexity of this incredible technology. The magic really is in how personalized and different each experience is.

### The journey of receiving the blessing to share these stories

There were many barriers to writing this book, due to the private and guarded nature of sharing about Iboga. Elders are strict in educating patients and initiates never to talk about their process to those outside the community. No other books currently exist about the "Iboga experience," as anyone who has authentically experienced Iboga is strongly encouraged not to share their experience with outsiders. As crazy as it sounds, Iboga told me that it was my job to write a book about it. I nervously raised this with the elders of the community who initiated me, fully expecting their response to be a firm "No."

One of the elders said to me "Who are you, to write about Iboga?" He raised a good point. As a young, white, Australian man without a relevant scholarly background, but who only worked with Iboga directly for one month in 2018, I am far from a logical candidate to talk extensively about the nature, traditions, or science of Iboga. However, I am very passionate about it, curious, and something of a "blank slate" with regards to Iboga. I wanted to write a book that truly helped Iboga and the people working with it. After 2 years of contributing to and supporting Blessings of the Forest and Ebando (the community where I was initiated), the elders were satisfied that I was aligned with Iboga and could approach this project with the purest intentions.

The culmination of many separate forces enabled the approval to write this book. Sensationalized YouTube accounts and forum posts about Iboga inseminated rampant misinformation online and a mystique of urban legend meant something major had to be done to clear up popular misconceptions. Prolific poaching and overharvesting of Iboga also meant that change was needed in how the West is consuming it. Additionally, I proposed that by having a group of high-quality (I'll let you be the judge) interviews compiled together, their summation would illustrate just how varied and personalized the Iboga experience is for each person.

We agreed that I would take every measure possible to avoid detailing the ceremony practices and rituals conducted in a traditional initiation. I would do my best not to precondition others, both by dispelling myths and collecting many different experiences. I would paint Iboga in an accurate, honest, and non-sensationalized light. Finally, 50% of the profits from the book, which was later revised to more than 50% of the profits (55% of royalties from Amazon), are donated to Blessings of the Forest, to help ensure the wellness and longevity of Iboga for a long time to come.

With all of these agreements in place, approval was given to me to write a book about *The Iboga Experience.*

## RANGE OF EXPERIENCES

This book is primarily focused on the experiences of westerners with Iboga. This group is the most likely to work with Iboga in modern methods and is generally unfamiliar with the cultural and broader background contexts of Iboga. Subsequently, this group is the most likely to both work with Iboga in risky situations, overconsume Iboga, acquire Iboga from unsustainable sources, and lack the necessary knowledge to have a beneficial experience.

People who only worked with Iboga or Ibogaine by themselves at home were deliberately excluded from this book. Upon editing and reflection, several completed interviews with people who had DIY Iboga experiences were not included. This is due to safety concerns, sustainability, and genuine concern for potential psychedelic adventurers who may think that they are experienced enough to do it. Let it be clear from the start that Iboga is not something you can safely consume at home without professional guidance! I cannot reiterate this too strongly.

**DO NOT CONSUME IBOGA BY YOURSELF OR WITH A FRIEND AT HOME.**

The included interviews will highlight how crucial extensive preparation and working with a professional facilitator are to having a constructive experience.

## THE QUESTIONS AND WHY THEY WERE CHOSEN.

The interviews generally consisted of 17 predetermined questions and organic follow-up questions when the conversation flowed. Below is a list of the questions. The detailed explanations to why each of them were chosen was removed for relevancy. If you'd like to know, feel free to contact the author on the website www.theibogaexperience.com for more information.

1. **Where did you first hear about Iboga? Where did Iboga first enter your awareness?**

2. **How were you called to Iboga? Did you feel spiritually called to it?**

3. **What was your life like before Iboga?**

4. **What is your life like after Iboga?**

5. **How did you prepare? Would you prepare differently a second time?**

6. **What precautions did you take to make sure it was a safe experience?**

7. **What was your intention?**

8. **How did you consume Iboga? What did you take and where? What form? Total dose?**

9. **Why did you decide to do it this way? Why did you pick this center?**

10. **What would be your advice to people considering Iboga?**

11. **What are your thoughts on micro-dosing? Did you micro-dose after a flood dose for integration?**

12. **Is there anything you wish you knew before doing Iboga about the process?**

13. **Would you do Iboga again?**

14. **Was there a memorable moment or particularly profound vision you had? Has it come true?**

15. **Has Iboga affected your spirituality?**

16. **What did Iboga teach or give you?**

17. **Anything else you'd like to add?**

**GENDER AND IDENTITY SPLIT.**

Throughout writing the book I was mindful of ensuring the most even gender split of participants as possible. Iboga is a medicine for potentially everybody, although (thankfully) not everyone may feel the need to work with it. The intention was for this book to have interviews and experiences that as many people as possible could relate to, with the widest range of conditions, identities, and motivations.

Considerably more men were interviewed than women for non-emergency reasons. (Un)fortunately, I believe this is most likely in line with the actual population-based numbers. Biological males, who may be more commonly predisposed to risk-taking behavior, were more likely to work with "risky" Iboga for spiritual growth or curiosity. Personally, I reflected that I had taken a huge risk in taking Iboga, one that my more sensible sisters and female friends have avoided.

If people are seeking Iboga for emergency purposes (defined as life-threatening drug addiction or another dire health condition), then the gender balance is likely to be more even. The misery of unhealed traumatic wounds can impact all people, equally. The risk equation is very different when dealing with a life-threatening situation versus psycho-spiritual growth. The gender composition for people working with Iboga for emergency purposes was far more balanced.

The majority of people interviewed grew up or spent a considerable amount of their life in the USA. They were chosen as the target audience is westerners who are working with plant medicines or thinking of working with Iboga at some point in the future. Within this, there was a wide range of educational backgrounds, income levels, and ages. I believe although important for context, the broader demographics are not as important as the age, conditions, and intentions of each interviewee. Each interviewee had something unique and worthwhile to share. You might be surprised by which stories impact you the most. There is some treasure in each one.

# HOUSEKEEPING.

## LIMITATIONS.

It's important to convey the scope and limitations of this book. It is limited by many things: primarily the range of people interviewed, the scope of the questions, and the author's limited interviewing skills. A broad goal for this book was to bring Iboga into the greater public awareness, in a conscious, respectful, and moderated way. It was important that this book dispelled misconceptions whilst maintaining respect and privacy for the traditions and practitioners who have traditionally worked with it. Traditionally, the initiation process and the rich spiritual world of Iboga are *never* shared with people who have not been initiated. The protocols, specific rites, and ceremony practices are deliberately withheld out of respect to facilitators and the tradition by explicit request. Additionally, by not sharing these components, it is intended that future participants will not have expectations around their experience. Finally, it was agreed that many of the visions and experiences shared in interviews would be omitted, so as to not precondition or predispose people to certain outcomes and experiences. Select personal visions were included to highlight the range of the psychedelic experience that can accompany working with Iboga. Hopefully, there is still a wide enough range of stories to cover a robust selection of outcomes.

Additionally, the interviewee's choice of words, metaphors, and general stance should be seen as a snapshot as to where they were at the time of the interview. As the book took over 2 years to write, it is natural that many interviewees' opinions and reflections may have changed since the interview. They were approved just prior to publication to check for accuracy.

The book strives to reflect an even gender balance and to include people from as many different walks of life as possible. Interviewees were chosen to generate the largest range of motivations from people of different cultural, genetic, and life backgrounds. Unfortunately, due to the author's non-existent French (and frankly, with the primary aim of this book to address open-minded westerners considering working with Iboga, at risk of choosing an unsafe or undesirable option), no endogenous Gabonese or Indigenous peoples of Central West Africa were interviewed. Subsequent and updated editions will hopefully include their experiences and knowledge.

It is important to note another limitation of this book. This book is geared towards the perspective of the Western, rational mind. It attempts to stay grounded in conversation and to discuss the practical aspects of working with Iboga. Mythos, spirits, genies, the nonlinear nature of time, and other ideas that surround Iboga are not thoroughly explored.

Addressing the spiritual dynamics and inexplicable layers of Iboga is beyond the scope of this book. However, the spiritual force is so central to Iboga's cultural tradition and the experiences of all individuals interviewed, including the author, that it will inevitably be acknowledged throughout. If this rubs you the wrong way or you feel hesitant to embrace this perspective, please take what resonates, and leave out the rest.

On the other hand, if you welcome the spirit of Iboga, you just might feel wild and unusual thoughts entering your awareness, and this may be Iboga beginning to work with you already.

**Why the limited discussion about the history, culture, and tradition around Iboga?**

Traditionally, in Gabon, the rich history of Iboga is rarely shared with people who have not been initiated into Iboga and Bwiti. It took 2 years of talking to my facilitators, and a global pandemic (!), for the elders who initiated me to allow me to write about Iboga. In Gabon, before people are initiated, they are often intrigued by the joy and kindness of the initiated people and know very little about the process. I sought to replicate that and limit the amount of information about the ceremony, tradition, culture, and rites of passage involved in a traditional initiation.

## Why no conversations with Gabonese medicine carriers?

Unfortunately, there are no conversations in this book with traditional, Gabonese-born medicine carriers. Practical matters including the difficulty of language barriers and personal connections meant that it was not realistic to feature them in this book. This book is focused on improving the experience and mitigating any potential damage for western people working with Iboga. It would have been great to have Gabonese elders featured, but unfortunately, the author's limited connections and the tradition of secrecy have not yet afforded this. It will take a long time and a significant improvement in my French to build substantial relationships with Gabonese-born medicine elders. The elders that gave me the blessing to write about this book were French-born, spoke English, and have lived in Gabon for many years. However, they are not biologically Gabonese. Hopefully, updated and future additions of the book will include interviews with Gabonese lineage holders.

## Are Iboga and Ibogaine facilitators interviewed?

Yes, this book includes many interviews with people who have facilitated and served Iboga to 1,000s of people. Conservatively, there is the collective wisdom of people overseeing over 10,000 plus Iboga journeys condensed and assimilated into this book.

For legal reasons, they are not specifically identified as facilitators, unless there are no legal restrictions in their home country. You may be able to figure out who they are, but most are not specifically mentioned as facilitators. Advice from facilitators and single-time participants is equally valid. Each story and voice included in this book has something unique and useful to share.

## INTENTIONS AND ALIGNMENT.

Before every interview, the intentions of this book were stated and potential participants were asked if it was in alignment with what they were willing to contribute to the project. The intentions were as follows:

1. The book will proactively avoid preconditioning people about their Iboga experience. It aims to dispel misconceptions about Iboga by providing a wide range of experiences and reasons for working with it. Additionally, ceremonial practices and protocols were not shared. This keeps readers open-minded and appropriately under-prepared for the ceremony.
2. More than 50% of profits from the book go directly to "Blessings of the Forest," a not-for-profit that focuses on Iboga conservation and reforestation. They are spearheading the quest for Iboga's longevity and health through many different avenues.
3. The interviewee has control over what is included in their specific interview section. Their interview will not be published without their absolute explicit consent and approval.
4. Interviews are to be an honest retelling of an experience with Iboga. No sensationalism.

The more open-minded or spiritually inclined reader may warm to the notion that the spirit of Iboga was guiding the interviews and interviewees. The experiences that needed to be included in this project naturally found the project. I had very few contacts in the Iboga world, beyond a handful of people I met during my month-long Iboga experience in Gabon. To secure additional interviewees, at the end of each interview, each participant was asked if they would like to invite someone who they felt should be included in the project. This snowballed until people were being politely turned down.

Several interviews with people who worked with Iboga at home, in a "do-it-yourself" context (or with a friend) were scrapped entirely. Although it is possible that people can have a beneficial experience working with Iboga at home by themselves, the odds are awfully stacked against them. Moreover, many experts warned against this as being highly problematic. Iboga is far more demanding and riskier than a heroic dose of mushrooms, or likely any other plant medicine. It is a very bad idea to do Iboga at home, without specific, professional guidance from people who have been trained in Iboga. Home-use or DIY work with Iboga is to be avoided, even for people who have professional training in other plant medicines!

There is no similar psychedelic experience home enthusiasts can measure Iboga against. It is important to insist that, the author vehemently discourages home usage. It is extremely dangerous to the health of the individual; a quick YouTube search reveals a shopping list of tragic, confusing, and seemingly unbeneficial home use experiences. Furthermore, home usage and sourcing Iboga from unsustainable sources place huge stress on the sustainability and survivability of Iboga. It truly is a lose-lose situation to work with Iboga at home.

The ordering of interviews was divided between "non-emergency purposes" and "emergency purposes." The first group represented a majority of people who chose to work with Iboga for "spiritual" or personal development reasons, and generally without drug and alcohol dependency. This was labeled "non-emergency" purposes, as the participants' lives were not at immediate risk if their pre-Iboga lives continued. Working with Iboga for drug or alcohol dependency issues has considerably different risks and precautionary steps. The second section is compiled from experiences for "emergency purposes," which includes people who worked with Iboga to treat life-threatening addiction.

This sequence was chosen to combat the perception in the plant medicine community that "Iboga is just for addiction!" I concede that there is considerable irony in using a selective ordering of the interviews (deliberate preconditioning) to combat preconditioning and misconceptions!

**BWITI.**

This book does not extensively explore the Bwiti tradition. Bwiti is a "cultural technology," or the "school of life," associated with Iboga use in Gabon and Central-West Africa. This is due to both respect and practicality. Bwiti is a spiritual way of living, a continual ritual. Although it contains enough information, rituals, customs, and wisdom to be considered a religion, many practitioners do not like this label. Bwiti is a comprehensive and complex technology, packed with knowledge to live a better life. Exploring it respectfully and adequately would take multiple dedicated volumes.

To be introduced to Bwiti, someone must first eat or consume Iboga. Bwiti is best described as a cultural technology, a traditional and adaptive practice which enables the full intelligence of Iboga to be invited into one's life. It is a series of techniques to help people deepen their relationship and understanding of Iboga. To quote a senior Bwiti practitioner, Tatayo Obiang Nzondo MaMissoba, "Bwiti is about happiness and humanity. It is hard for a human to be happy if we are sick. Bwiti helps man liberate themselves from disease. A man (or woman) liberated from sickness can find his way to happiness. Many people practice different forms and styles of Bwiti, but the aim is always the same, to be wise and happy."

The vast majority of people interviewed were not regular, deliberate practitioners of Bwiti. Some had been exposed to it while traveling to Gabon or during their initiation, and others are facilitators who utilize it regularly. However, Bwiti will not be explored in depth. Bwiti is typically passed on through spoken tradition, with lessons and teachings shared by the elders and initiated members of the community. For people interested in learning more about Bwiti, traveling to Gabon or Central-West Africa is your best option. The comprehensive and expensive textbook *Bwiti: An Ethnography of the Religious Imagination in Africa* by J.W Fernandez is another in-depth resource for people wishing to learn more.

Moreover, a strict agreement was made for this book not to explore or discuss Bwiti beyond what is absolutely necessary or unless an elder mentioned it in their interview. This is out of respect, privacy, and to safeguard this powerful cultural technology.

**Author's Note**

If you are reading this book for pleasure and do not intend to work with Iboga, Ibogaine, or other plant medicines, then feel free to skip straight to the interviews from here. The "emergency purposes" (addiction) interviews are particularly moving. The "summary of advice" section is filled with technical advice for people looking to work with plant medicines.

## SUMMARY OF ADVICE.

The following is a summary of the advice collected directly from interviewees and experts. Many of the points were reiterated throughout multiple interviews.

Please note, this is not medical or formal advice. The following section (and all "advice" within this book) is a summary of the reflections and ideas from others who have worked with Iboga and Ibogaine. Always consult with your appropriate medical practitioner before engaging with any of the ideas mentioned throughout this book.

If you are not planning on working with Iboga, Ibogaine, or other plant medicines for "emergency purposes," there is still a lot of value and extra information for added safety.

### HOW TO FIND A FACILITATOR.

1. Make sure that the person who is offering you the medicine is genuine. You need to *feel* that they are genuine, authentic, and focused on you. Ideally, they should be someone who is connected to the tradition in the sense that they have received training from the place where the medicine originally comes from (Gabon, Cameroon, The Congo Basin, etc.)
   i. Ask them what their link to the traditions of Iboga is?
   ii. Who did they study with? How long did they train for?
   iii. How many clients have they worked with? How many other people will they be working with, whilst working with you?
2. Ideally, the facilitator should be steady and settled in their own life. What does their personal life look like? Do they have a partner? Children? This is important in the environment and energy that they will bring into the experience and how they will treat you.
   i. Abuse of vulnerable people is rife in many industries and Iboga is unfortunately no exception. Someone who is settled, grounded, and happy in their own life is less likely to take advantage of you.
   ii. What is their personal story? Why did they start working with Iboga? What is their motivation now?

3. The best recommendation, in finding somewhere or someone to work with, is a recommendation from a trusted friend, who has previously worked with this medicine person, facilitator, community, or group for a similar intention to you.
   i. Ask your friends for honest advice and guidance. Share your intention with them and see if they would recommend the place they went to for that intention.
4. Many people spoke about "The right time is the perfect time." This means that everything aligns for you to work with Iboga at exactly the right time for you. Many interviewees observed that "You shouldn't have to hustle or really force your way to work with this medicine." Many people believe that at the right time, things will align perfectly for you. With that said, it is important to be vigilant, screen facilitators thoroughly, and follow all the other advice in this book. If you find yourself "pushing" too hard to work with Iboga, then it is most likely not the right time for you.
5. In terms of mental, spiritual, physical, and emotional safety, really try to connect with the facilitators and have a conversation well before you commit to working with them. Ask them about themselves, as well as these types of questions:
   i. How did they set up their center? How did they develop their approach to serving the medicine?
   ii. How do they work in terms of holding space for people? What do they do to make sure you are safe? You will learn a lot just from that conversation.
   iii. Are the facilitators doing their own healing and deep work? Are they continually working on themselves and engaging with a beginner's mindset? Or do they know everything and don't need to learn more?! (Wrong answer!)
   iv. Do they think that they are the ones doing the healing? Do they have a savior complex? Or do they get out of the way and allow the medicine (Iboga) and the participants to do the work together?
   v. Do they hold your hand and give you a hug, if you need it, or do they just leave you in a room to figure it out? What do you want from a facilitator in terms of support?
   vi. Have they created a (warm) family-like environment or are they running a medical clinic?

6. With both facilitators and integration coaches, look for someone with whom you can be open, honest, and resonant with. You want to find someone who you can be completely yourself around.
   i. Could you yell, cry or throw a tantrum in front of them? Can you disclose your medical history, current medicines, and life story to them? Do you feel they would judge you for this?
7. Look for these signs of a good facilitator:
   i. Early on they should start assessing where a person's vulnerabilities are, where their strengths are, and what this experience means for them. They will also start asking and determining what your needs are and how to best prepare you to fulfill these needs.
   ii. They should offer reviews and past clients to talk to, preferably with similar intentions to you or from similar cultural backgrounds or countries.
8. Sustainability and sourcing of Iboga is another important topic to discuss with your facilitator. The following questions may be useful to ask:
   i. Where do you get your Iboga from? How do you source it?
   ii. If you are working with Ibogaine (not Iboga root bark) was their Ibogaine extracted from Voacanga (plentiful in supply) and not the Iboga tree (critically endangered in the wild and commonly poached)?
   iii. Can I visit the place where the Iboga comes from? This is most likely to be a no, but it is a good conversation starter around the medicine you will work with.
   iv. How do the communities and people that you bought Iboga from benefit? Are they victims of poaching or are they supported?
   v. Are you personally doing anything to promote sustainability? Iboga is critically endangered in the wild, so this conservation is extremely important.
9. It is useful to think of Iboga as heart surgery or brain surgery. Do you want your surgery to be performed by a lobotomist with no training, or an expert who has spent many years training, practicing, and facilitating? It is truly worth it to work with someone who has studied with great teachers and practiced for a long time. Both brain surgeons and lobotomists exist! Choose wisely!

10. If at any point of meeting and screening a facilitator you feel something off, listen to your intuition and honor that. While fear and hesitancy are normal emotions, the ego's defense mechanism to avoid challenging inner work, this is distinct from the feeling that something is strange! Listen closely to your instinct and intuition, and practice discerning that voice.

This is a brief summary of how to find a suitable facilitator or center. For more in-depth articles, with additional (and better) questions, both resources from Juliana Mulligan, the "Guide to Finding a Safe Ibogaine Clinic," and "Warning Signs When Selecting a Psychedelic Facilitator with Juliana Mulligan," are great places to start. Links can be found in the appendix: resources section.

## REVIEW OF SAFETY PRECAUTIONS.

### Essential Safety Precautions for Everyone.

1. Disclose all medications and supplements you are using to your facilitator, community, or center. Be 100% transparent and honest. This is crucial.
2. A good blanket rule is to presume that a medication will interact with Iboga and be contraindicated unless you are certain otherwise.
   i. If you can't trust your facilitator with all the medicines you are currently taking, then you're not at the point of trust to be working with them.
   ii. A famous expression within the community is "If you lie, you die..."
   iii. Consult with a specialist pharmacist, psychiatrist, or MD about contraindications for any of your medications, and determine a plan for being able to work with Iboga if appropriate.
3. Undertake a thorough heart examination. An EKG (aka: Electrocardiogram or ECG) is the bare minimum.
   i. Additionally, you should screen for conditions such as bradycardia or a prolonged QT interval.
   ii. It may be worthwhile to consult with a cardiologist for a thorough screening of your heart, especially if you have a personal or family history of heart issues.
4. Have a comprehensive liver panel done by your doctor and review it for any signs that you have an inflamed or damaged liver.
   i. Iboga places a lot of demands on the liver. This is especially important for people with a history of alcohol, drug, or food misuse or abuse.
5. Have a comprehensive, long-form physical examination done by your doctor to assess if you have any underlying or unknown health conditions that may prevent you from working with Iboga.
6. Undertake a thorough pre-screening and interview with your facilitator. This should consist of a medical history form, motivations, and a detailed exploration of who you are and where you are coming from.
   i. It should also screen you out if you have an existing contraindicated mental health condition.

7. If you are working with Iboga in an area prone to malaria (Gabon), have a plan and suitable medication in place to manage malaria.
   i. Death can result from complications and contraindications with malaria medication.
   ii. Talk to your doctor to develop a plan to manage malaria.
8. Review your family history to determine if you have an underlying predisposition to psychiatric disorders such as schizophrenia, bipolar, mania, etc.
   i. It is also useful to learn about your family tree and start exploring your ancestral history. Where did your ancestors come from? What spiritual practices would they have practiced? What are the names of your grandparents and ancestors? Do you know the broad history of your ancestors?
9. Develop your cardiovascular health. Start exercising safely and preparing your body physically. The better physical condition you are in, the less you have to worry about physically when you work with Iboga.
10. Even small doses of Iboga can have severe interactions with medications or pre-existing conditions. It is possible to have a serious cardiac event with very low doses of Iboga. For this reason, it is wise that anyone who is interested in micro-dosing Iboga, undergo all of the same medical screening and testing that is done prior to a flood dose.

**Safety Precautions for "Emergency use" of Iboga and Ibogaine (Drug and Alcohol Dependency).**

1. Undertake all precautions listed in the above section.
2. Additional EKG (Electrocardiogram also known as an ECG) screening over numerous days to detect any irregular heart activity that may be missed in an initial screening.
    i. The heart's activity may change as drugs and medicines are removed from your diet and as you prepare for your treatment or initiation. Running tests over multiple days can help catch underlying issues that might have been missed in an initial assessment when your body was adjusted to your old life and patterns.
3. Ask your facilitator about what they will do to "stabilize you" leading into your treatment.
    i. What is the plan in the days and weeks leading up to the ceremony or treatment to ensure you are as safe as possible?
    ii. Have they worked with people with similar conditions to you? How did it go? What are the common issues that can occur? What have they learned from people with similar conditions to you?
4. Have a plan in place to avoid constipation. For many people working with Iboga for opiate dependency, constipation is a major issue and can be life-threatening if not addressed.
    i. Consider natural remedies such as psyllium husk and traditional purgatives and "vomitivos" (a South American word for treatments that induce purging). This should be done well before your treatment. Your bowels should be moving normally when you undergo treatment.
    ii. Your facilitator, medicine person, or community should have a treatment plan in place to manage constipation. Ask them what it is!
5. Have a plan in place for hydration. Constipation, purging, and detoxing from substances can deplete you of electrolytes. Dehydration can be fatal.
    i. This may involve using an IV electrolyte solution. Is your facilitator equipped to administer this? Who is supplying it?
    ii. Check with your facilitator if supplementing with electrolytes and supplements like magnesium is appropriate or advised.

iii. Check with your facilitator if your hydration plan is acceptable to them.

6. Do your research, work with a trusted and reputable facilitator, and then trust them. Follow their protocols and directions explicitly. Do not deviate from their instructions and plan.

**Additional Safety Precautions and Advice.**

1. Iboga or its alkaloids is a medicine **YOU SHOULD NOT DO** by yourself or with an inexperienced "trip sitter." Iboga is not like psilocybin or LSD. It is best considered to be akin to serious brain, heart, and soul surgery. Prepare accordingly.
2. Try to establish a rapport with your facilitator beforehand. Trusting them and having a genuine relationship may allow you to surrender more fully and have a deeper experience. If you feel a disconnect or that there is not a genuine relationship there, they are likely not the right facilitator or community for you.
3. The best providers will begin communicating at least 2-3 months before you intend to work with Iboga, to better understand you and treat you. This also gives them the time to understand you as a person, what your patterns are, and how they can best help you.
4. If you can, try not to rush the experience. Take your time, prepare thoroughly, and slow down. Make decisions based on safety, trust, and connection rather than desperation, fear, or urgency.

## GENERAL TIPS FOR HOW TO PREPARE.

The following have been compiled from the interviews and conversations in this book and summarized into an easy-to-find resource. This a broad overview of useful tips to think about on your journey of working with Iboga.

### General Tips for Non-Emergency Purposes (Non-addiction).

1. For most people, Iboga should be a last resort. It is good advice to try other appropriate healing modalities and spiritual practices before you decide to work with Iboga. There may be more appropriate and culturally familiar practices, closer and more accessible to you.
   i. Iboga is best seen as "graduate school" or "post graduate school" in terms of plant medicines, primarily because of the intensity, duration, and depth of the experience.
   ii. Other psychedelic medicines may prepare and teach you to better work with Iboga. Additionally, you may find that through working with other psychedelic medicines, you no longer have need to work with Iboga.
   iii. It's useful to start thinking, how can I be in balance with Iboga? How can I ensure I am not consuming it in a way that leads to its demise physically or culturally? What am I doing to ensure this is a sustainable practice? How can I be in reciprocity with the plant?
   iv. What spiritual practices are near to you that you can implement in conjunction with Iboga? This means, what is geographically close to you, ancestrally relevant to you, and biologically familiar to you? As an example, if you are Celtic, is there a druid practice you can explore? Can you talk to your "everyday" life elders, parents, and grandparents about their spiritual practices?
2. Dedicate deliberate periods of mindfulness, prayer, intention, and gratitude leading up to the experience.
   i. Try to get in touch with whatever faith, spirituality, or higher states of consciousness that are familiar to you. This might be visiting churches or temples, spending intentional time with loved ones, listening to your favorite teachers, or spending time in nature... Whatever works for you.

   ii. Setting an intention early, and continuing to refine it based on your values can help immensely in your experience.
3. The people who have the most transformational experiences tend to do the most work both before and afterwards. For those who receive the most benefit, the challenging and transformational work begins well before they physically ingest Iboga.
   i. Generally speaking, people who have devoted and invested more of themselves (and this is not meaning financially) to work with Iboga and into the process experience the biggest transformations and healings.
   ii. The sacrifices made towards the experience can act to generate humility, which helps with accepting and processing the treatment.
   iii. In the author's own experience, I "sacrificed" my own artificial happiness and many false beliefs that were based on this. It would have been useful to work with a therapist beforehand to dismantle some false beliefs prior to working with Iboga.
4. Be prepared to slow down and for your life to take a considerably different pace.
5. Deep introspection, intention-setting, and self-reflection can be invaluable in preparing the soil of your mind to work with Iboga. Determine what you are trying to achieve, what areas you want to focus on.
   i. Become very clear about why you are doing this. What do you personally want to achieve or realize through working with Iboga?
   ii. If you could only have one goal in working with Iboga, what would it be? Be very precise. Once you are clear on your primary reason to work with Iboga, you can think about the secondary and ancillary reasons that you want to work with it.
6. Be discerning and selective about what you read about Iboga. More information is not necessarily better. Be careful with what you choose to learn. For instance, it may be useful to read a book (this one!) that's been endorsed by a trusted friend, but it might not be useful to read online forum posts, watch YouTube videos, or watch TikTok videos on Iboga. They are likely to bias you to a certain outcome that doesn't reflect the plant or your process accurately.
7. If you are in good health, and have a good relationship with food, in the months leading up to your experience, consider safely fasting from food and

teaching your body to go extended periods of time (1-2 days) without eating. Consult with your doctor before attempting any fasts.

8. Clean up your diet to the best of your ability: limit alcohol, sugar, fast foods, excess salts, spices, and other foods that can alter your brain chemistry.
    i. It is particularly useful to limit sugar and processed foods, as the dopamine and serotonin these foods release can alter your brain chemistry.
    ii. Similarly abstaining from sexual activity can also prepare your brain and body for the transformation too, primarily through helping to modulate (or resetting) your dopamine receptors. Some practitioners believe that abstaining from sex also helps cultivate "chi" or life force, our primal energies, which can be channeled towards transformation.
9. Consider exploring complementary practices that interest you.
    i. Vipassana meditation retreats appear particularly useful as they help you sit with discomfort and teach surrender over an extended period of time.
    ii. Breathwork, deep breathing practices, yoga, and tantra were also recommended by interviewees.
10. Schedule fun into your life both before and after the experience.
    i. For many people, coming from addiction backgrounds, or a fast-paced, depressive life, having fun can be an afterthought. Having fun and knowing what activities you like (painting, hiking, playing board games, etc.) are vital parts of recovering and integrating post-treatment.
    ii. Set aside the time to actually have fun and do it!
11. Often the first time working with Iboga is the strongest and most impactful. This is why many people stress the importance of preparing as best as you can.
    i. Without adequate preparation, you can only get so far. If approached from an earnest place of authenticity, the experience will still give you what you need, but it may not be as smooth or easy to process.
    ii. Ideally, someone will have already broken down many of their internal barriers beforehand and have a laser-focused, specific intention that can be explored, in full trust and surrender. The experience will get through what it can get through, it is most useful

to be precise in what you are looking for but open to the sometimes odd and challenging answers that will come through.

12. Journaling before and after your experience can be very useful to help prepare and then digest emotions and experiences that come up.

**Why should people work with a therapist, coach, or counselor around Iboga?**

Having a professional who is traveling through the entire experience with you can be extremely valuable. A good coach or therapist will not establish a hierarchical relationship, but rather share useful experiences and advice, to help you make the most of your journey. It's very useful to have someone who can hold the bigger picture of your life and intentions for you, and who can see through the day-to-day roller coaster of your life. A good therapist can hold the greater narrative for you and help you get out of the everyday monkey-mind story. They may also push you or help you venture into challenging places and memories that you may be scared to explore. They can help you get the most out of your experience. Working with a good coach, counselor, or therapist throughout your Iboga journey may have the power to potentiate a single treatment to have the same transformative effect as doing many!

Put simply, a good therapist, counselor, or coach can help you have the most transformative and supportive experience possible for you. They can both laser-focus you on what's important to your intentions and help weave together the bigger picture, as unexpected revelations emerge. Uncovering unexpected truths about yourself might rattle you and set you "off-course." A therapist or coach can help you integrate your new findings and ensure you neatly tie your experience all together, with minimal blood. Furthermore, it is useful to work with a professional to help refine and set your intentions and to have an integration program in place beforehand too. Many people interviewed explicitly wished they had worked with a therapist or coach to help set their intentions, push and help them with integration, or they were very grateful that they had done so.

Traditionally, it took an entire community of people to help someone process and integrate their Iboga experience. In Gabon, a village that has known someone for a very long time would support and assist them psychologically, through friendship and understanding. The village would help someone before, during, and after their experience. Traditionally, it may take a whole village, or at least a family to help someone integrate. In the western world, this might not be as realistic. A therapist, coach, or counselor can be a modern-day substitution for having an entire village to talk to and support you.

**Brief Intention Setting Tips.**

1. Write a broad list of everything you would like from your Iboga experience. This doesn't have to be specific, but think of it as a brainstorming exercise. Get in touch with what you want and why you are choosing to work with Iboga. Review this list with a professional coach, therapist, counselor, or trusted friend, and seek their guidance in refining it and determining what is realistic. Prioritize what you would like most from the experience after you have written out everything possible. It may be useful to settle on one main motivation and be very precise about that.
2. For example, an intention such as, "I want to stop being depressed" is useful, but it's much more efficient to set an intention such as, "Take me to the pain, the event, the behavioral pattern or the environment that is making me depressed. Please show me and help me explore and understand my depression. What is not working for me?"
   i. Set specific, clear intentions that take you to the root of your issues and intentions.
   ii. The more work beforehand you can do, to understand and explore your intention the better.
3. Have specific, well-thought-out intentions, but be prepared to leave them "at the front of the temple door." Pick your intentions back up on your way out of the ceremony. Don't hold onto them too rigidly during your experience, and let Iboga work with you, however it needs to work to fulfill your intention.
   i. By holding onto intentions too rigidly, we can limit the information we are willing to see and be exposed to. When we hold on too rigidly, we deny certain parcels of information from being accepted or received and limit our capacity for healing.
4. Your intention should be about what you want and need from Iboga. No one should be telling you what you are trying to achieve. Your intention HAS to be self-motivated and very clear to you.

**Additional "Emergency Purposes" Specific Preparation Tips (Addiction)**

1. It is essential to follow the advice and guidance of your facilitator and doctor. If they tell you to transition to shorter-acting opiates or alternative medicines, you really must follow their advice. It can be extremely dangerous not to do so.
2. Set an intention that is specific to you. Not your friends, family, or anyone that wants you to just "get off drugs."
   i. Be very clear about why YOU want to work with Iboga, doing it for yourself is infinitely more powerful than doing it because other people say "you have to do it." Get in touch with what YOU want, not about what your society or family wants, which is usually total abstinence from drugs.
3. Try to find a "sponsor" or guide to support you through the process, someone that has been through the experience and genuinely wants the best for you. Ideally, the sponsor would help you find a center or facilitator, and guide you in preparation and integration, but probably not physically help you through the ceremony. A supportive friend, who has been through the process before can be valuable in helping assist you through the process as well.
4. It's especially important to start building a community, rather than just relying on a significant other or a family member to be your safety net. A positive and supportive community around you can help you rebuild yourself and life following the experience.
   i. A supportive community is crucial to avoid being pulled back into old patterns, relationships, and behaviors associated with loneliness or an unsupportive community. In this way, you can fill your time and life with people who want the best for you and not succumb to old patterns.
   ii. If you think it will be challenging to build your own community, then it can be useful to tag along to existing communities, such as AA, NA, religious groups, etc. If they are not available to you, then online groups on Facebook and Reddit, coupled with recommendations/referrals from your facilitator of people who live near to you, who have worked with them and Iboga may be useful. Try to begin this well before you begin your treatment.

   iii. Many facilitators spoke about a challenging process: "Sending someone home from a clinic to an environment that they were living in beforehand, where they don't have any good friends, where they have no community. It sets people up for relapse or a very challenging integration period." Try to establish a small community beforehand to help with integration and building a new life.
5. Recognize that this is a long process and not a miracle cure.
   i. Some practitioners said that 3 months is the ideal time for healing addiction to opiates. 30 days of preparation, 30 days during treatment, and then 30 days following treatment. Withdrawal from modern opiates can take up to 6 weeks to physically leave your system. The mental patterns and habits may take even longer.
   ii. You need to prepare yourself mentally to work as hard on your recovery post-Iboga or Ibogaine, as you did previously to fuel your addiction. If you are not prepared to do the work, you are going to end up exactly where you were, but much poorer. You may potentially feel terrible because you may feel like you have failed or that this "miracle" cure didn't work for you. It does not mean you are a failure, or you suck, it just means there is more work, healing, and acceptance to do. It takes real work, over a long period of time, to break strong patterns.
6. If possible, try to start shifting your mindset to one of gratitude. What has this substance misuse or addiction protected you from? What has it helped you with? Are you ready to face what you have been escaping from? Are you ready to be grateful for this old life and move on?
   i. Are you stuck in the mindset of, "As long as I'm using, I'm a bad person. I'm in a bad place and I'm not getting better"? Are you truly trapped here? Is there anything you can start changing already?
   ii. You can start making positive changes in your life well before you work with Iboga, Ibogaine, or other plant medicines. You don't have to wait until after you've taken Iboga or Ibogaine, or until you're off other substances. You can start making healthy changes, NOW. Do small, simple things: try to get yourself into a routine, go to bed at the same time, get up at the same time, do something for yourself every day, do some meditation, deep breathing, start volunteering, try to find something that engages you and gives you purpose.

iii. Try to focus on shifting the way you think about yourself. Transitioning from "I'm a hopeless or bad person" to "I'm sick right now, but I'm healing. I'm ready to change and I'm grateful for this period of my life."

## WHAT PEOPLE WISH THEY KNEW BEFOREHAND.

Most interviewees stressed the importance of not knowing too much about the experience before working with Iboga. In fact, so many of them highlighted the importance of not researching or knowing more than what is essential, it made me reconsider writing this book! With that said, here is the summary of the most frequently made and useful points.

### Recommended Prior Knowledge (Non-emergency Purposes).

1. It's better either to know very little about the experience or to know enough that everyone's experience with Iboga and Ibogaine is radically different. The worst situation going in is to be aware of only a few experiences, myths, or tall stories without context. Less information is better than bad information!
2. Although some people see the movie of their life, only a few people interviewed saw this. Seeing this movie or having very clear visions is actually quite rare.
3. Each person will interact with the medicine differently. Some people may experience what feels like an internal conversation, others "blackout" and experience nothing, some see visions, and some only have feelings.
4. The strongest experience working with Iboga is more often than not the first, hence why preparation for the first time is stressed so heavily by many people. With that said, some people had more powerful experiences with subsequent journeys.
5. Don't expect there to be some huge external change in the circumstances of your life. Often Iboga works by changing the trajectory of your life by 1-2 degrees and not by catapulting you somewhere totally different.
6. Openness, honesty, surrender, courage, trust, and sacrifice to the experience were common ideas that interviewees highlighted as being crucial to having a transformative experience.
7. If you are casually considering doing Iboga, it's not for you. Additionally, if you are considering Iboga for psycho-spiritual growth or general personal development, there are a lot of other options you should consider working with first. It's a good idea to explore other options, before committing to working with Iboga.

8. The experience begins much earlier than you would expect and continues for a much longer time afterwards. Many people noticed their life and psyche changing after committing to work with Iboga and well before they physically consumed Iboga. Additionally, some facilitators shared that it can take a lifetime to fully understand and integrate an Iboga experience. One facilitator said that it took 10 years to understand their first experience!
9. The most consistent theme emerging through the experiences was Iboga showing people their blind spots, which can be very confronting and potentially shattering.
10. Many testimonials online are offered by people healing from addiction. This is a very different experience and has a wildly different physical toll than working with Iboga for non-emergency (non-addiction) purposes. So, understand that the medicine can be very gentle, nurturing, and loving. It does not have to be an "ass-kicker." You also don't have to take heroic doses in order to get what you need. If Iboga is in your awareness, it's because it wants to meet you. It may be time for that transformation to happen. Use your discretion.
11. Despite Iboga working primarily internally, it also has the capacity to rapidly change your external life, although this is uncommon. It can shake your world to the core and it can help things leave your life very quickly.
12. The deep changes that Iboga generates within you can disturb formerly harmonious relationships with your friends and family. You could change "too quickly" in the eyes of your close relations. Sometimes the distance can be so large between you and your loved ones that following your experience, you become incompatible with them.
    i. Many interviewees spoke about cutting ties with people they loved but were no longer in alignment with, following their experience. After they healed from traumatic experiences or addressed "toxic" patterns within themselves, a lot of relationships were no longer beneficial to either party.
13. People well-versed in Ayahuasca can have some of the hardest experiences when working with Iboga. Working extensively with other psychedelic medicines does not guarantee that the Iboga experience will be an easy one. In fact, it appears that it may make it a more challenging and deeper one.
14. Within the ceremonial experience it can be useful to Say "yes" to the things you are shown. Try to examine and explore everything you are shown.

Don't shy away from the things you are shown in your Iboga experience. Do the work in selecting a facilitator early so you can build trust with them, and trust that what Iboga is showing you is for your healing.

15. Confrontation is often a major part of the healing process. You will likely face conflict within yourself, calling yourself out or being called out by other people. Learn the lessons from the conflict and don't fight more or less than you need to. But understand that conflict is a natural part of the process.
16. Generally, don't read too much about Iboga beforehand ;)

**Additional Recommended Prior Knowledge Specific for Emergency-use (Drug and Alcohol Dependency)**

1. After the treatment or ceremony, you may initially feel good. Ibogaine is useful in mitigating receptor withdrawal. But when detoxing from opiates, you are still likely to have opiate metabolites in your fat cells. As it slowly metabolizes out of that, you may have a prolonged withdrawal process.
2. A lot of the relationships you may have had previously, based on co-dependency or mutual escapism, most likely will dissolve. Liberation from co-dependency or mutually destructive patterns is not easy. Sometimes the harder segments of Iboga treatment are found in the sober dissolving of relationships afterwards and not the ceremony itself.
3. One facilitator said, “If we let someone rush right in to be treated, it doesn’t mean it will be bad for them, but we don’t see as vibrant (grand) of an outcome. This is compared to people who really take the time to prepare. Generally speaking, the more someone puts into and energetically gives to the experience, the greater the healing will be.”
    i. Sometimes sacrifice of the comforts of old beliefs, behaviors, and patterns open people to receive greater healing.
4. Look at it as a minimum 3-month process. Ideally, put a plan in for 30 days before and 2 months after. Know how and where you are going to prepare, consume, and integrate Iboga. Have a plan, people, and locations organized beforehand.
5. Make sure that this is what you want. Iboga is not going to change your will. Sometimes people work with Iboga because their spouse or family want them to. This is not a good motivation if someone has no real desire to work with Iboga themselves. Do you truly want to work with Iboga? Do you really want to change?
6. Iboga requires a very different mindset than the one most people searching for Iboga are used to. Often, people are desperate to get out of their addiction loop and have been for a long period of time. They have conditioned their mind to seek instant gratification and instant relief. Often, when people find out about Iboga they think, "This is amazing! This is exactly what I've been looking for. It's the answer to all my problems." Iboga is not a magic pill and requires a considerable mental shift away from easy fixes and instant solutions to be effective.

7. Iboga is not a cure for addiction. Rather, an entry point into a deeper and embodied understanding of the why. Why am I choosing to drink to excess? Why am I choosing to misuse drugs? What am I escaping? What is hidden deeper? Am I ready to make peace with this? Do I want to?
8. For people who have complex PTSD, less Iboga can be more. For a nervous system that is overwhelmed and stuck in a state of hypervigilance, going into a peak, intense experience and white-knuckling through it can sometimes be less valuable than building trust and safety, working with smaller and medium-sized doses over a longer period of time. "Breaking though," or having a huge "blowout" experience you think you need might not be the answer to your problems.
9. Sometimes, people dealing with addiction are dealing with control issues. They need to control what emotions they are feeling, what experiences they are having, or what memories they are revisiting. Iboga, coupled with trust in a supportive team can help you to lessen the grip (control) you have on your life, which may give you the healing you are seeking. Trusting and depending on others, who want the best for you, can be a healing experience in and of itself.

## INTEGRATION ADVICE.

**Authors note:**

Integration is commonly overlooked by people working in the plant medicine world. It is arguably more important and "harder work" than the actual psychedelic experience itself. The challenges that arise in integrating and applying a big experience and transformation are commonly much more challenging than the hardest moment of altered consciousness.

Many people race from one gigantic psychedelic experience to another, without giving themselves the time or opportunity to process and apply what they have learnt. With adequate integration, lives are regularly and benevolently transformed. Without integration, people run the risk of putting themselves in danger: physically, mentally, and emotionally. Doing a lot of psychedelic medicine work without integration is similar to buying many cars and never driving them, enjoying them, or fixing them. Just collecting experiences (cars) without using them to take you further on the journey of life. The real magic of plant medicines comes from the unsexy work of applying lessons and knowledge gained from ceremonies, elders, friends, and experiences in our lives. When we apply what we learn, over a long period of time, miracles and dramatic transformations can occur.

Additionally, this integration advice is broadly useful for anyone working with plant medicines, psychedelic medicines, or seriously walking on a spiritual path. Although specific to Iboga, there is a lot of useful advice to be gleaned from this section for all types of spiritual work.

**Integration Advice Summary.**

1. Understand that Iboga and Ibogaine are tools. They are very effective tools, but they require us consistently to do the work to benefit fully from them. They don't do "the work" for us.
   i. "The work" can be broadly summarized as facing oneself. This means not shying away from uncomfortable emotions, conversations, memories, and experiences. Following challenging experiences,

thoughts, and memories all the way to the lesson that is embedded within them is considered "doing the work." It is also known as facing oneself and seeing ourselves even in the most unpleasant, uncomfortable, and truthful light.

ii. A deep commitment to doing the work, before, during, and after the experience is required to see deep, lasting change.

2. The integration process after Iboga can be very challenging. Both your internal world and external world can change very rapidly. If your life is not "in service to you" (alignment) and things need to go, Iboga may accelerate their departure. If you don't have the proper support, friends, family, or a professional therapist, this can be a very challenging period.
3. Do your best to embrace what you are receiving. Do not focus on what you're not receiving or missing out on. Stay away from what you didn't get. You will receive a lot. If you look at what you didn't get, you are missing the wisdom and healing you did receive. Trust that you did the necessary preparation, fully committed, and embraced your journey. If you do this, Iboga will facilitate the perfect experience for you.
4. Listening to recordings of ceremonial music, meditating, and reflecting on your experience can be powerful tools to help integrate after the experience.
   i. This can potentially be more useful than micro-dosing, without the complications, legality, and sustainability issues that micro-dosing can involve.
5. Some of the biggest transformations occur over time, through integration. They don't commonly occur during the ceremony. Yes, some issues can be resolved quickly. Thought patterns, behaviors, and perceptions can "magically" disappear. You might notice "I don't want to watch horror movies, I want to eat better." However, the deep, excavating, life-changing work normally doesn't happen in the ceremony. It happens after. If you don't have support doing this longer-term work, it's harder to really capture the breadth of the power that comes out of the Iboga experience.
6. Schedule time each week (or every day) to have fun. Simple, childish fun. Often, before working with Iboga, people are stuck in patterns of working, addiction, or the fast pace of modern life. Many of us have forgotten to have fun, and joy is an essential part of any healing process.

   i. This activity is not about "making progress." It should just be something enjoyable. Many of us have been raised in environments where our self-worth is tied to productivity and what we are doing.
   ii. One of the hardest things to do when leaving a life of substance dependency behind is to relearn how to have fun because for so long people have associated having fun with doing drugs.
7. Iboga can make you far more aware and hypersensitive to the world around you. This can cause major changes in your relationship with others and the world around you. To integrate the experience, it is necessary to be tolerant, open-minded, and to be fluid with what changes in your life based on what Iboga shows you.
8. The gap between what you saw or felt during your experience with Iboga and "regular life" can be stark. Sometimes, periods described by facilitators as "decompensation" can arise, which are psychologically brutal. This may present as a feeling of inability to realize one's "dream" and a feeling of extreme isolation. Iboga calls for discipline and patience, but also for support from a team to weather this storm.
   i. Many interviewees spoke about the year following their initial experience being beautiful but very challenging.
   ii. For the author, the 6 months following Iboga were very challenging. I both wanted to talk to others, couldn't communicate what I had experienced, and felt Iboga radically rearranging my life. Going slow, practicing patience, and being gentle with myself were useful during this time. It was a very uncomfortable and isolating period. I continued with my meditation, health, and spiritual practices through the hardest times and trusted that things would get better eventually.
9. In the modern western environment, there is a huge focus on sharing all details of our lives. Many communities and facilitators advise the participants not to share their experience with anyone outside the community and to be very slow (many years) in sharing their experience with the wider world. This is part of the traditional approach to Iboga, where knowledge and experiences gained from Iboga are not shared with anyone who has not been initiated.
   i. What is shown to you during the experience belongs to you and to you alone. It can be useful to share it with a competent facilitator,

elder, or therapist, but sharing and interpreting the visions is best seen as a delicate art form.

ii. One interviewee said: visions are timeless, multi-dimensional, and symbolic, and therefore very difficult to interpret through the prism of our basic and untrained cultural understanding. Understanding visions is an art and a science.

10. Iboga is neither a miracle solution for everyone nor easy to integrate, especially if one is socially isolated. Traditionally it takes a village to support someone in the months following their experience. Close friends, family, and trained psychological professionals are less ideal than a village that has known you your whole life, but the most realistic option for people living in the western world.
11. Take the time to set your intentions for integration. Planning what your integration practices are going to be (journaling, talking, painting, writing, walking, etc.) and mapping out your support network is important. Create rituals around the week or weeks approaching the ceremony to continue in the weeks and months afterwards.
12. After you have successfully completed your treatment and given your body and mind adequate time to rest, slowly begin to ask other people about their experiences. How they explain their process, and the commonalities with your own process will likely aid you in integrating and understanding your own treatment or initiation. Be slow with your sharing, and only share with trusted friends who understand plant medicines and ideally understand Iboga. Reading the experiences section of this book will be very useful now.

**Additional Addiction-Specific Integration Advice**

When talking with your facilitator or counselor (or anyone who helps you professionally with integration), be very clear on what you are intending to integrate and heal, and what you're not going to cover. You should both be clear on what you are working towards. Be specific. Example: Are you healing the root cause of your addiction? Or are you healing relationship patterns? Be clear on what you want to integrate and address.

1. It's useful to think of integration as a holistic process. A journey of reuniting all the disconnected, neglected, and unique parts of yourself into a whole being. In particular,

i. It's helpful to begin in the physical space, focusing on the body. The road to emotional, mental, and spiritual healing begins with being physically safe.
ii. Learning to regulate your nervous system, and learning how to "BE" in a new way is part of the process. This takes time and Iboga is very useful for resetting the nervous system.
iii. As a starting point, feeling safe in a physical sense creates space to process other feelings. Once you feel physically safe and healthy, it can allow values, desires, and beliefs to change. This ultimately deepens the connection to a spiritual path and allows more healing to occur.
iv. It's a circle or seasonal understanding of oneself, rather than a linear one. As we do more work and go deeper, we may revisit old traumas and beliefs in a new more profound way.
v. Integration is not a straightforward path upwards, but rather a drill, circulating downwards to understand the different parts of yourself and how they are all interwoven. Normally, things tend to "click" together when you understand more about your story and life.

2. The physical process of integration is similar to building an airplane out of an old car or the transformation a caterpillar goes through to become a butterfly.
   i. To take the masculine analogy of building an airplane from an old car, you wouldn't rush the building process and you definitely wouldn't do it alone or without professionals. All the small parts need to function as intended, so the new machine can fly and reach greater heights. You wouldn't try to fly until you were sure that the wings weren't wobbly and the engine wouldn't fall apart. You would take your time to be sure, go slowly, and listen to the experts. Only when everything checks out and you pass all the pre-flight safety tests, then would you consider getting out on the runway.
   ii. To take the feminine analogy of a caterpillar transforming into a butterfly, it's a natural process that can't be rushed. It all begins with an internal transformation and a period of the caterpillar becoming goo! After being totally reformed, the butterfly emerges from the cocoon, shedding its old life, and is ready to enjoy its new existence.

If the butterfly tries to leave the cocoon too early, there will just be a lot of goo on the floor!

3. People often feel a rush to integrate. They want to stop waiting around and have their next experience already. Many people feel like their consciousness is behind "where it should be" and want to catch up. But, if we move forward with loose bolts, what's going to happen? Accidents. Tragedies.
4. People should try to get out of unhealthy relationships before they start working with Iboga, and prepare a safe space, which minimizes exposures to unhelpful relationships and triggers. It is especially important for post-treatment to integrate in a new place. This allows for the medicine to reach in and start creating a new life filled with new patterns, relationships, and habits that work for you.
   i. It's very hard to maintain sobriety and new habits in an old environment, with old relationships that trigger old patterns. It's best to build and solidify new mental habits and patterns in a new environment, before exposing yourself to old triggers.
5. Some facilitators believe that the first 12-24 days after the treatment are vital. They said "12-24 days after the treatment are the key to the foundation to your new life. Ideally, someone would be in a container with other people who have just taken Iboga. They would be creatively building and imagining their new life, brainstorming together as a team. This is where people start to set the foundation, and as they re-emerge after those two weeks, then the Noribogaine is active. The body and mind are recovering on the physical plane, and you can integrate back into the regular world."
   i. The facilitator continued: "That would be my advice, you come into a facility, you don't want to take Iboga in the same place you live. You go somewhere to take Iboga. After that process is done, you have to leave. You're basically coming out of the old life, and entering a new life. Separation from the scene of the crime, so to speak. After the detox, you have to switch environments, this will take an additional week or 2 for integration. We call it the 'crystallization' period."
6. Slow is fast. Don't risk retraumatizing yourself by flooding the nervous system with something it can't handle.

## A WARNING: STOP HERE!

This is a polite, but firm request to not continue reading on if you broadly plan to work with Iboga soon and know very little about it. Soon is defined as "within 5 years". The information up to this point is useful in helping you to optimize your experience. It will be most useful to you to read the "Experiences" section *after* your own Iboga experience, as it will help you integrate, assimilate, and process your own experience. If you read the "Experiences" section too soon, it may precondition you and alter your experience.

If you plan to consume Iboga within 1 year and *know little about Iboga*, it is especially essential you **DO NOT READ ANY FURTHER.** Reading further may jeopardize your mindset and predispose you to having experiences similar to those found within this book. Every Iboga experience is different. 23 people were interviewed and 23 very different experiences were recorded. If 500 people were interviewed, then it's likely that there would be 500 different experiences. You will likely benefit a lot more from reading the experiences after you have worked with Iboga.

However, if you have already researched Iboga, or heard in-depth stories about peoples' experiences, then I'd recommend continuing to read. Reading will help show the huge range of experiences people have and help dispel misconceptions and predispositions about the experience. If you know a small-medium amount about Iboga, then reading ahead will help you a lot.

On the sum of things, the ideal approach to working with Iboga (as a westerner, who is culturally foreign to Iboga) would be as follows:

1. Either you know very little about Iboga, trust your well-trained and aligned facilitator, and follow all their directions to the best of your ability – so as to not precondition you, and you follow their advice precisely.

   OR

2. You have heard a few stories about Iboga but have researched enough: through reading this book and others, talking to other people, and learning how you learn. In doing this, you can remove your preconceptions, and go into the experience expecting nothing, with full trust in your facilitator.

I am trying to caution against what happened to me. I watched a few YouTube interviews, read a book about Iboga which I didn't understand at all, and read a few forum posts. I had not researched my facilitator enough, nor had anyone in my "regular life" recommended the facilitator. I didn't fully trust the facilitator or the community at the time of my initiation. As a result, this made my experience much harder than it needed to be. I struggled to surrender to the process and was clutching to the steering wheel of control too tightly. I ended up having a profoundly positive experience, but it was much more challenging than it needed to be.

If you know you have no intention to work with Iboga, please continue reading. I hope you enjoy the experiences, transformations, lessons, and learning about Iboga.

## A SEPARATE POINT ABOUT WORKING WITH IBOGA FOR EMERGENCY OR ADDICTION REASONS.

Discard the above advice.

IF YOU ARE WORKING WITH IBOGA FOR ADDICTION REASONS or are planning to work with Iboga at any time for addiction, be it in the near or distant future, **I PLEAD WITH YOU TO READ THE ADDICTION EXPERIENCES, AT LEAST. Read the introduction, start, summaries of advice, and the experiences of people who also worked with Iboga for addiction/emergency purposes.**

There are very common themes about preparation and safety advice. A few hours of reading may save you a lifetime of pain. Feel free to read the 'non-emergency purposes' section too, if you have time.

If you are working with Iboga for emergency purposes (addiction), then on the sum of things, it is better that you are fully educated and aware of the dangers of inadequate preparation.

# THE EXPERIENCES.

## PSYCHO-SPIRITUAL DEVELOPMENT AND NON-ADDICTION (NON-EMERGENCY)

**Tatayo...... Curiosity and Spiritual Growth.**

***Bio:*** Tatayo Obiang Nzondo MaMissoba, *24 when first initiated with Iboga, male, French-born but living in Gabon for 50+ years, 25-30 handfuls of Iboga root bark for first initiation. Motivated by curiosity, friendship, and seeing the happiness of people that had worked and lived with Iboga.*

**Author's Introduction:** An embodiment of the benevolent spirit of Iboga, Tatayo is described by one friend as a cartoon, a clown who may have taken acid. He is one of the funniest, kindest, most generous, and playful people I have ever met. Whilst I was in Gabon, one of his troubled young friends was arrested for drug possession and taken to jail. He visited her in jail frequently, taking food, water, cards, and coloring books to help her. Tatayo lives from the heart and helps countless people all the time.

Tatayo was chosen as the first interview to be presented as he initiated many of the participants in this book, including the author. He is considered to be the first westerner to be fully initiated into Iboga (specifically the lineage of Fang Bwiti) and in addition to this, he successfully completed a ten-year traditional training to initiate people into Iboga.

**Where did you first hear about Iboga?**

When I came to Gabon in 1971.

In 1976, in August in Gabon, I had a car breakdown with an old Land rover. I had to take a spare part to the other side of a river, 100 miles away. When the car blew out, I was lost in the dark, in the night, in the middle of nowhere. I saw a little light, off in the distance, and walked towards it. I met Papa Andre, the Bwiti Father who initiated me 3 years later. It was a very nice meeting, Papa Andre was my friend up to his death.

We were smoking weed at that time, I was a young man of 21, smoking weed with an old man of 45 years. It was very unusual for me as a French man! That led me to have an initiation 3 years later. People told me, "They are going to eat you! They are cannibals! Iboga is evil." All of this was shit. Psychedelics have always scared people. But now, that seems to be changing.

**What made you want to do Iboga?**

I took LSD in 1971, the same period I went to Gabon. From 1971-1975, I had a few experiences with very good-quality LSD. It was LSD before amphetamines, it was pure. I had very important experiences with LSD.

What was said about Iboga was scary, but I was friends with Papa Andre and his people. They were so nice, so brotherly, so generous, so funny, just really wonderful friends. It was not a call, but I wanted to do it. I wanted to understand what made these people so nice? What made them so happy? I decided to do it.

It took me 3 years, from the time I met them, to the time I ate Iboga. The confidence was there, but it needed time. Three years is a long time in your 20s. I ate Iboga in 1979, and I met them in 1976. I was 29 when I had Iboga for the first time.

**What was your life like before Iboga?**

I came to Gabon in 1971 for 2 weeks, that was 50 years ago. In 1973, we bought an old Land Rover, with two French friends who were teachers. We went back to France by car. It took one and a half years to get back to France! Hahaha! We had many breakdowns along the way. We had to stop in a lot of places, where we spent a lot of time, there were no spare parts. But it was a good time. That was the "hippy" era, there were a lot of travelers. We met a lot of people from all over the world, we enjoyed it.

Because of that trip, I understood African roads. A friend of my mother said, "You are familiar with African roads now, bring me a car from Europe to Gabon." I bought a truck from Europe back with me and began working for him. It was working for him that I had the car breakdown where I met Papa Andre and met the village where I would discover Iboga.

My life was a life of adventure. I invented myself into being a photographer, at that time it was easy to find a job in Gabon, it was a very simple and friendly country. I became a photographer and was taking photos in helicopters and planes.

**Were you happy in your life?**
Yes. It was the life of a young, crazy, heavy weed smoker. It was a fun time.

**What is your life like after Iboga?**
I had a really, really big experience with Iboga. A very intense and interesting experience.

After the ceremony, I was living in a wooden house by the beach. I was cared for by two brothers from the village, a French painter, a Gabonese French woman, who was in love with me. She was feeding me very well, every day. For three months I was like a buddha on the beach. Hahaha!

I thought of an idea. There were people coming to see me. Libreville was a small town then, everybody knew that I had an experience with Iboga. I think I was one of the first westerners (or outsiders) if not the first one to do it (a full initiation into Iboga/Bwiti). People were very interested and came to see me. I told my "keepers," if people want to see me, they have to pay 5 francs. That's a very small amount of money, similar to a penny. Most of the people said "This guy is crazy. Why should I pay to see him?" It ensured that a lot of people didn't disturb me.

We decided with this girl to go to France, to find money to make co-operatives in the villages. We were going to plant bananas, other crops and develop craft work. Her father was an advisor to the previous president. We wrote a letter to the president, proposing what we would do and he gave us his approval, but no money.

So, we went to France to find money to start these co-operatives. We spent $15,000 to earn $1,000. Hahahaha! It was crazy. We were not respected people, we hadn't been to university, we just had this letter from the president. That was in 1980. That was the year Bob Marley came to Gabon. The only year I wasn't here, I missed him! If I was in Gabon, I would have told him to eat Iboga.

I came back to Gabon, from 1981-1983 I was working. We brought 3 trucks from the Algerian war to Gabon. We crossed the desert with three trucks. When we reached Libreville, I was using one of them to sleep in and the others to buy fruit in the villages and sell it in the hotels. This lasted about 3 years.

Then I bought another truck and did long-line transport with trailers. Trailers on muddy roads are a very good experience. You have time to smoke, time to get patient. The roads were very bad, but it was a great adventure. I did that for 16 years. I built an enterprise of transport, eventually taking cars on boats. I never lost contact with my village that initiated me.

In 1994, I was initiated in the southern rites ritual, "Missoku." It was 15 years after my first initiation with the people from the north. I wanted to be initiated by people from the North and the South. The first experience was the strongest.

**How did you prepare? Would you prepare differently a second time?**
The first initiation, I prepared for three years. I was really well prepared.

The second initiation, one year before I did it, the mother of our children did her initiation with another village. She didn't want to belong to the same family as I, which was clever. She went to another family of Bwiti people. That's where I met the Missoku village. One year after she did it, I did it too.

The southern ritual was more masculine. It is traditionally for men. It's centered around masculine energy. It's very aesthetic, it's very pure, it's very beautiful. But the quality of the people is not always as good as the people from the north. In the sense, people from the northern rituals are more open-minded. In my opinion, they are less harsh, less strict, and more welcoming. They are all welcoming, but in the Missoku rituals, it is very competitive amongst the temples.

**What was your intention?**
The first time it was to understand how these people were so happy. I wanted to know "Why are they so happy?" I wanted to be as happy as they were.

The second one was to know a different ritual. The first experience was the strongest, of course.

**Were those intentions successful?**
Yes. It takes time. It took me years to find the right temperance or mindset. I was very much like many people. I was quite sectarian, I thought, "If you are not initiated, then you are stupid." Which, I don't think anymore. I have met many initiated, very stupid people and many non-initiated, very clever people. Hahaha! Initiation into Iboga and cleverness have nothing to do with each other.

**How did you consume Iboga? What did you take and where? What form? Total dose?**
It was not spoons then, it was little, little round handfuls from a plate. I think I took 25-35 handfuls. I took plenty. I did really strange things! Hahaha! Like you did too! (Tatayo initiated the author.)

If people want to learn more about my experience they can listen to a podcast interview I did (link can be found in the appendix).

**What would be your advice to people considering Iboga?**
My advice is the same advice Dimitri Mugianis gives to people, "One spoon of Iboga might be good fun, but a big quantity of Iboga is a very strong experience." It's not a game. It's not for fun. It's normally done for the improvement of yourself. It can take one second or thirty years to integrate and understand. We are all different and unique. The experience of one person can be very different from someone else.

The quantity of a flood dose can be very different. The strength of the experience can vary greatly between people. You have to know that. You have to be humble, you have to have perseverance, be dedicated, and be generous to yourself and the people around you.

My advice is to take the experience very seriously. It can be a life-changing experience, or it can be a very simple experience. It depends on what life you have had and what age you are.

**Has Iboga affected your spirituality?**
No. It has just reinforced it. I was very involved in Zen philosophy and Tibetan Buddhism before Iboga. I was introduced to all of that from LSD. I had an atheist school education, but LSD made me see that the "Love energy" is the creative energy. Iboga improved my spirituality. It gave me the link to my higher self, forever.

**Is there anything you wish you knew before doing Iboga about the process?**
Iboga consumption has to be done in an environment of trust. If you do not trust (the facilitator and community around you), then you will have a bad trip. That's why we have to lessen the shock between cultures (for westerners coming to Gabon for an initiation). Most people in Africa have very good intentions, when they see people coming to appreciate and join their culture (of Iboga) they enjoy it. But there are a lot of cultural differences that have to be managed, to help people trust the experience.

Sound is like a vehicle, with no sound you go nowhere, lost. Sound (music) provides the direction in a ceremony. Iboga without music, means you don't go somewhere deliberately. The music carries you to the bottom of our soul, or to the bottom of the universe. The music carries you to where you have to go, or where you are called to go.

The team around you is very important. They are singing, playing music, and caring for you, much like a team rowing a boat. They are rowing and working to take you to where you need to go.

**Did you have a profound vision and has this vision come true?**
Yes. I had profound visions. The vision I had was about the eternity of spirit, which as I'm not dead yet in this life, it's yet to be proven wrong. One of the main visions I had was about the eternity of spirit and the fact that I found a spirit in the ocean. The spirit was directly in front of me. Your future is in front of you. This vision came true.

I went to the ocean to wash my dog and I found god! Hahaha! This is what I mean, the fleas of the dog led me to the sea, where I went was just in front of my house. I found an ancient ceremonial mask in between me and the legs of the dog. Someone had given it as an offering to the water spirits, it's not a mask you would ever find in a shop. It's certainly one of the most powerful experiences in my life. What are the chances, it's incredible to happen.

**What did Iboga Teach or give you?**
Iboga taught me that we are as important as a grain of sand and as important as the sun. Hahahaha! We are nothing and everything at the same time.

Iboga made me a much better person. It made me more tolerant. It took time because I was young. When you are young and stupid it can take time for you to become happy, fun, and generous.

I think I was always generous, in the sense that I used to say, "We have been crucified in the past, so that's why we can't keep money in our hand!" Hahaha! I am more than generous. I can be a stupid man. I don't always give to the right person. Who is the right person? I don't know. I should have someone close to me to say, "No! Yes! No! Yes!" to each person that asks for something. For me, if I have something and you ask, I will give it to you. I can't help giving.

The mother of my children used to say, "When somebody has a problem, you only give money. Maybe the money will make the problem bigger. Instead of giving good advice, you just give money." She would tell me that I am wrong to give the person money, because often money makes the problem bigger.

If you have no doubt on what to do, then you are not very clever. Doubt helps you to be humble.

**Anything else you'd like to add?**
Iboga breaks your Ego, it makes you reconstruct it. But, Iboga is love, some people like to call it god, but I prefer the word love. Iboga is supposed to be love, depending on who does (facilitates) it.

Look at the history of wine. It started in the Mediterranean, in Greece and over 2,000-3,000 years it spread around the world. But Greece is bankrupt. It looks like Gabon will go the same way with Iboga. Charities (non for profits) like

Blessings of the Forest are important to ensure that the Gabonese people can have a good standard of life and protect Iboga.

Iboga is more than a simple plant, Iboga is love. Iboga is a treasure, some people in Gabon don't understand that they are sitting on a treasure, some do and some people are shitting on the treasure. Iboga is not a miracle cure, but it can allow you to be healed from some very deep issue, like childhood abuse, with time. It can help you to realize and eventually accept the trauma, and that's how Iboga heals. That's what I've seen.

Our future is in our hands. The Muslims pray looking at their hands, in French we say "domar" which means two hands, which means tomorrow. Our future is in our hands, depending on how we act. We make our own future.

Here in Gabon, we don't say "Shaman" we say "Nganga," which means the one who has been saved and can save others. The secret of Bwiti is the knowledge of plants and the power of plants.

**Author's note.**

Transporting and connecting people and goods has been the broad story of Tatayo's professional life. It seems synchronistic that his gift for connection has led him to serve as a guide to help transport people to a deeper understanding of their own lives and healing.

Tatayo lives in Libreville, Gabon, and has been based there for more than 35+ years. Tatayo founded the spiritual community of Ebando, which aids some of the most disadvantaged and troubled youth of Gabon. Ebando has initiated over 700 people into Iboga and Bwiti, including many local Gabonese people who Tatayo has helped reconnect with their culture and empower them by reminding them of their innate wisdom and joy.

**Thomas...... Mental Health and Exploration.**

***Bio:*** *Thomas Henning. 27 when first working with Iboga, 38 now. Identified as male at the time of working with Iboga, identifies as it/that/you now. Australian. Approximately 35 handfuls of Iboga root bark. Thomas is an artist, filmmaker, producer, and performer. He works mostly between live performance and theater, film, live visuals, and multidisciplinary immersive installations. He lives in South East Asia. Motivated by mental health (depression, anxiety) and exploration, "I wanted to work out what was wrong with me, really, and to also break reality."*

**Author's Introduction:** Thomas took a truly heroic, gigantic dose of Iboga under the guidance of Tatayo at Ebando in Gabon. Thomas's dose of Iboga was the largest discussed in this book. Although he had a profound and benevolent experience, without the guidance of a facilitator such as Tatayo or a prolonged period of preparation, a beneficial experience may be unlikely and is not advised.

Connected to the path by Tatayo, and uncannily similar in spirit, Thomas is an adventurous creative, who lives his life off the beaten path. Thomas' experience is a journey of self-exploration, authenticity, and approaching challenges with humor.

**Where did you first hear about Iboga?**

The first time I heard of Iboga was in the book *Fear and Loathing on the Campaign Trail*, in that really obscure claim from Hunter S. Thompson, that Ed Musky was taking Ibogaine. This was around when I was 20. It was a very obscure reference, I remember going off and looking it up.

Later, I was researching about altered states of consciousness in 2008. Some of the things I was reading about were DMT, Ayahuasca, etc. This was before everyone was going off to do Ayahuasca. I started reading about Iboga. In 2009 or so, I started to get very interested in Iboga and Bwiti. I then got into Terrence Mckenna and the stoned ape theory; looking at psychedelics being the road to human consciousness. I wanted to explore that.

Then I had my first paid job ever, I had never really earned much money at all for my work. Suddenly, I had 3-4 months of paid work, and I came out of it with some actual savings. A friend and I set out to travel by land to Jerusalem. It became this very weird pilgrimage, to have Christmas in Bethlehem. But a bunch of things went wrong, we couldn't travel from India into Pakistan, there were sanctions on Iran (I couldn't transfer money from an Australian bank to pay for an Iranian visa). It went messy. Anyway, we ended up flying to Turkey and traveling through Iraq, down through to Syria to Jordan. I met my girlfriend there, in Jordan. We then traveled through Israel and into Bethlehem, Palestine, for Christmas. We went for a second Christmas in Lalibela, Ethiopia. So, it was this weird, slow pilgrimage.

**How were you called to Iboga? Did you feel spiritually called to it?**
I don't know, maybe? I definitely found it really, really interesting, it was really fascinating. I was fixated on the idea of psychedelics and altered states and how that intertwined with human consciousness.

And also, I have a really odd brain.... Maybe you'd call it a mental illness? Just a very odd brain. I didn't know if this was because of trauma, or ADHD or something else. I wanted to poke around in there a little bit, see if I could open it up a little bit.

**What was your life like before Iboga?**
It was pretty similar. I was an artist, actor, a writer, and director in theater. I had made a lot of odd stuff. I had taken a fair bit of psychedelics and stuff like that already. I was pretty neurotic. I was very up and down. I was very uncertain, I would go from being confident to very self-loathing.

**What is your life like after Iboga?**
It's hard to quantify. Maybe things became less dour and less uncertain. I didn't notice any short-term extreme shifts, but long term there was definitely a change. Definitely. There was less self-loathing, more openness, less feeling fixed and trapped in a certain character.

At the moment, I feel more joyful day to day. Since January 2011 (when Thomas was in Gabon and working with Iboga) things have changed. In 2011, I became quite transient. Then from 2012 onwards I started living and working in foreign countries and that in itself brought about a lot of change.

The shadow turned out to not be so dark. I said bullshit like that on both sides of Iboga. Hahaha!

**How did you prepare? Would you prepare differently a second time?**
I prepared by going to temples across the world; from Buddhist temples in Thailand, Hindu temples in India, mosques in Syria and Turkey, Coptic churches in Jordan, Christmas in Bethlehem, new years in Ramallah, second Christmas in Lalibela. It was like a long, weird pilgrimage to get to Gabon. It was pretty "Eat, pray, love," but with a lot of alcohol, idiocy, and a video camera. I also washed in the Ganges. Gabon was the final point.

Next time I would be less high-minded, I would go a bit slower. I would have tried to see more of Gabon, more of the natural landscape, more of the villages. Iboga is a root, when I took it, it was physically talking to me. It was a root, part of a tree! That link to a natural spirit, that was moving around inside my body and could shift things, depending on what I would show it. Walking around, spending more time around the trees and the people, would be good! Most of Gabon is registered as a nature sanctuary. I would be interested to learn more about where it comes from and spend more time there. Also, I'd like to learn more about the daily life of the people that created the culture around Iboga.

When I was there, I went to the final initiation for a woman, who was a Polish visual artist. She was being initiated by someone very high up in the Bwiti practice. There were lots of interesting people there. The way everyone was dressed was in this fascinating, turn of the 18th century, French clothing. The women were in hooped dresses, with bodices. There were dervishes, everyone's faces were painted up. It was a really strange combination of "Courtly 18th century France" and traditional Fang (a particular sect of Bwiti, in Gabon and surrounding areas). It was this strange collision of cultures that had happened centuries ago and somehow that created this unique belief system.

It would be good to be there for longer and see more of Gabon. When I was there, things had just kicked off in Tunisia (2011). There were big protests in

Gabon at the time. The opposition leader tried to overthrow the government on my birthday. It was a strange time.

**What precautions did you take to make sure it was a safe experience?**
As much as I could. I spent a lot of time talking to Tatayo (the facilitator) in the lead up and he seemed quite kind. He put me in touch with some other references. I researched other different routes I could go down, the person who gave me the best communication and clearest information was Tatayo. He seemed to be easiest to understand and trust. I had also seen him on TV. Most of the documentation around the time featured Tatayo, so I figured he had a reputation to uphold. He has had a lot of people come through already, he seemed very solid.

Back then, there wasn't much information available. People hadn't started looking at it much as a treatment for getting people off drugs. People knew about it, but it wasn't as popular. There was a lot of fear surrounding it as well. Lots of people were saying that if it goes wrong, your heart will stop, you'll die. I spent a fair bit of time reading what I could.

**What was your intention?**
If there was something fucked up inside of me, I wanted to know what it was. I wanted to be able to stabilize whatever was off inside myself. With all of the spiritual build-up, I guess it was a spiritual pilgrimage. I must have put some mystical bullshit on it as well. I guess I was looking for some holy revelation too. Ultimately, it was exploring the hidden parts of myself and understanding myself more.

It definitely worked towards this. It was very odd. There was nothing but imagination. I didn't open up any traumas until much later (2020). And that wasn't with Iboga. At the time, it was generally pretty delightful. I could see how my mind moved, and how my mind could create things for myself. It seeded things for a few years later, where I went a bit nuts with that. My entire world became imaginary in 2015.

It made everything very simple. It made the amount of influence my imagination has on my reality very clear. How my "self" is quite absent from most things.

**How did you consume Iboga? What did you take and where? What form? Total dose?**

Shaved root bark that had been pounded into a powder. I would have a handful at a time and then some water to wash it down. I think all up it was 34 handfuls (spoonfuls) of Iboga. (Author: I estimate this to be about 120-140 grams!) Then they took me on a walk because I was just having a nice time and wanted to sit by the fire and smoke cigarettes. The facilitators were like "WHAT ARE YOU DOING?! HOW!??!" So we went for a quick little walk, and then bubbles and lights started coming out of everything. We came back to the space and I had a little more Iboga and then vomited.

Some people might only take 1-2 handfuls and then vomit.

**Why did you decide to do it this way? Why did you pick this center?**

At the time, some people were doing it in sessions in Mexico and people were doing it in houses in Holland. I thought that all these sounded far more unsafe and dubious to me, than a system that has existed for thousands of years. People who have been dealing with this plant for thousands of years would probably know more about how to look after a person through all of this.

I didn't want to be put in a room with pre-recorded whale sounds on headphones, in some kind of sterilized hospital. I didn't want a medical thing. I thought it would be far healthier, beneficial, and interesting to follow a traditional practice. I wanted to learn and see the belief system. I think it should be taken as a sacrament and not a medication.

**What would be your advice to people considering Iboga?**

Why are you doing it? That's the most important thing. It's not a novelty thing. You don't do it just for a laugh or for the experience. You should be willing to die... If you have to. If you are doing it to look at parts of yourself that really need to be examined, or opened up, then it's good.

The guy who I was initiated with, he didn't think about what he was going into. He was very arrogant, he just wanted to get off cocaine. He didn't give a shit about the world. He was just concerned and involved with himself. He didn't prepare and didn't follow the instructions from the community. He just vomited the entire time. He wanted to do it again, and he took a greater amount of root bark and vomited a lot. He then had it inserted into his anus, to get the required dose. I can't remember who said it but they said, "He eats with his arse and shits with his mouth." Later on in the night he tried to throw himself into the fire. He didn't take it seriously, he only thought about what it could do for him, not what it would do to him. I think the machismo of this guy's own ego was something that terrified him. He was trying to be someone that he was frightened of. And he couldn't acknowledge that he wasn't. When he finally had the capacity to look at that, I think it fucked him up.

If you are okay with having your psyche ripped open, you'll probably be okay. If you're not sure about it, don't do it.

**What are your thoughts on micro-dosing? Did you micro-dose after a flood dose for integration?**

Before actually... On the first night that I was in Gabon and staying with Tatayo, there was a ceremony going on. In ceremonies, it is a sacrament, people take 1-2 handfuls (spoonfuls). It's just a heightened state, you are more alert and connected. It was great. It's not a tree you ever want to see die out. I don't think we ever want to get to the point where people are taking a spoon or a "bump" of it before work. Sure, for that person it might make their life better, but it would probably kill the tree.

In that ceremony, it was great. Everything was a bit bent, you are very alert and connected. People sing all night and it is very powerful. As a small amount, it was a fun and beautiful experience. We want a huge amount of it to exist before people start using it widely. If Iboga was treated like Ayahuasca, it would be really bad. I don't think it (Iboga) can handle it (mass consumption). It's a really excellent medicine, people are desperately seeking this medicine. It's a fantastic tool for healing and helping the mind. It's a while away from being able to be used frequently or widely.

**Is there anything you wish you knew before doing Iboga about the process?**
No. Not really. I think my younger self needed the learning experience. I would have wanted to know more about Bwiti and the belief system behind Iboga.

**Would you do Iboga again?**
Yes, for sure. Absolutely. I would need a clear goal, a reason, a good visa into Gabon and money. I would also want 2-3 months to travel around Gabon and learn more about it. It would be good to take it, understanding the context around it. I'm not interested in it as a western medicine. It can definitely treat western problems. But in the western context of a sterile, isolated room, which is all about the individual, I don't see that involving learning anything. If there's a context, where I could be useful (art and film), then I would love to do it.

It was one of the most beautiful spiritual practices I have ever seen. It was amazing.

**Was there a memorable moment or particularly profound vision you had? Has it come true?**
I met God. God was an inflatable idea. We were standing inside a giant triangle and we walked, arm in arm, outside of the triangle, into itself. The whole world was coming out of God's navel. It was an absence of substance that was connected to everything. It was about me, linked to this conceptual object, which is actually all things. Rendering it into a person was entirely imaginary. Sure, I could link arms with it, but it was actually everything.

Also, I found there was no problem with me. There was no fear. I could talk to this root bark and it would ask "Okay, what have you got in here?" It would swim around in my imagination. Depending on whatever I put out, it would guide the way. I would show it fear, so it would give me something to be afraid of. It was a conversation about how "The echo of my imagination creates my world." It wasn't about my memory, it was about everything being caused by my imaginary outlook, my subconscious reaction. Depending on what I felt or what reaction I gave, is how it responded. There is always a choice. There was then a lack of fear. I realized that there is no problem with anything. For me it was just this delightful time, talking with this conscious plant, that was inside my head!

I was expecting a huge psychic purge, and it didn't come. I was a little disappointed. I felt that I hadn't organized myself well enough to dig into what's going on in my psyche. But maybe I didn't actually need to see any of that. My brain or Iboga could have said, "You don't have to be shown that, it's not relevant." All that stuff you're worrying about, that's not necessary. It gave me what I needed, not what I wanted. I feel like I was looking for something that was really serious and really dark. But I didn't find that. Instead it said, "You're doing the right thing generally, but your imagination is ruining/creating this." It really showed me how much my imagination was impacting my reality.

**Has Iboga affected your spirituality?**

Absolutely. I was already interested in psychedelics as a spiritual medium. That sense of being able to unlock parts of myself pretty easily was great.

Other experiences afterwards were much more extreme. Iboga helped me to differentiate between the bullshit between wanting spiritual connection, and then manufacturing it for yourself and where that can go. The long journey I had in getting there, and then the Iboga ceremony itself being a pretty bananas good time. There's a fictitious idea of spiritual self-satisfaction that goes from tree wizards through to Gweneth Paltrow, this morally high grounded, fake, crap. It helped me see through all that. I realized that all I was really doing was tripping balls, next to the ocean in Gabon. That's all it was, and there's nothing bad about that. You're not learning to speak the language of the birds. You're just high and in the jungle. The pageantry is necessary for the psyche. The theater of it, makes reality altered. When you are in a hallucinatory state, the theater is real, and the performance of being a person is visibly an act. And, I guess it's about getting comfortable with things being both real and not real simultaneously. It helped me be comfortable with navigating the road where things are both real and not real. Whether we dress things with a spiritual or scientific facade, it's all down to perception and imagination.

I was also trying to believe in some singular truth and it fucked that up. It was like, "You're never going to find that, just give up on that." It helped to break that up a bit.

**Anything else you'd like to add**

It's been exactly 10 years since I was in Gabon. I would have been in Gabon this time exactly 10 years ago. I would really like to go back. Gabon was really magical, in this completely odd way. You presume the magic is in front of you and you're walking towards it. For example: the Pope has the magic touch, let's walk towards the Vatican. Actually, all the power is coming from some strange cupboard in the corner. The thing that made it so spectacular was the comedy of it all. Everything had this touch of humor and banality, whilst this grand magical process was going on. It was a bizarre ride.

**Author's note.**

This interview illustrates that Iboga is both a customized healing program, perfectly tailored to each person and their intention, and also an amplifier of the unique qualities of each participant. A humorous, open-minded, adventurous person (like Thomas) is more likely to have a humorous and wild type of experience. It is almost as if Iboga is a liberator of consciousness, unshackling us from our chains to become freer versions of ourselves.

Thomas is a professional artist and his write-up of his experience in Gabon was one of the most entertaining and insightful documents on Iboga that I have read. Although Iboga is not something to be done for enjoyment, Thomas reveled in and captured the joy and humor that can surround ceremony with it. If you are considering working with Iboga, have worked with Iboga, or are thinking of working with Tatayo, Thomas may be able to send you his personal reflection.

## Chrissy…… Healing Depression and an Eating Disorder.

***Bio:*** *Chrissy Sandwen. 28 when working with Iboga, 32 now. Woman, uses she/they. USA. Consumed Iboga root bark, 2 x flood doses. Motivated by mental health (healing depression and an eating disorder).*

**Author's Introduction:** Chrissy is a psychedelic integration coach and co-leader of "The East Bay Psychedelic Healing Collective," which brings together events for the psychedelic community in Oakland, California. Chrissy was chosen as one of the earlier interviews, as hers is an unconventional success story with Iboga. Although she didn't heal what she initially set out to heal with her Iboga experience, it opened the door for her healing to come later. The clarity and perspective she gained from working with Iboga helped her to connect to a greater purpose. Her inspired path of continued healing has taught her the tough lessons she needed and enabled her to take on a role of supporting others as an integration coach.

**Where did you first hear about Iboga?**

When I heard about Iboga, I was living in Costa Rica. At the time, I was really depressed and kind of in a desperate situation. I was working, supporting child health and education projects, in the middle of nowhere. I heard about Iboga through an Ayahuasca center that was near where I was living. It was in the context of it being this really intense thing and I thought "Who in their right mind would do that!?" Can you imagine 36 hours of hallucinations?" But the seed was planted. I filed it away under, "Wow, people are really up to some wild things these days….." And, hilariously, about six months later I went and did it myself. I guess I'm a little wilder than I thought!

I used some psychedelics in my youth, but not very consciously. I certainly knew there was something there, in terms of expanding beyond ordinary states of consciousness being important and potentially healing. I had this inkling that I wanted to continue that kind of expansion but didn't really know much about it.

**Did you feel called to Iboga?**

I would say "yes." A big reason I decided to work with Iboga was that I was dealing with an eating disorder and depression.

The decision was twofold. One aspect being this beautiful desire to do anything for myself. I knew I didn't want to live like I was anymore. I knew I had a light, I just had to bring into the world somehow.

And then on the other hand there was also the egoic mindset that was constantly screaming "Fix me! Anything to fix me! And FAST!"

Certainly, there was a deeper spiritual component and I believe there was a spiritual call.

I have to recognize that I was in a very human experience of suffering. I think that was also a huge motivating factor. I don't think I would have chosen to do something that sounds so intense that not many people in my world had done, if I wasn't deeply desperate.

I had a spiritual call but also there was the human side of, "Wow, Fuck! Anything other than this!"

**What was your life like before Iboga?**

Before encountering plant medicines, I always felt like a deeply lonely person. I moved around a lot. I lived in several different countries in my 20s. I was that “fun friend” who came from god knows where with all the stories. Yet, I could be in a room full of people, and I felt so utterly alone. I really felt this pervasive sense of meaninglessness. I felt a lack of connection to life itself. That's not to say it was all bad. I had ups and downs certainly but there was always this inner voice that was whispering, "There is more to life than this."

Like a lot of people who find Iboga and other plant medicines, I think I was born pretty sensitive in a world that doesn't always treat sensitive people very well. It isn't designed for sensitive people. I had a rough go of it, I felt like the black sheep. It started in my family and then that became the blueprint for the rest of my relationships. I was always into things no one else was into. I was more spiritual than others and an internal processor. That wasn't valued.

I became a social worker and was really invested in helping others. That felt like a deep calling. Certainly, Ayahuasca was my first big opening before Iboga. I don't think I would have gone to Iboga had I not experienced Ayahuasca before. Once I had the Ayahuasca experience, I had a spiritual awakening. Things got worse before they got better. I didn't have any support. I didn't have anyone to integrate with. No one I knew had done Ayahuasca. I came into Iboga with that. It felt like there was something unfinished. It felt like there was a last piece to click. I still was dealing with disordered eating. I know what the "more" is that I had been missing, but I was looking for a deeper "click."

**What is your life like after Iboga?**

The Iboga experience itself was evocative. It's hard to say the main differences because during this time I was doing a lot of work. This includes things like: working on conscious sexuality, getting a coach, there are a lot of other things.

On the "healing journey" I hesitate to say, "It was just the Iboga that did all this." I think that's why integration support is so important. It can be an incredible opening experience, but every day can be a ceremony. The tedious, unsexy work of showing up every day as who I want to be feels like where so many of the changes have actually come from.

In terms of what Iboga opened for me, absolutely a connection to my true self. I'm doing work now (as a psychedelic integration coach) that I feel really deeply impacts people. When I was a social worker, which is wonderful work, but for me personally I felt like I was just moving people around on a chess board that I hadn't designed. I deeply wondered if I was even helping. Now, I feel really connected to a deep understanding of what spiritual awakening is. Because of this, I can support others to get in touch with their own innate healing intelligence. That brings me a lot of meaning.

Before, when people talked about loving themselves completely I thought "C'mon, like completely? Really?... I dunno." And now, I can honestly say I love who I am. I think that has given me the foundation and stability to love others well and find a community that is more aligned. It has opened so much for me. There are a million other things too.

The biggest two takeaways are that sense of meaning and self-love. I used to have this image that I was a leaf blowing in the wind. I rarely had a partner, I had no best friend. I was just doing my own thing and I felt untethered and questioned "What was my purpose?" Now I feel my purpose is to live this life. To live it! To experience duality, to experience suffering, joy, awkwardness, farts, sex and all the weird things. That feels enough for me. As well as supporting other people through that for themselves.

The self-love piece sounds like a hallmark card and kind of trite, but it changed my life. In my experience, having that love, it changes everything about the way I show up and the way I live my life. I really wouldn't have gotten to this point without the opening that was provided by doing work with Iboga and Ayahuasca.

**Do you feel smarter or wiser?**

A lot of my clients feel that way. I don't know if I feel sharper, but in a way, I feel more connected to my inner wisdom. I have better discernment of my thought patterns, which may be related to the Iboga experience. I can go "meta" on myself. I do meditation, which is supportive. I feel that I believe my thoughts a lot less and I am able to have better discernment on what is my inner wisdom and what is the ego or sub personalities, that have experienced traumas and see the world in a certain view. I think I have a much better idea of what "the true self talking" sounds like. That does feel like a certain type of intelligence and wisdom.

**How did you prepare? Would you prepare differently a second time?**

I did two ceremonies with "Awaken your soul". In terms of preparation, I certainly would have prepared differently. Again, I didn't know many people who had worked with Iboga before. I didn't know how important integration and preparation was. I stuck to the recommended diets and the regular practicalities. I journaled.

I came in with the approach, "I just want to get rid of my eating disorder." That was my intention.

What I would do differently and what I encourage people to do, is to start more "upstream" of the problem. My "problem" wasn't actually the eating disorder – that was just the coping mechanism.

In my experience with clients, it's vital to contemplate and work around the unexpressed emotions, unprocessed traumas, etc., that created the need for parts of them to compensate through coping mechanisms. It's also really important to create a plan on how to support oneself after the experience. Who are you going to share with? How do you create a net of other work around this intention and not expect the medicine to solve it?

My approach was almost like, "Okay, Miracle, I'm ready!" I think what I would do differently is talking to someone, professionally, and planning for the period afterwards. A coach or a therapist. Someone who has had this experience, either Iboga, Ayahuasca or whatever experience that you are going to have is super helpful.

**What precautions did you take to make sure it was a safe experience?**
I'm relatively healthy. At the time I was 29. I was in good health. They didn't request a liver panel, but they did an EKG when I was there. At the first ceremony they had medical staff present. They did a mental health screening. It felt sufficient for my personal background. They weren't working with people who are trying to get off opiates or more complex cases. Certainly, I would encourage anyone who is going to do it, to do it in a supervised container.

I think having the medical staff present on the first night is very important, because there are some cardiac risks. You want to be sure that you are safe. It worries me when I hear about people buying Iboga off the internet and doing it on their own. In my experience, I needed that support afterwards.

**What was your intention?**
My intention was to get rid of my eating disorder. Then I think the secondary intention was spiritual connection. At that point, I already had a spiritual awakening experience. I believed in the beauty of these plant teachers. I was also coming with this beautiful desire to connect more to that spiritual space, but primarily I was trying to heal my eating disorder.

**How did you consume Iboga? What did you take and where? What form? Total dose?**
There were 6 of us in the ceremony at "Awaken your soul." On the first night of the ceremony, we all took the same amount of bark (Iboga wood bark shavings). They observe you and see how you go. I couldn't stomach more bark, so then they gave me the alkaloid (Total Alkaloid extract).

The second night I did more than anyone else there. I did a tremendous amount. This may be why Amber (the founder of Awaken your soul) remembers me. I felt like I wasn't breaking through. I wasn't having any visions, so I just kept taking more. This was a big lesson. Certainly, that was more of a herculean pursuit. That was both root bark and TA.

**Why did you decide to do it this way? Why did you pick this center?**
I was living in Costa Rica at the time, it seemed like it had the best reviews and it wasn't super far from where I lived. It was mostly based on my own research.

**What would be your advice to people considering Iboga?**
Each night is so different. I had this amazing, cosmic, going around the universe with an Alien experience on the first night. On the second night, I kept taking more and more Iboga and all I was doing was shaking and feeling incredibly ill. I was the sickest I had ever been. I was so sick and had no visions. Afterwards, I couldn't sleep for 5 days. It was a really intense experience.

You never want to scare people or give people false expectations, I think people need to hold it all lightly and realize that your experience is going to be exactly what you need. That goes for each night. The texture, feel and emotions of each night were so different. I got my ass beat on the second night, and the first night was one of the most beautiful experiences I've had.

Integration is the most important thing. Especially with something like Iboga, where it is opening you up a tremendous amount. I talk to people who go to an Ayahuasca retreat or an Iboga retreat and then go back to work on Monday in downtown Manhattan. They can be completely lost. It can be so scary. We are divorced from the traditional way these medicines are used.

The original keepers of Iboga usually use the medicine in close-knit communities. There is community support and understanding. There is a slower style of life. I think it is up to us, as consumers of plant medicine, to recognize that the medicine is a huge part of it, but the integration is vital. In my experience, it helps get so much more out of it and keep you accountable to the new way of life you want to create.

Also, I think with Iboga it's important to know who your provider is. Do a lot of research on them, ask for testimonials and ask to talk to people directly. If they do pre-integration calls (or talks), go to those. It's up to our own discernment and intuition, but definitely do your research! Especially with something like Iboga.

**What are your thoughts on micro-dosing? Did you micro-dose after a flood dose for integration?**

I did micro-dose. The person who gave me the medicine is a different Iboga provider, who gives people Iboga on her property. I got the micro-doses from her. I'm quite sensitive and I think they were a little too strong for me. I was starting to get little tracers. It wasn't under the limit before I started getting a bit too out there. So I stopped. I know many people who have great results with micro-dosing, especially if they are working on addiction issues.

**Is there anything you wish you knew before doing Iboga about the process?**

The answer might be no. I think either way it's better that I didn't know how sick I would feel. I didn't know how intense it would be on my body. Everyone's experience is so different but I was just not prepared. My body was recovering for weeks afterwards I would say. Especially because I couldn't sleep for several days after the last flood.

**Would you do Iboga again?**

I remain open to working with it in Gabon. I'm not sure when or if that will be. For me right now, the barrier is mostly the expense. It would certainly have to feel like a deep calling, since it was so intense for me.

**Was there a memorable moment or particularly profound vision you had? Has it come true?**

The first night the most profound vision was being with a little alien who brought me out into the universe. I went to this part of the universe that felt like the "stepford wives." There was no duality. Everything was perfect and everyone was happy. I looked around and it was joy, joy, joy! I hung out there for a while with this alien and it felt like the deepest recognition of "Oh, I needed to suffer. I needed to feel that deep grief. That pain. In order to truly appreciate the joy and to experience gratitude." I am really happy that I'm human and don't have this perfect existence. I have this capacity to feel everything. After that, I bounced in and out of different people's lives all over the universe for the rest of the night. It felt like this really interesting embodied way of experiencing that deep beauty of the bittersweet nature of human life. Things are so precious and so hard. It felt very much like a spiritual teaching that has stayed in my bones.

It made me see previous pain and suffering in a different way. To learn to appreciate it. It's a lesson that keeps unfolding. I'm human and I think of course part of our conditioning is this addiction to pleasure and aversion to pain. It feels like something that continues to resonate, that there can also be joy in the sorrow. There is an underlying layer of grace and peace, even when challenging things are happening in my life.

**What did Iboga Teach or give you?**

I think it got me in touch with my own inner warrior energy. Just to do something so physical. I am imagining gladiators or high-level athletes. People that don't blink an eye about going into the thick of things.

I was a tiny, blond social worker. And yet, I made it through that. It felt like a warrior initiation. I cannot believe I made it through my second night. It was the most miserable I had been in my life and then I didn't sleep for 5 days. It was just "Holy fuck!" The way I showed up for myself and the way I could embody that energy of "I don't care what is happening, it's for my healing. I am not giving up!" That was a powerful teaching.

Through taking so much Iboga, I got a little warning on my own egoic "fix me!"-type fast-food mentality around healing. I assumed that more was better. That is a really important teaching too. I see people who do plant medicine ceremonies very regularly. Or people, whenever something is happening in their life think “Okay, I'm just going to take a bag of mushrooms" I think a big part of the lesson I have is that everyone is different. But, we need to recognize when our own ego patterns hide themselves into the plant medicine space and into this disempowerment of thinking that there is something outside of us that can completely fix us. When so much is really a window into our own power. I think that was a good but difficult lesson. I do not recommend to anyone that they take three times as much Iboga as everyone else in the room!

Maybe I had to learn that lesson to teach other people it. I feel that a beautiful part of this work is sharing the teachings with other people. I hope that with the people I support I can save them from making some of the mistakes that I made. But of course we learn from our mistakes, and I don't regret it at all, especially now that I'm not sick and shivering.

The lessons that any of us get from this work are passed onto others.

**Do you feel that you resolved your intention? Did it resolve your eating disorder?**

It’s an interesting one. That's why I hesitated with this interview, because I didn't know what your angle would be. Because, it didn't resolve my eating disorder. Now, I have resolved it. Iboga opened up so much that it provided me the path to do it, potentially. I think it's really important for people to know that. Because sometimes those experiences happen where it flips a switch. We know of those, YouTube has those. But I think more often, what I encounter is that it is still a lot of work. It is not a magic pill. I think it's good to see all of those experiences as super valid. I think afterwards I thought "What the fuck is wrong with me? Am I beyond healing? I did the most intense psychoactive substance I know of and I still have this issue!" Again, if I had more integration support, I would have had more context. But I really went in and I feel that the facilitators said, “We have seen all of these amazing things.” And of course, they have. But for me it was a longer road than just one ceremony. I am so grateful, because I think that is another lesson I can pass onto other people.

The lesson is: it's not just the plant medicine. There are so many other ways we can expand our consciousness or work on ourselves. Who knows if I would be here without Iboga? I don't think I would be, in terms of recovery. But it wasn't like flipping a switch for me.

**Did it teach you anything specific about it? Or did it open a door for later on?**

Definitely more opening of a door. I had a period of recovery afterwards and then I slipped back. The way someone would with other kinds of addictions. There are relapses and that can be part of the growth. It did provide that opening. If I did have more integration, support and a plan then perhaps it could have been sustained. That was valuable for getting my training wheels. I was going back to the same patterns around the same people. I think that is what made it more challenging.

**Why should people work with a therapist, coach or counselor around Iboga?**

Having someone who is traveling that path with you is really valuable. When I coach clients, it's not a hierarchical relationship. I'm sharing my experience with them. I think one of the biggest benefits people get is having someone in their corner who knows what is going on with them, who is really caring. I think sometimes we forget what a special relationship that is, to have someone who is just there for you. Who is completely invested in your journey.

I think the second thing is having someone who can hold the greater picture. When we are so in our own lives, it can be hard to get out of it and see the bigger picture. I thought I was always going to have this eating disorder, I was always going to have this whole mind jungle. What I try to provide for people is the ability to get out of their day to day life, tinker with what's going on with them and also to remind them that, "This too shall pass." There is so much we can do, there are so many resources. Providing that ability to get out of our own mind story and see the bigger picture is really valuable.

Working with a coach, you get the most out of your plant medicine experience. I see a lot of people that are constantly engaged with plant medicines and not getting that far, they are still struggling. Whereas when people are really well prepared for it and integrate their experience really well, through having support before and after, they can move more quickly. It's hard to compare because everyone is so different, but a well-supported person who does one ceremony could have more impact than someone who does 10 ceremonies without support.

I think what Iboga can really teach us is so profound. But I don't think it's a medicine you want to do a lot of times! To really respect the medicine so much that you really prepare for it and do everything you can to really receive the messages. To do everything you can afterwards, to do something in this human life to make my and the community's life better. It's nice to think we can do this ourselves but it's much easier to work with someone who is also on the path and can help shine the light. They can remind you, "Hey, you're doing the right thing. Keep going!"

I think people often have negative experiences with therapy in the past or they feel like I am spending all my money on the medicine, I don't have the cash to do the support work as well. There are certainly barriers, but there are a lot of great people out there doing the work. I hear again and again that it is worth it. I have never had someone come to me and say "Man, I wish I didn't do integration (coaching and post ceremony support)!" Hahaha!

It's important to have someone remind you that you are doing the work. It's easy to give up on the hero's journey. You are going to see many dragons. If you really are your own hero, it's really about having the courage to continue anyway. That courage often comes from having the right support.

**Anything else you'd like to add?**

I knew people that went to music festivals not that long after Iboga or people that really had to go straight back to their day-to-day life. Sometimes it is just the reality. However, with Iboga it can be such an undertaking for your body, mind, spirit, and emotions. I think if people are considering doing it, they should also consider allowing some spaciousness and time in their life if they can, in addition to the support of working with someone (professionally, afterwards). Get ready to slow down. Some of us can't and that's okay. But if you can, try to!

After Iboga, I was very open for a few months. That's a beautiful time to gain a lot of insight, especially in the first two weeks. I remember trying to go back to work and thinking "This shit is pointless. I'm an alien being. I am consciousness itself! What am I doing here!?" Hahaha! It felt so ridiculous. I know sometimes we have to pretend and do the earth thing. I always encourage people, if they can, to take some time off after. Nourish your body. Not all of us can take that much time off. If you are thinking of undertaking Iboga, try to do it, the best you can.

Going back to the paperwork and minutiae of everyday life can be so tough and feel so pointless. Recognize that working with Iboga is a real spiritual initiation. Treat it that way. It's not just this experience to be had or to consume. It's a look into your very soul and being. That means some slowing down.

**Author's Note:**

There was a softness and lack of judgment that came through in Chrissy's interview, almost as if someone who had spent their life trying to impress others had truly accepted and impressed herself and no longer had much to prove. The big themes in Chrissy's experience were letting go of expectations, taking a long-term approach, and the importance of continual integration.

Working with Iboga, as with any healing modality, is not necessarily about consuming a big dose, seeking more or cramming it all in. But, as Chrissy shared, true healing and transformation occur with the "tedious, unsexy work of showing up every day." By getting to really understand ourselves, our coping mechanisms, and how they pop up over time, we can connect to the lessons within our challenges. Then, we can begin opening ourselves to the idea that healing really is possible.

While the healing potential of Iboga is immense, we must be really willing to put in the work ourselves, meeting the medicine or spirit more than halfway. Though the work may be unsexy, our lives become very sexy when we can open our hearts and become honest with ourselves.

Chrissy is an integration expert and coach, for those interested in working with her professionally, her details can be found in the appendix section.

**David...... Healing Chronic Stress Forming Depression.**

***Bio:*** *David Nassim, 35 when first working with Iboga, 43 now. Male. British. 5-8 spoons of Iboga root bark. David is a consultant, teacher, and writer on the health energetics of Chinese medicine, Taiji, and Nei Gong. David is also Co-director of the organization "Blessings of the Forest CIC" based in the UK, focused on helping the Indigenous Gabonese secure sustainability and reciprocity for Iboga and its forest bio-culture, within the UN international mandates (Nagoya protocol). David was motivated to work with Iboga to heal "chronic stress forming depression."*

**Author's Introduction:** As one of the founders of Blessings of the Forest, David is passionate about the sustainability of Iboga and ensuring that the totality of the plant and culture survives and is protected. In this interview, he makes a prescient point about the re-introduction of plant medicines into the western health paradigm. Psychonauts and psychedelic plant medicine enthusiasts can be seen using medicines like Ayahuasca, San Pedro, Mushrooms, and Iboga prolifically, placing enormous strain on their longevity. Westerners tend to use psychedelics like a hammer, smashing at any condition to see what happens. Hopefully, as time goes on, and as the infatuation and obsession with psychedelics tapers, the holistic and traditional knowledge of plants, herbs, and natural medicines can be specifically and precisely used to treat individual ailments. Until then, supporting Blessings of the Forest and being conscious about our medicine usage is a great step!

**Where did you first hear about Iboga?**

The first time was whilst I was going through a very deep, depressive period in my life. Basically, I was trying to go towards plant medicines as a key to wanting to find some resolution for the depression. It was mainly in circles where there was Ayahuasca.

I made one connection to another and it was towards a man who was working with Iboga. I went towards that. I didn't know anything about it. I was told that if you want to go on to the next step, this is the plant. I had a single experience, one experience over 2 days. What I understand now as being a "cure dosage," it was quite a strong dose but not an initiative-level dose. It completely broke the fundamental structure of my personality. It was such a huge experience that within one day I let go of the work I was doing and the place I was living. I changed everything in one day. It was a very strong process.

That drew me towards immediately wanting to work towards initiation. Maybe 3-4 months after that first experience, I did an initiation. That was with Tatayo in Gabon. It was conducted by Tatayo and his initiating father Papa Andre. They both did the ceremony together. It was quite a powerful thing!

However, nothing has been as powerful as that first experience. There is nothing that touches the experience I had the first time. With less wood, less medicine. The first experience was by far the strongest. Even with other Ngangas, in the middle of the forest, nothing touches that first time.

I later understood that it is quite normal for the first time one meets the plant to be the strongest for many people. This is why in the traditions, the first experience is held with such esteem. I think it took me at least 6 years to really engage and understand that first experience. To really integrate that and deal with it.

From my perspective, there are people in the west who are taking way too much medicine and doing this in a very "regular" way. They are bypassing experiences of the medicine. I think Iboga is something that really needs deep integration.

**How were you called to Iboga?**

People talk about a calling to the medicine. From my perspective, I couldn't say what that is, being "called" to Iboga. A lot of the time it sounds like a person is just drawn towards Iboga instinctively. I don't believe in spiritual callings or reasons behind instinct, so for me, it was just a process of moving towards things that might help me, that I knew nothing about. Iboga was at that time another plant for me to investigate.

What I knew I wanted, was a strong experience. I knew that whatever I was carrying, the pain and difficulty I was carrying, was so complex and so deep that it needed an experience that was extremely strong. That's the only kind of feeling or calling that I knew. I got the sense that the medicines and other modalities I had worked with couldn't touch certain depths.

One of the reasons for that, was the origin of the hidden problem that I uncovered with Iboga was something that had been going on throughout my life, from a very young age. When something is "pre-verbal," this is what Iboga is particularly brilliant at. Even if something is preverbal or cannot be verbally expressed or engaged with, Iboga can get underneath that and bring out kinaesthetic or energetic qualities of the problem that was there. It allows for something that is impossible to be described to be recognized, understood and explored. It's especially important when you are dealing with trauma. For me, this was something the other medicines couldn't touch. It was deeper.

**Interviewer: It's almost like it is shifting and sorting through your subconscious. It is finding things that are deep and hidden. You might not be able to find them yourself. In a way it precisely targets them, unlocks them and then you can integrate it. Does that resonate for you?**

I think that's true but what I would say is that it "hits the blind spot." The main thing is even if someone has a complete understanding of their psychological state or personality, there is always going to be a gap or spot you can't find. You can't feel it or see it because you are inside your character. What this can do is it brings the blindside into focus. When you can see it, the identity or personality around the problem can start to crumble. There is a chink in the armor. Iboga goes into that chink and explodes it from the inside.

Iboga is very often associated with "light" within the darkness. It is the quality of yang energy. Iboga or light penetrates a place that is quite hidden. Anything that is hidden is brought up. There are no shadows in the midday sun. It does it from the darkest and most inner depths. You get this trojan horse that comes into the body and looks at everything from the inside. It lights up the inside. These images come to me when I think about the wood.

**What was your life like before Iboga?**

Well, my entire life was focused around one major issue. My father had multiple sclerosis from two years before I was born. That drew me into the process of being a carer from a very young age. It basically involved me being in the process of being a carer on and on, throughout my life.

Moving into my adult life, I started to engage with Chinese medicine and moved into being a practitioner. I continued this trait of being a carer into my adult life. It was all about care, treatment and medicine. That was the whole of my life. What Iboga showed me was that it was my obsession and a kind of addiction. I was a person who was addicted to being in that role. I was always in that role.

All of my depression and discomfort came from being attached to being somebody who was in that role and was unable to see outside that. It is an extremely difficult thing to have an addiction for that long. Usually, when people have addictive patterns it is something that could be associated with a substance. This isn't a substance, because it is a pattern of behavior. It is so old that it was like a structure of my personality.

When I took the wood (Iboga), it broke that. That was absolutely devastating, it took away everything it possibly could. Including about 80% of the people in my life, my relationship to them was me being a healer. As I broke away from that pattern, a lot of people who were in my life, I couldn't engage with them anymore. It was a huge process to go through.

**What is your life like after Iboga?**

There are a few points that I'd like to make. First of all, Iboga's nature is already part of the natural function of the particular human working with it. It stimulates that which is already your natural state. It fundamentally unblocks the flow of natural energy, which is a form of detoxification, but at a very deep level, much deeper than the other medicine I've come across. Through this it shows you what you think is "yourself." It's like a mirror, a very clear mirror. It shows you what you think you are. What I got from that is that I was able to recognize the pattern of "myself" more clearly and understand it in a bigger sense.

My life before, was that "I was a carer." My life after, I stopped "being a carer." It's not that I have stopped engaging with the medicine. I still work with people in consultation, both in Chinese medicine and Tai chi & Qigong. These are my passions. What happened is I am no longer in a "carer" role. I am not addicted to being in that role, where I was trying to help people who were in very difficult situations or were just codependent and did not want to help themselves but wanted a hero to save them. l fit that role and joined into that codependency. They loved me to be in that role of savior and so I was praised for it and felt needed. But, I knew that I couldn't live up to people's demands and that every step was eating at my life force. I was also trying to heal and save my father through engaging with other people. That identity and role has broken and continues to die away.

What I generally say to people when they engage with Iboga and when they engage with plants is don't expect there to be this enormous change that is external. It is the very small change of the rudder of your life, which is happening on the inside. It is a little change but it adds up. If you take a jumbo jet, and you take that change, if you turn the rudder about 2 degrees and then you go down to the end of the runway, that is quite a big distance by the time you get to lift off. When you get these little nudges, at a very deep level, it can be an enormous change. It takes time to manifest that. Anything that makes an enormous shift and the person totally changes in a few days, commonly the original issues come back again. They don't just suddenly drop out, the issues come back again. But you are looking at the issues from a slightly different perspective, you are looking at them and no longer believing that they are absolutes anymore.

The thing that breaks the mold is actually the aftermath, 3 months, 6 months, a year, 6 years after. Then you can really see where Iboga has taken you.

**How did you prepare? Would you prepare differently a second time?**
I followed the diet I was told to follow. One important thing that happened, unintentionally, was that I had no conversations and no engagement with anybody or any stories associated with taking the wood (Iboga). I think that was brilliant. That was absolutely perfect. I didn't engage with any thoughts or ideas about what the experience was like. Personally, I think that is a very important thing.

Also, I know with initiative experiences as the general principle, this is one of the reasons they don't very often allow people to have these conversations about this. In a lot of the different tribal groups in Gabon, a lot of the things you may see or experience are not talked about. They are very often kept to yourself.

In the west, there is a huge focus on sharing, but in fact there is a lot to be said for not sharing things too early. Sometimes, it takes a lot of time for things to be clear with Iboga and if other people's ideas are mixed into what you experience, it can lead to massive confusion and a lengthening of the process. Especially, if the person or people speaking to you have no sense of humility but want to involve themselves.

A lot of the time in the west there is the approach of not liking the mystery of something. Of wanting to understand it. Looking at the mystery and wanting to explain it. Actually, having something as a mystery is very useful to close the mind down, so you can feel what is going on.

**Interviewer: I agree. And I think that ideally that is what we would always have, is total mystery going into it. But people read online, they will watch YouTube videos, read blogs and forum posts etc. This book is aimed at correcting those preconceptions and opening people back up to the unknown or magic. Ideally, I agree you should go into this as a blank slate, but I don't know how realistic that is for everyone?**

David: I get it. And I totally understand where you're coming from. But it's all the little things that make this experience powerful. The most important is to come in with that unknown sense. It's important to meet the medicine from that place.

**Interviewer: There has to be a sacrifice, a bite. There has to be a reverence, a deep respect for the medicine. And there has to be surrender. Those three things automatically come if you haven't heard anything about it and you go in with a blank slate. If you have heard a little bit about it, you probably need to be told "Surrender, reverence, sacrifice."**

David: That resonates with me. It's like meeting the reaper. There's an ominous quality and you have no idea about what that energy or quality is. It's mysterious and immediately you have this feeling of meeting something.

**What precautions did you take to make sure it was a safe experience?**
Myself, none, because I just trusted the people I was being connected with, I was quite naive to the whole thing and I was desperate. I had a little on the phone interview with the person who was giving this to me. The level of engagement, the full understanding of the medicine and its safety were not something that I believe the facilitators had full awareness of. They weren't trained in the tradition but did offer what they had gleaned and the person holding the ceremony had a quality of deep dedication and care to what he was doing. They knew that it was dangerous and you had to be careful with certain people and refuse others. I was considered a safer person to work with. Now I know what this medicine is, I would have a much more cautious approach in hindsight but I will always be grateful to the people and process.

The depth of psychological effect of the medicine, the quality of the requirements for engagement after the experience and what is necessary to ensure someone is psychologically well and held after the process, didn't exist. It still doesn't exist, in general. It doesn't exist where people are giving the medicine in the west. To fully do this, takes a village. Generally, people from western context don't understand community-village culture now, they understand individualism that might purport to be community minded but isn't.

**What was your intention?**
I didn't spend a long time really going into that intention, or really trying to direct things. Once again, I think that it's the openness you need. It's not so much prayer or intention, I think from my perspective those things are about an alignment to what is really happening, what is really happening inside your body. If you can be very honest, that is the most important thing. So, I believe in engaging with full honesty when working with this medicine. That's it.

I was very open and just trying to be honest about what I felt.

**How did you consume Iboga? What did you take and where? What form? Total dose?**

The first time I had a symbolic spoon of wood bark, so that I could taste it and recognize what it felt like. After that I was given capsules. All in all, I think I would have had 5-7 full spoons. That's maybe around 30-50 grams of Iboga.

For subsequent ceremonies, where I have been taking Iboga, have been initiative experiences. With Tatayo I had probably twice that amount (10-14 spoons total). With Adumangana, associated with the Babongo pygmies, much less. He doesn't initiate on very much wood.

**Why did you decide to do it this way? Why did you pick this center?**

The first experience was a referral through a friend I was connected to. The second one was my initiation to Bwiti which was a referral, as the person who had given me the wood was connected to Tatayo. I went to see Tatayo in Gabon and was initiated by him because of that original connection. The last one, with Adumangana, was because I wanted to have a connection to the Babongo. It was a very specific desire to connect to that because I found that I didn't connect to the other types of traditions associated with Iboga the same way.

**What would be your advice to people considering Iboga?**

Make sure that the person that is offering you the medicine is genuine. You need to feel that they are genuine and focused on you. They should be focused on you and not on them. They should be someone who is connected to the tradition in the sense that they have got training from the place where the medicine originally comes from. They should have a link to that tradition. The facilitator should be steady and settled in their life. In their own personal life, they should be settled and steady. Ideally, they should have a family, children, and a place that they are working from.

**What are your thoughts on micro-dosing? Did you micro-dose after a flood dose for integration?**

I did that, because I was told that was a good idea, "You take some more of the medicine afterwards to integrate." But, I actually completely disagree with that practice. I don't believe in micro-dosing after you do a flood dose. I think that the flood dose is enough to give you the information and the understanding that you need. You have to integrate from that. If you need to do micro-dosing, that should be a separate occasion where you have a particular time where you are deliberately micro-dosing.

Micro-dosing is extremely powerful in its own right. It is another useful and much safer way to engage with the medicine. I don't think about micro-dosing for integration. I think you should take the medicine and then integrate from it (in a ceremonial dose). Micro-dosing is another different form of engaging with it.

Side note, I think that people can way over take this medicine and that there are some people that are taking this medicine, where they shouldn't be taking it. It is inappropriate for them to be taking it. People say, "You can't be addicted to psychotropic medicine. You can't get addicted to Iboga." You can be! For sure! I have seen it happen many times. Especially in the psychotropic world, there are lots and lots of people that are using these medicines to avoid issues. You can do that with Iboga too.

**Is there anything you wish you knew before doing Iboga about the process?**
It's good not to know anything. In a lot of ways, the less you know the better.

What I would like to stress is how important it is to have a careful space holder for the process. I was lucky in my initial engagement. It was luck more than judgment.

**Would you do Iboga again?**
I haven't taken that medicine for years now. I would say I would take that medicine again, if it was necessary for me to take it. If I felt a point where it was really necessary for me, I would engage with it again, yes.

But, remembering that in the forest the names of the plants are, "The one that resolves burns," "The one that heals bruises," and "The one that does this and that." Iboga is, "The one that cures or saves." If you really need to be saved, that's the time to take Iboga. I hope that I don't need it.

**Interviewer: It is a blessing not to need it. To be in a place where you don't need to be saved.**

**David**: That's it, exactly. I've heard them say in Gabon, "Ngangas don't need wood!" If you really have touched something and it shows you yourself, and you are comfortable in yourself, how much Iboga do you need? I am not saying that I am by the way, I'm just saying I look at it with total reverence. If I need it, I will use it.

**Has Iboga affected your spirituality?**

From my perspective, I don't see where spirituality begins and non-spirituality ends. For me, at some level there is a sense that in natural reality there is absolute neutrality of what we call good/bad, right/wrong, including war, horror or love, joy and all the rest of it. It is all one, it's all nothing being everything. For me, Iboga doesn't show me something that I didn't sense about that. It can allow me to recognize that oneness is there, even if I am in the way of it. But, you don't need Iboga for that, for me Iboga can break down some of the tension that means that the daylight is let in more easily.

It can show something a little bit beyond the self-identity.

That question is a little bit difficult for me, because I don't have a sense that there is anything called "spirituality."

**Was there a memorable moment or particularly profound vision you had? Has it come true?**

The first time I had the wood, I had visions with my eyes open and closed. I had visions, but the visions weren't the thing that broke me. They didn't change me considerably. It was much more auditory and kinaesthetic "visions" that were very powerful. It was a combination of those kinds of things that affected me and really changed things for me. No one specific thing did it.

**What did Iboga Teach or give you?**

It showed me out of myself. It showed me outside of the picture I have of myself, so that I could realize that the self, the identity was not as real as I thought it was.

**Did it free you from your old self? Or show you a pathway to a higher self?**
No it didn't. It showed me something. I have to walk on now with that change of perception. After it broke the image I had of myself, it had made its mark. I had to take that realization with me and walk through the rest of my life. The image of myself was not as real as I thought it was. I didn't need to take the idea of who I thought I was so seriously. That brought me relief and of course a huge process of change, but some deep relief. I didn't have to be that person.

**What was the image or idea it broke you with? Do you feel comfortable sharing it?**
It was a very difficult process, Iboga was using the voice of a very aggressive teacher I'd had, he was constantly berating me for about 5-6 hours. It was about being totally wrong and bad and that my thinking was all messed up and that nothing I would do would ever amount to anything. It was this process that needed to come in to get me to the point of giving up, of stopping this steam-train energy of being a carer, I had to see that my whole life's work was, in a way, a side-line or coming to a dead end or exhaustion, that along the journey of focusing on being a carer for my father, primarily, and then thousands of others after that, I had completely bypassed my instinctual senses. This was so awful to release it still gives me shudders now, but if I hadn't have understood it, I may never have been able to see outside the track I was in.

**Anything else you'd like to add?**
The world is changing and things are changing with medicine. I am definitely not a traditionalist. I don't have a religious perspective on this at all. What I do begin to have is an understanding of the energetics of this plant, it is very complex. The forest people of Gabon have an understanding of the energetics of this plant, which go back to an ancient time in history. I think it is very important for people to engage with that understanding of the energetics of Iboga because it is about long term understanding of the safe use of Iboga. By energetics, I mean the properties of the medicine, so just like any other herb, you know who it is suitable for and why and when and it's not a one-size-fits-all approach. It is fundamentally about understanding the ways the medicine can change the mind. Both to your benefit and detriment.

When you have an herb in traditional medicine, from understanding the energetics you know who will most benefit from this medicine and who will least benefit and why.

Iboga does have some quality of adaptogenic nature but it is not good for everybody. In traditional herbal medicine, in all the countries that have a medical system where a psychotropic plant is the figurehead or considered a very important medicine, you have 800 or so other medicines which are supporting that. A traditional herbalist will take a look at you, understand what is going on with you and prescribe the appropriate plant. It is not always Iboga.

What is going on in the west, is we are taking Ayahuasca or Iboga and we are using it like a sledgehammer, to break every nut. It's the only tool in the tool box. It is like having a big hammer and hitting everything with it. It is a total distortion of traditional medicine. It is basically a kind of mad and arrogant way of looking at it.

For me, Iboga is brain surgery. It should be considered like brain surgery. When you have a brain surgeon in the room you want to have a very good assistant to that brain surgeon, that is taking care of that situation. There are a lot of people around, who have experience and understanding. If you have that in your mind, as a basic analysis of what is going on, then you have a respect for why somebody would train for 10 years within the tradition in order to offer it. That is why someone who is protecting the tradition, someone like Yann Guignon, has a 10-year protocol on protecting the rites. There are a lot of things that are a clash of cultures, where people cannot see the ancient, traditional approach to something as intricate and in depth and as energetic subtleties, as going to learn brain surgery in the west. Until there is an understanding of that and a realization that there can be cultural equality, we are going to have a little difficulty.

**Interviewer: The image that comes to mind is the contrast between a great brain surgeon and a lobotomist. On one hand, people that have been training for 10 years and understand the deep energetics, herbalism and traditions and on the other we have lobotomists. They both will change**

**your life, they are both doing surgery on your head, which one do you want to work with?**

**David:** The key thing is a difference between someone who is centered on the patient, and someone who is centered on themselves. This is the big difference in how to verify which practitioner to go to. Someone who is really focused on the people taking the medicine, they will want to go to some lengths to try to figure out how to really engage with Iboga. The self-centered type people are publicists and want to show that they can do it, that they can play the Mungongo or Ngombi harp or be the "medicine giver" or Shaman. That they are worthy of being the center of attention. That's the big difference.

This is not something that is localized in western society only, there are lots of people multiculturally including Gabon who are focused on being at this central position, it happens everywhere. There is nothing right or wrong with it fundamentally, it is just something else for the plant to overcome in the process, which it usually does. However, a plant that gives power is only truly a blessing in the hands of the meek or gentle and a poison that accentuates the ego and corrupts absolutely in the hands of the harsh or arrogant.

**Author's Note:**

David's experience is all about cultivating humility, surrender, and letting go. When someone is ready to transform their life, Iboga can be a powerful tool for illuminating the blind spots and helping to fan the flames of transformation. Oftentimes, in the healing journey, there can be a shattering of the identity– blindspots are torched, old beliefs and programs are burnt off. If this – miracle – happens, it is up to us to continue the process over a long period of time, and repeatedly rebuild our identities as we evolve through the many chapters of our lives. When we allow ourselves to trust in the process of nature and remember our place in it, we are able to live in the greatest service and inner peace.

**Vivek...... Self-realization.**

***Bio:*** *Vivek. 29 the first time working with Iboga, 33 a second time to volunteer and learn, 37 now. 8 spoons of shaved Iboga root bark. Male. Born in India, grew up in the USA. Vivek's intention was "Self-realization."*

**Author's Introduction:** Vivek became a personal friend of mine when I was initiated in 2018, and it has been wonderful to watch his journey. He continues to learn and study with many different masters, joyfully sharing his lessons with others. During the author's Iboga experience, Vivek offered brotherly care in the toughest times. He taught me what it really means to support someone without judgment or agenda as they face themselves and go through their own process.

**Where did you first hear about Iboga?**

I first read about Iboga in early 2012, when I was researching the spiritual potency of sacred plants like Ayahuasca and their ability to awaken one's kundalini energy. There was very little written online about Iboga back then, but somehow, I came across a BBC documentary of Bruce Parry called 'Going Tribal', where he participates in an intense Iboga initiation with the Babongo pygmies in Gabon. Despite Bruce's extreme near-death experience, my curiosity grew until I discovered and contacted the driver in the documentary, Tatayo, a French-Gabonese man who co-founded Ebando, the place where I had my Bwiti initiation in December 2014.

**How were you called to Iboga?**

My inner calling has unfolded through following various streams of curiosity and gathering clues, from chance encounters, that I often realize when I look back and try to connect the dots. However, there's no one cause I can pinpoint, instead, it's been a slow culmination and convergence of destiny with certain inflection points along the way that seem to catapult me into new chapters of self-exploration.

One of those major inflection points was my first Ayahuasca journey in 2013 at Blue Morpho in the Amazon. After that journey, my so-called spiritual path started unfolding in a profoundly accelerated way, with the next major calling just six months later to Mount Kailash and Lake Mansarovar at 15,000 feet in

Tibet to meet Sadhguru, a yogi and mystic. The pilgrimage to Mount Kailash, which is considered the abode of Shiva, brought a new level of balanced stillness to my breath. Over the next several months, my longing to know 'WHO AM I?' intensified to a point where nothing else truly mattered in my life, my thirst to go deeper and deeper grew profoundly, and the following year in late 2014, I booked my trip to Gabon.

**What was your life like before Iboga?**

Outwardly successful but still seeking something inwardly. I was in my late 20s, single, living alone, driving a BMW coupe, working for a Fortune 500 company in a corporate sales role, pursuing my MBA part-time, partying with friends, and enjoying time with family. On the surface, I was content with the so-called material fruits of life, yet there was something within me that was looking for more, not worldly but spiritually. I realized I was in a rare phase of my life where I had three precious things together: time, money, and freedom. I decided to maximize those three things by focusing on the fourth treasure, 'Wisdom through the pursuit of spiritual experiences'.

**What is your life like after Iboga?**

Iboga for me was the Dawn of Stillness. The journey left me with such a profound revelation that there was no room for doubt or misinterpretation of its brutal directness. The truth was naked, and its immediate impact on my being was incredibly silencing. There was a new kind of effortless and dispassionate equanimity towards everything. It was a deep and natural neutrality that was free of any contrived ideology about compassion or non-judgment. Before Iboga, I would notice the gaps between my thoughts, after Iboga, I noticed my thoughts between the gaps. What was in the background was now in the foreground. The whole thing had flipped, as if I was the sky looking down at the small fluffy clouds, versus being on Earth and looking up at the clouds, only to get entangled in trying to anxiously forecast the weather. The expansiveness of being the witnessing sky was the dawn of stillness.

**How did you prepare? Would you prepare differently a second time?**

Deep introspection and honest self-reflection helped prepare the soil for Iboga to be planted in my life. Iboga for me was not the first chapter in my journey of self-exploration. Since I was living on my own, I started experimenting with self-guided meditation practice every night, chanting various mantras, lighting incense, and exploring different crystals. I was reading, listening, contemplating, and digesting teachings from different masters and Indian mystics such as: Osho, Jiddu Krishnamurti, Ramana Maharishi, Nisargadatta Mahajraj, Alan Watts, and more. I was also deeply influenced by the talks of Terence McKenna and his insights into Shamanism. In a way, I was a student without a teacher, just following my own childlike curiosity, wanting to know about the deeper mysteries of life, nature of consciousness, and my place in the vastness of the cosmos. All these things allowed me to explore more freely and naturally in order to become clear and focused about my intent leading up to my calling for Iboga.

In terms of preparing differently, I would say just like with Ayahuasca, you don't choose the plant, the plant chooses you when it's right for you, meaning your inner climate has to be receptive and ripe for transformation, otherwise there's no smooth symbiosis. So, in that sense, there is no second time with Iboga, whenever it happens for you, know that it's a major turning point in the trajectory of your consciousness, and so it should be approached with utmost respect, a pure heart, an open mind, and deep trust in the 'youniverse'. Iboga can be a tremendous catalyst if and when you're truly ready to face yourself, otherwise, it can be a rude awakening if you simply go into it without proper self-assessment.

**What precautions did you take to make sure it was a safe experience?**
**Laughing** there are no precautions to consider when you're compelled to take a leap of faith into the unknown in search of the truth. Luckily, I had no pre-existing health issues, drug dependencies nor was I on any kind of medications that would've counteracted or been a concern. I was young and in good overall health so I was not worried. But as a recommendation, it's probably a good idea to enhance your cardiac health, establish deep breathing practices, and boost physical endurance so you're strong enough to handle a flood dose of Iboga and the night-long ceremony.

**What was your intention?**
**SELF-REALIZATION** I remember typing those two words in my questionnaire form in a very large 24-point font size, bold and all caps. On the

day of the ceremony, Tatayo, who was my initiator at Ebando, had printed out the form to read through the questionnaire, and as he came across what was written for my intention, he looked at it, paused with a soft smile, and said, "Well, that is very clear."

**How did you consume Iboga? What did you take and where? What form? Total dose?**

I was given 8 spoons of shaved root bark of Iboga by Tatayo at Ebando in Gabon as part of a traditional Bwiti Initiation ceremony.

**Why did you decide to do it this way? Why did you pick this center?**

I was called to Gabon for the same reasons I was called to the Amazon to do Ayahuasca. The plant is native to that place and the spiritual traditions that are tied to it are also deeply rooted to that part of the world. It's the motherland for that plant, for that medicine, and I wanted to ensure I had the deepest, most authentic experience possible. Since, I was fortunate enough to have the time, money and freedom to do it in Gabon, it just felt right.

**What would be your advice to people considering Iboga?**

If you're casually considering Iboga, it's not for you. Plain and simple. Unless and until every cell in your being is compelled and ready to leap into the unknown to discover the truth of "WHO AM I?" it's probably premature and foolish to consider it. It's not for everyone. If you're not ready to be a "jungle warrior" inside and out, then do not consider it. If you're not ready to go through the total mind-shattering chaos of a category level 5 hurricane in order to radically transform yourself, then do not consider it. That is my recommendation for those "considering" Iboga in the Bwiti tradition in Gabon.

For those whose intention is to recover from a drug addiction or dependency I imagine it is a very different story, as it's more about Ibogaine's neuro-resetting properties rather than the true heart spirit of Iboga. I would still say that it is important to assess and reassess the level of openness and receptivity you have before going into it. Make sure you do a thorough analysis of yourself before you go into it, otherwise the plant will do it for you. And things will come up that you had no idea about. The integration process can be extremely tough if you're not ready for it. Imagine what it would be like if Neo takes the red pill in the Matrix over and over again 8 times.

**What are your thoughts on micro-dosing? Did you micro-dose after a flood dose for integration?**

I didn't micro-dose right away after my initiation because I didn't feel right taking it back with me from Gabon, nor did I sense a need at the time. As I said before, Iboga was the dawn of stillness. After the dawn, the light of stillness continued to grow within me. I think if your intention is clear enough and pure enough, you can get what you are looking for with one flood dose ceremony. At the same time, I do think micro-dosing could be beneficial to help Iboga spread and deepen its roots into your being more harmoniously. About a year after my ceremony, I did come across a little supply of wood (Iboga) through a friend, and I would take a tiny pinch before my meditation at night. I'm not sure why I took it, but intuitively it felt like the right thing to do. My point is if you're meant to micro-dose you'll have some of it come to you when it's needed through synchronicity. I would add that listening to some ceremonial Bwiti music is also a powerful way to activate and integrate the medicine without having to take the wood, it depends on how sensitive and receptive you are after your ceremony.

**Is there anything you wish you knew before doing Iboga about the process?**

Iboga is a root so it continues to grow and deepen even after the initiation. It's all about how you come across Iboga and your intention going into it. It's a very different path to go into it trying to heal something versus wanting to go beyond the sense of personhood, that's a completely different path. If you just want to stay in the realm of identity of "this is my mind, this is my body, this is my story, these are my memories, this my person" that process can take lifetimes. If you are willing to suspend that identity and say "Show me the truth, at any cost" then it unfolds more directly and immediately. There are really only two choices: You can be an ambitious and anxious raccoon sorting through the garbage of the world looking for crumbs of joy, and talking about what you found yesterday, what you hope to find tomorrow, and comparing it with your raccoon friends. Or you can be a truth-seeking pyro racoon that torches the entire dumpster of identity on fire, and discovers what remains true. That choice is bound to be made sooner or later, so choose wisely before your racoon body deteriorates.

**Would you do Iboga again?**
Iboga is typically taken only once in Gabon as a flood dose initiation, if done right there shouldn't be a need to do it again and again. At this point, there's no intention of trying to strap on the Iboga rocket and blast off only to journey back to nowhere.

**Was there a memorable moment or particularly profound vision you had? Has it come true?**
**Silence** You've asked a question that is so deep that I can't answer with words. I can only answer that through falling into silence, and silence beyond the word silence or the attempt to be silent.

**Has Iboga affected your spirituality?**
I think of spirituality as a file inside a folder. The folder being the person, so if "Vivek" is the folder and you open the folder then Vivek spirituality is still just another file inside of it. Iboga can sort the files inside the folder or it can dismantle that folder completely. So how has Iboga affected my spirituality? It has dismantled the folder. There is no separation. All barriers and lines defining spirituality have been erased. It's no longer a file, but rather the all-pervading space that was always there.

**Anything else you'd like to add**
"Seek TRUTH and LOVE will follow." The American Dream is about the pursuit of happiness, ironically that's all it is for most people, a blind perpetual pursuit of happiness, without a fruitful realization of it. Rare are those who pursue the truth of who they are. And even if you seek love, it has so many masks, so many conditions, so many false promises. All those masks are ephemeral and transient. What you really want is THAT which is eternal and everlasting, THAT which transcends time and space, and once you touch THAT within you, love flows to you and from you.

**Author's Note.**

Vivek's experience illustrates the power of setting and maintaining a very clear intention. His intention was one of "self-realization" and more broadly "self-discovery." His story offers a reminder that it is not necessary to take a huge dose to experience profound insight and transformation. His experience highlights the importance of surrendering and trusting in the process. A clear intention and dedication ultimately determine the healing potential far more than the size of the dose.

In a previous conversation, Vivek remarked that 2020 was the year of the raccoon, which meant sorting through our own garbage, focusing on cleanliness, and ultimately discarding things that are no longer of service to us. There are many similarities to working with Iboga and the spirit of the "pyro raccoon." It invites us to sort through our own garbage and ultimately can present the opportunity to burn off a lot of what doesn't nourish or aid us. Fittingly, a common discovery myth about Iboga is that a small rodent or marsupial had eaten Iboga, and was then consumed by a human, thereby uncovering the magic of Iboga.

**Tricia...... Psycho-spiritual Growth and Healing an Eating Disorder.**
***Bio:*** *Tricia Eastman. Female. Mestiza (South American Indigenous and European mix). Iboga root bark. Tricia is a medicine woman, author, and Indigenous and plant medicine preservation advocate. Tricia was motivated by psycho-spiritual growth and healing an eating disorder.*

**Author's Introduction:** Tricia's experience is a remarkable one and a testament to the power of facing oneself earnestly, doing the work, and taking a longer-term approach to healing. Her journey is nothing short of miraculous and can be attributed to her tenacity, courage, and trust. Miracles happen, but often over a long period of time with continued work and dedication.

**Where did you first hear about Iboga?**
The first time I heard about Iboga was through a close friend of mine who was working at a plant medicine retreat center in Costa Rica. My curiosity was immediately piqued. I started to research and really try to understand the medicine. Some of the statistics raised alarms for me initially.

I read an article that one in 300 people died whilst taking this medicine, but then later learned that these numbers were not only skewed, but were a sample of people who were specifically taking Ibogaine for opiate detox and were not in ideal health beforehand.

Another friend of mine joined Crossroads Ibogaine, piloting their initial 'psychospiritual' program. This was a non-addiction program spread across a weekend. It involved a night with Ibogaine at a psychospiritual dosage, much lower than the dose used for opiate detox, followed by a day of rest.

I've noticed that when something is significant, it often surfaces in multiple areas of life. I was open and alert to these signs.

Later, I met Dr. Martin Polanco at an event. He was the owner of the clinic in Mexico where my friend worked. I shared my struggles with eating disorders that I had since I was ten. I asked him about the potential of Ibogaine to address food addiction.

His reply was cautious yet open, "I'm not sure, but perhaps we could explore this further together." I ran into Dr. Palanco again, this time with my partner Dr. Joseph Barsuglia at a festival. Martin asked me if I wanted to come to the clinic, as we had discussed in our last conversation.

At that point, I had experienced enough signs that I was convinced it was time for me to meet Iboga.

**Did you feel spiritually called to Iboga, or how were you called to Iboga?**
About a year before delving deeper into Iboga, I had the opportunity to micro-dose with it. However, I tread carefully in sharing this, as I don't wish to promote micro-dosing given the sustainability concerns. Iboga is limited in supply, and it should be preserved for initiations and therapeutic healings until we have a sustainable source.

Around the same time, a close friend began exploring Iboga in more clandestine circles. This coincided with, or perhaps preceded, the release of James Fadiman's "The Psychedelic Explorer's Guide," which popularized the term "micro-dosing." Back then, it wasn't a widely discussed topic.

It was my first time micro-dosing so she instructed me, "Consider connecting with the plant's spirit to determine if it aligns with you." She provided a few capsules, instructing me to consume one on an empty stomach in the morning, and then to wait an hour before eating. She emphasized not taking all the capsules at once, warning of its potency.

I took it on my own, in the morning. I said a prayer with an intention to connect with the spirit of Iboga. After about 90 minutes I felt this sense of presence, I felt rooted. I could feel that this was medicine for me. I felt a sense of trust that it could support me with the struggles that I was experiencing at that time in my life.

**Were you already working with other plant medicines at this stage, or was Iboga the first one you worked with?**
In my college years, I worked at a counter-culture bookstore that housed an array of psychedelic classics from TiHKAL and PiHKAL to writings by Ram Dass and

Timothy Leary. This immersion into the counterculture scene also led to participation in raves, experimenting with substances like ecstasy and Psilocybin.

After a decade-long hiatus, I reconnected with MDMA, a decision driven by an undercurrent of what I'd later recognize as an existential crisis. Around this time, "Plant Spirit Medicine" by Pam Montgomery found its way into my hands. Though the book discussed various plants, not exclusively psychedelics, I was drawn into its chapters on Ayahuasca.

Rekindling my bond with psychedelics ushered in a profound mystical journey, akin to a kundalini awakening. This transformative experience made me realize the need for drastic changes in my life. I left behind the familiar - my marriage, my home, and embarked on a soul-searching journey, reminiscent of the narrative in 'Eat, Pray, Love'. My travels spanned across Europe and Argentina, eventually drawing me to Venice Beach, California. Here, after considerable introspection, I finally found my community at Café Gratitude, a vegan café just up the street from the beach filled with people who were interested in consciousness and plant medicine. And it was there, of all places I could have imagined, that I first received an invitation to work with Ayahuasca.

Marking my entry into the world of shamanic plant medicine, I continued my path walking the traditional ways, which brought me back to my own ancestral roots in Mexico. Strangely, this would be the place where I would first meet the spirit of Iboga. I guess I had to return to my roots to meet the root.

**What was your life like before Iboga? What was your life emotionally like before Iboga?**

I've long grappled with profound ancestral trauma. Drawing insights from Gabor Maté, it's evident that many mental health conditions, ranging from ADHD to Schizophrenia, are deeply rooted in trauma. This inheritance of ancestral pain manifested in me as intense anxiety and ADHD. In my younger days, I displayed mild traits synonymous with the autism spectrum and incredible sensitivity. My journey became one of self-healing, predominantly through alternative therapies and holistic practices. The landscape of my inner world was characterized by a restless mind, pervasive anxiety, a lack of presence, and an internal cacophony. I was relentlessly self-critical and perfectionistic.

**What is your life like after Iboga?**

My interactions with Iboga were transformative, each instance propelling me forward dramatically. My initial experience was at Crossroads, involving a non-initiation session with Ibogaine. Subsequently, I undertook two more sessions in Costa Rica with the full plant, Iboga. I undertook four initiations in the Fang tradition, which were all under Atome Ribenga's family lineage and one initiation in the Ngonde Missoko tradition. Each had profound impacts, which I'll detail.

As I embarked on my journey of facing my trauma, akin to the hero's adventure, my physical well-being seemed to unravel. My attempt at facing my eating disorders led to a weight gain of 50 lbs, despite maintaining a healthy vegan diet. Concurrently, my skin suffered severe acne outbreaks. These distressing changes induced even more tremendous stress, leading to adrenal fatigue. My financial stability crumbled; from owning multiple properties to living on friends' couches. It was almost as if I poked a bees' nest and was being dive bombed by the entire hive at once. It was hard to find my way out, so I am grateful that each of the journeys helped me unlock a piece and led me back to genuine holistic wealth.

After my first session, I felt empowered and experienced newfound clarity and presence. Subsequent sessions led to physical improvements: I lost weight after each session, even regaining the health of my kidneys. By my fourth session, coinciding with my initiation into the Fang tradition of Bwiti, I reclaimed my financial stability and manifested a stable home of my own. By the end of all the sessions, not only had my skin cleared up, but I also felt whole again. Not to mention how greatly prepared I was for the future storms ahead.

This six-year period of my life had many deaths and rebirths. These years also marked the strengthening of my relationship with my partner. Our bond deepened, weathering the storms of individual and collective challenges. The continuous work with Iboga fortified our relationship, helping it endure and blossom to this day.

**It sounds like those plant medicines helped unlock a lot of chaos and trauma, and that's why those things bubbled up, you gained weight, and then your skin broke out, and your life kind of went out of order?**
Yes, and it feels that a word of caution is in order. I delved into this journey with the impetuousness of a novice. For those bearing the weight of trauma, gentleness and patience with oneself are crucial. It's essential not to disturb too much, too soon. Fortunately, I possessed the resilience to navigate through the challenges. I do feel that Iboga was like a life preserver in the chaos that I created.

**It sounds like Iboga gradually helped you get your life in order, like piece-by-piece, step-by-step it kind of helped you filter down. Is that accurate?**
Yes, exactly.

**How did you prepare, and would you prepare differently for subsequent times?**
At Crossroads, they had a commendable approach, particularly geared towards opiate detox. Their program introduced specific breathing techniques, many sourced from the 'HeartMath Institute', emphasizing heart coherence. These techniques were invaluable in my preparation.

Although I hadn't consciously geared it as a prelude to Iboga, my experience with Vipassana meditations—intensive 10-day silent retreats—was instrumental. If there was any preparation that truly grounded me for the extended journey with Iboga, it was Vipassana. The meditation helped me to find my center and find peace in the length of the journey, because it's truly a long journey.

**What medical precautions did you take to make sure it was a safe experience, or what medical precautions do you advise people to take?**
At Crossroads, the precautions taken included an EKG, a pre-administered saline IV drip, and continuous heart monitoring — which is very different from the traditional Bwiti approach. I'm not saying that in any way to downplay the wisdom these masters of Bwiti possess, spending 10 to 25 years in study to be able to give initiations. I mean, some of the most profound spiritual masters that I've ever met are Nemas, who can give initiations or Nema Kombo, which in

some traditions of Bwiti is considered the highest level of training. Yet, some of them have still had deaths, and in some cases I think they were preventable.

We all can make errors in judgment. No matter how good you are, no matter how connected you are to the medicine or spirit... We go through periods where we can be really connected, and then sometimes we can be a little bit less connected. We have to constantly be doing our work and maintaining that connection. I've known individuals who sadly passed away from Ibogaine, and some from complicated interactions with other conditions like malaria, in environments that lacked medical infrastructure.

In my capacity as an Iboga provider, I believe in thorough pre-screening. We assess potential risks, including mental health conditions that could lead to complications. We require an EKG, and we're not just looking at an EKG and saying, the doctor said "your heart's reading is normal so you are good to go." Instead, have our doctor, who's been working with this medicine for 10 years in a medical and psychospiritual setting, review the EKG and make sure that there aren't any abnormalities or any indicators, such as bradycardia or QT prolongation, but there are other abnormal readings that could put you in a high-risk group. Even if someone is healthy and all their biomarkers are within the healthy range, we still have a doctor on site for safety. If you are in a high-risk group, that doesn't mean you can't work with Iboga. You just have to be monitored.

A person with certain abnormalities isn't always ruled out. It just means that they're much better off to be in an environment where they're monitored so that if something does come up, you have to react quickly. We do keep a defibrillator on site and Atropine, although we've never needed it. We have IVs on site. We have almost everything that we feel would keep us from having to call in an emergency medic, to be able to deal with everything in-house with our own medical team. And knock-on wood, we haven't had anything come up. Ultimately by doing all of these things, we are creating a safer environment and preventing those things with proper screening and preparation in the beginning.

**What was your intention each time you worked with the medicine?**
For me, I think the biggest intentions that I've always had working with the medicine were wanting to heal my body with everything that I was going through. The second one was really about empowerment, whether that was financially or within the work that I was doing, but really it was about reclaiming my power. Then, the other major intention was liberation. I think just emptying myself, being free, and having greater clarity.

**How did you consume Iboga? What did you take and where? What was the form and the total dose, if you can remember?**
The first time I took a single capsule of Ibogaine HCL, I don't know what the exact milligrams were, but it was a very conservative dosage that was calculated by my weight at the time by a doctor. Then, when I was in Costa Rica, I took root bark and Total alkaloid extract, which laid me out completely for several days. I took two heaping spoonfuls of root bark, and then a capsule filled with a half a gram of very strong TA.

**Why did you pick this method or center? What drew you to working with this particular center, people, or method?**
I think it found me. I think that was really what it was at the beginning. I mean, each one of these found me. It was really a blessing.

**What would be your general advice to people considering Iboga?**
I really feel like these experiences are not something that you seek out. I feel like they find you, so the most important thing is to ask for signs, and to be quiet and listen for them, because being called to something and it being the right time for you are two different things. I think that going to Gabon is an especially big thing.

It's a big thing in that it destroys a culture when you have a lot of Westerners coming in, and it's disruptive to the culture when you have lots of psychedelic tourism, especially when they don't understand the cultural customs within how things are done in the village. It can actually cause conflict amongst the villages, because there's a lot of competition and jealousy.

You have to be really careful. I do believe that if you go at the right time, meaning the time that you're destined to go, the time when you're not pushing to go, you'll be protected. But I feel like if you force it, and you're seeking it out with your own will like, "I have to do it," I feel like those are the people that don't make it. They're the ones that have things happen that are not pleasant, like getting malaria, getting some other parasite, ending up in the hospital, or even dying. I saw it happen. They were a tourist group who thought "Oh. Let's all go to Africa together and have this experience." I will just say, it was not a story that they wanted to share with their friends about when they got home. Many of them got very sick.

It's not something you go and do with your friends. It's something that you do because it's time for you to do it. Maybe if you're in a relationship with somebody, like one other person or there's someone who you're really close with, that's an exception.

But it's also really important, that if you're a Westerner that you have a guide that is from Gabon. Someone like Tatayo, who is watching out for you, and also translating and making sure that you're not getting taken advantage of in any way and ensuring your safety.

**Is there anything you wish you knew before doing Iboga about the process?**
Within the Bwiti tradition, there's a fundamental principle: the experiences encountered during these ceremonies are deeply personal and often ineffable or unexplainable. Attempting to convey these experiences in words might not only diminish their profundity but could also misrepresent the experience to others or leave them expecting something. Furthermore, by vocalizing these experiences, there's a risk of diluting the personal meaning and the transformative impact they carry for the individual.

With that being said, many people, including myself, have publicly shared information about the process or their experiences. It is just a new evolution of the Western approach to this work, as our culture carries quite a bit of trauma and I think needs some context to feel safe.

I think the key in knowing what you need to know beforehand is that the facilitator is able to meet you and address the underlying fear or whatever it is that you are experiencing. In some cases, I could say I would have appreciated being met but I trust that the experience that I had in my preparation was part of the journey, which essentially taught me what to do and not do with my work with others.

**Would you do Iboga again?**
With respect and honor to the medicine, I am always open when I am shown the signs that it is time to dive into my own inner work. Also, as an initiate, I will continue my studies and learning at every opportunity that I am given.

**Would you feel called to do another flood dose or another big initiation any time soon?**
My initiations bring me immense blessings and growth. Annually, I try to continue my initiations to keep learning, and detoxing my internal space. While I abstain from substances like alcohol and cannabis, Iboga stands out as my teacher, guiding and strengthening me. It grants me a reset, cleansing away the accumulated impurities in my system, and processing of any stuck emotions.

My sensitivity, coupled with my interactions with many who release intense energies, necessitates frequent personal cleansing. Through my non-profit, Ancestral Heart, I've connected with esteemed elders, such as Luisah Teish of the Yoruba tradition. Like Bwiti, the Yoruba, linked to Bantu peoples, emphasize annual rituals to purge fear and other negative energies. I regularly perform cleansing rituals even outside my work with Iboga, which has brought me significant healing. It is the daily work that really helps maintain the opening post Iboga or Ibogaine.

I hope to embark on a pilgrimage back to Gabon, perhaps this upcoming summer.

**How has Iboga affected your spirituality?**
From the initiatory standpoint, Iboga is about creating a deep connection to your soul and remembering to engage with it on a regular basis, using it as your north star to move through things. To me, that has been the essence of my

journey. Ever since then, that's where my manifestation has come from. During Covid, I was guided to build a retreat center in Azores. We've done all the architectural designs. We're now in the permitting process and the final approval for financing to make this a reality. If it wasn't for that deep connection to my soul, I wouldn't be able to create at the level that I can now.

I do believe that every day that I wake up in the morning and I feel like connecting to myself, I've always had practice, but I feel like my practice is more meaningful in having my connection with Iboga.

**It sounds like maybe it's given a 'groundedness' and a centeredness to your practice. Is that accurate?**
Yeah, when I give offerings or when I do prayers, I really see nature, the spirits in nature, and the ancestors working with me in day-to-day life. I feel in complete awe and wonder of the beauty of the creative forces working around us and supporting us at all times.

**Was there a memorable moment or particularly profound vision you had? Has it come true?**
Bwiti's essence resonates deeply with the theme of liberation. This connection is vividly depicted in its symbolism that emphasizes balancing duality, encompassing the harmony of masculine and feminine forces, represented by the colors white and red. The very name of Gabon's capital, Libreville, hints at this theme of freedom.

A striking parallel I observed was in a book by Laurent Sazy that documented a Fang ceremony. Among the photographs of various Fang initiations, one showcased women donned in white, bearing torches crafted from Akoume and crowned with plants. Their posture and symbolism bore an uncanny resemblance to the Statue of Liberty.

Considering that the Statue of Liberty, a gift from the French people to Americans, stands as an emblem of freedom, and given the whispered connections of artists like Picasso with Iboga, the correlations become more intriguing. Such interlinkages underscore Iboga's message of the intricate web of connections that bind seemingly disparate elements.

Iboga's teachings hint at the deeper interconnectivity in our world, suggesting that it has a destined role in addressing the U.S's opioid crisis and potentially heralding a broader human liberation. This idea echoes the Bodhisattva vow, emphasizing collective liberation.

While I'm optimistic about the expanding influence of Iboga in the psychedelic movement, I also harbor reservations. My concern stems from the novice spiritual journey of many Westerners and their potential lack of reverence for the sacredness of Bwiti and Iboga. Gabon, roughly the size of Colorado with merely 200 villages, is the heartland of Iboga. However, the global demand overshadows supply, considering the plant's seven-year maturation period to produce medicinal alkaloids. This growth of interest is both promising for humanity's collective healing and alarming in terms of sustainability and respect for tradition.

**What did Iboga teach or give you?**

I'm writing a book called “Seeding Consciousness: Plant Medicine, Ancestral Wisdom, and the Path to Transcendence.” I downloaded the book and the layout of it during my Iboga initiations. It's a mystery school, because it's really understanding these principles of nature, the laws of nature, working with the soul, working with the ego. I feel that in order for us to be true masters of ourselves and also masters of our reality, we must master our own internal landscape because our reality is an expression of our inner environment.

I really feel like Iboga has kind of taken me through a mystery school within myself, and it really has taught me the secrets of the mysteries of life of being able to be a master of myself, a master of my mind, and a master of my creative power.

I laugh at myself because Iboga also has humbled me to the dirt. Many times over. It wants us all to be humble. Yes, it has shown me the keys to mastery but I must continue to practice every day what I have learned. I feel anyone that has been given that gift to meet the spirit of Iboga should show respect by honoring what the plant has shared and doing your best to do the homework that you were given. It doesn't mean you will do it perfectly, but it is about the intention that you put into your daily life after being given such grace.

**Author's note.**

Tricia is extremely passionate about the health of Iboga and the wider community surrounding it. She is involved in many projects to ensure Iboga not only thrives, but the cultures enveloping it are treated with reverence by the wider plant medicine world.

Tricia raised fair concerns about disclosing the dosages of Iboga people worked with, sharing that it could be dangerous and possibly encourage people to seek doses far beyond what is necessary. Her perspective is motivated by concerns regarding sustainability, safety, respect, and compassion for other people. After much contemplation and deliberation, I decided it was important to share the dosage amounts to portray the wide range of experiences and healing benefits from various ranges of doses, while also depicting the enormous healing potential with only small doses (and the brutal challenges of working with too much Iboga).

**Keith...... Depression, Cutting Karmic Cords, and Expansion of Consciousness.**

***Bio:*** *Keith Walters, 37 when first working with Iboga, 45 now. 24 spoons of Iboga root bark the second time. Male. USA, living in Sedona, Arizona. Keith is a healer, ceremonial facilitator, life coach, writer and is currently working at a holistic healing center. Motivated to work with Iboga for "Depression, cutting karmic cords, and expansion of consciousness."*

**Author's Introduction:** Keith and I were initiated at the same time in Gabon, in 2018, through Tatayo. It was Keith's second time working with Iboga, having worked with Iboga earlier in Central America. We share a very strong bond, similar to being brothers because of our joint initiation. As an Ayahuasquero (someone who works with Ayahuasca) Keith was familiar with altered states of consciousness and the tough work plant medicines can facilitate. Though even for people that have worked a lot with Ayahuasca or other plant medicines, the Iboga experience can be very tough. People who have worked with a lot of Ayahuasca, tend to be very open and well versed to handle the visionary state. This can enable Iboga to push them very far. Keith's experience took him to some very dark places but was ultimately liberating.

**Where did you first hear about Iboga?**

I first heard about Iboga in 2014. A couple of my friends had already done it and another friend wanted to go to Iboga quest in Mexico, so I ended up learning about Iboga from her and going with her.

I've worked with Iboga 2 times at a center and a couple of times on my own.

**How were you called to Iboga?**

I was called to it and really motivated by the expansion of consciousness. Also, I had worked with Ayahuasca quite a bit and my friends had said it's really good for cleaning up the brain, cleaning up any damage caused by Ayahuasca or any ungroundedness. My two main goals were expanding my awareness practices and cleaning up the brain.

I definitely knew I was called, I was definitely called by the spirit.

**What was your life like before Iboga?**
I was very open, my heart and third eye were very open from the Ayahuasca work. But in a very ungrounded way. I was leaking energy. I ended up being too open and too vulnerable. I had been having it really backfire on me by opening up to people too much who really weren't able to meet me at that level. Iboga helped me to anchor, to ground and to become more integrated.

**What is your life like after Iboga?**
Being an Ayahuasquero, serving medicine, and holding space is my life. Iboga has really allowed me to expand that and really be able to hold a deeper, cleaner, stronger container. It has made me more resilient in all dimensions that come with serving medicine. There are a lot of things it helped with, but it definitely stripped my life apart. The year after was very difficult. It broke me down and then built me back up again.

**How did you prepare? Would you prepare differently a second time?**
My whole life has been constantly preparing in a way; eating as cleanly as possible, spending time in nature, exercising. Also trusting, just trusting, not having to do a whole lot. Iboga found me at the right time and everything was meant to be.

At the time, I was working on a lot of energy medicine work. The person I went to Iboga Quest with (my first time) was a Tantra teacher, we were working on a lot of tantra. Learning how to integrate masculine and feminine aspects.

I went into it, in a really good place.

**What precautions did you take to make sure it was a safe experience?**
I did an EKG (ECG) and took a liver panel for safety.
I would recommend at a minimum, for everyone doing Iboga to get an EKG (ECG).

**What was your intention?**
*Talking about his Second time, at Ebando, using root bark and a traditional Bwiti initiation.*

When I went into Ebando, I had decided to disconnect from my family of origin. The intention going in was to completely cut all ties, chords and energies to the family of origin, my lineage ancestors. To set everyone free. And also, to be able to better serve plant medicines. Learn how to hold space better for other people and learn to be a carrier of Iboga.

I was happy with how the intention was met, but it was really, really difficult. I realized that family of origin connection, in my experience, is one of the stickiest and deepest connections. It's a super sticky and strong energy, it's hard to undo.

**How did you consume Iboga? What did you take and where? What form? Total dose?**
At Iboga Quest, I took Total Alkaloid extract (TA). It was titrated up to a traditional flood dose, administered and supervised by a doctor.

At Ebando I took Iboga in the traditional root bark form, in a traditional Bwiti ceremony. My flood dose was 24 spoons.

My experience with the TA was a lot more controlled. You can manage the dosage easily. It was an equal or better psycho spiritual experience than taking the root bark. I thought it would have been the opposite.

The root bark to me is very savage and intense. A lot of people are not ready for that level of intensity. It is really unpredictable and hard to manage as far as the dosage goes.

**Why did you decide to do it this way? Why did you pick this center?**
I chose Iboga Quest because my really good friend was also a teacher, a Buddhist practitioner and Tantrica. She followed a lot of clean, ancient lineages. And the owner of Iboga quest is a practicing Dzogchen Buddhist. Which is a really ancient form of meditation. It follows the meditation on the nature of the mind, the great perfection.

I didn't want to go to a hospital or clinic setting. I wasn't doing for addiction. The owner was very conscious.

Ebando for my second time was highly recommended by two trusted friends.

**What would be your advice to people considering Iboga?**
Just don't read anything about it. Erase your mind from any preconditioning you have about it. That's not your experience, it's based on someone else's projection of their own experience and consciousness. If you can let go of that and trust that the medicine finds you exactly when it is supposed to. It is very divinely orchestrated. All you need to do is try to stay clean with your mind and body.

**What are your thoughts on micro-dosing? Did you micro-dose after a flood dose for integration?**
Yes, I did it (micro-dosed) afterwards. I didn't really enjoy it. I dunno, I was a little too sensitive to the energies when I was on it. It made me very tense and anxious. Overall, it was a useful tool in integration and healing.

**Is there anything you wish you knew before doing Iboga about the process?**
Not really. If I would have known I probably wouldn't have done it. Hahaha. If I knew what I had to go through… It's kind of like anything that is worthwhile.

**Would you do Iboga again?**
Yes. I plan to work with it again in 6 months or so. I will probably do TA again, I don't know if I'll go back and do the root bark again. It's possible that I may do root bark again.

**Was there a memorable moment or particularly profound vision you had? Has it come true?**
Yes. There wasn't a lot I can recall consciously. One of them was really letting go of all structures and systems, especially this 'god program'. It's just you and this consciousness. Who are you when everything is gone that you believed in? It's just you. There is nobody there, no loved ones, no god, no angels, masters, breath techniques, any technique. Part of my memory is just being a bacterium in an underground car parking garage. Just a little bacteria, that's stuck. All I

could do was completely surrender and trust that everything is temporary and eventually it would end.

I don't remember much of the visions too clearly. It was humbling.

**Has Iboga affected your spirituality?**
Yes, definitely. I think it has made me a lot more real, and a lot clearer. I feel more integrated and present.

Even though it was humbling, it broke me down and it was very depressing, it helped me understand the 'suicide dimension'. A lot of people I talk to who have done Iboga have gone through this. I think it's part of a matrix we have to pass through in order to go to the next level. In order to raise our vibration, we have to pass through this darker dimension. The more we raise our vibration, the more we get tested.

It's a game and we all have opportunity. If you chose to do that (suicide) you're going to be in a time out for a long fucking time. The shamans used to tell me, if you commit suicide, it's a long way to get back to this present moment… No matter what happens I'm not going to fall for that (suicide) program that's stuck in the collective matrix.

It has given me the confidence to hold space for myself and everyone else.

**Anything else you'd like to add**
These medicines are sacred. We have to make sure that they are held in a really safe and impeccable way. It's important that they are preserved and we give back. It's not for everybody. It finds people at the right time. It's not just for addiction. But everybody is addicted to something, thoughts, food, phones. It breaks the pattern of attachments and wanting. Iboga breaks old conditioning.

**Author's Note:**

Keith and I had not met before being initiated in Gabon. Despite our intentions and goals for working with Iboga being vastly different, they became interwoven, weaving into one big intention. Interestingly, there was some transference of our intentions throughout the ceremony, we both received and continue to receive messages and lessons for each other. Our 'combined' initiation gifted us a very deep experience and strong bond. Our connection is a reminder of the relationships and bonds we form with people who we sit in ceremony with. These interactions can teach and trigger us, nudging us along to odd and wonderful places. Often, the medicine may not bring us what we want or what we think we need, but what and whom we truly need.

From my perspective, Iboga provided Keith with profound healing and sense of groundedness that work with other plant medicines had not enabled. Whereas for me, Iboga was not grounding at all. The medicine opened a door for Keith to wrestle deeply with his mind and pass through some very dark places. He passed through "The Bardo" first and then guided me through it. Luckily for Keith, he was working at a healing center afterwards and could integrate his experience with meditation, yoga, counsel from other healers and time in nature. Having a place to rest, ground and integrate after working withIboga is crucial to processing the experience and bringing the lessons into practice.

**Chris...... Developing Extraction Methods for and Spiritual Curiosity.**

***Bio:*** *Dr. Christopher William Jenks, 28 when first using Iboga, 54 now. Male. USA. Up to 1.5 grams of Iboga PTA HCl. Chris is a chemist and alternative energy specialist, a parent to two generations, living near Sacramento, California. Chris was initially motivated to work with Iboga for "Development of extraction and synthesis procedures to make Ibogaine available using low technology at low cost and for spiritual curiosity."*

**Author's Introduction:** The work of Dr. Christopher Jenks is truly revolutionary in the field of Iboga and plant medicines, both through expanding access to the total alkaloid extract of Iboga, and inventing a method to extract Ibogaine from the abundant Voacanga Africana tree, and spare the critically endangered Tabernanthe Iboga tree. Dr. Jenks has applied his vast wealth of chemistry knowledge to both improve the lives of countless people and also give Iboga some "breathing room". Through the alternative extraction of Ibogaine from Voacanga, Dr. Jenks has helped ensure that Iboga can survive into the future whilst other sustainable approaches are developed. The plant medicine movement has been hugely aided by the contributions of Dr. Jenks.

**Where did you first hear about Iboga?**

I'm not really sure. I was an atheist back when I was a teenager and I was very depressed. I ended up attempting suicide late in my teens. So, I was sent to a psychiatric hospital. And when I was released from there, I was put on antidepressants. Back then, it was desipramine, a tricyclic (correct) antidepressant. That's what they had back in the '80s. I was also put on Xanax, alprazolam, it's a benzo. It is used to control the tremors that are caused by the desipramine.

But at the time, I also had some anxiety. I noticed that I felt very calm when I took the Xanax without taking it every day. If I took it every day, the anxiety-relieving effect would go away. So, I learned that if I didn't take it, except maybe once a week, I could still experience that benefit. So, I would take it on a Friday or Saturday night because then I could sleep in the next morning also.

But I noticed that in the mornings, when I slept in, I experienced this REM rebound because the desipramine would prevent sleeping very well. It wasn't just extra dreams. I actually would find myself basically awake, not like a lucid dream, because I wasn't attempting to have lucid dreams. I was finding myself in this mind state where I could see a dream around me, it felt like I was awake. And it was just a fantastic experience. And that started my interest in psychoactive drugs in general. That's why, although I already had interest in chemistry from about the age of 13, I turned my interest to psychoactive drugs. I was looking for a way to have the same experience for more than a few minutes without having to wait a whole week.

I probably heard about Ibogaine back then, but probably didn't dwell on it because I was looking for something I could actually obtain. I was more interested in things like morning glory seeds, which was the first thing I experienced.

The interesting thing about the morning glory seeds, when I finally ended up taking those - I was hoping to have visionary experiences. I was looking for the visuals commonly reported by others because I thought they would be like the REM rebound that I had experienced. But I didn't actually have visuals. I don't tend to get visuals with most psychedelics. What I did get was a philosophical insight. This was when I was at a college dorm waiting for an epistemology final exam. I took these morning glory seeds the day before, hoping to have visual experiences. They didn't wear off because I had taken 600 of them!

I went to bed after the trip was supposed to end, and I was going in between sleep and wakefulness. I had this insight that I couldn't experience falling asleep without subsequently experiencing waking up. In the experience of falling asleep, the only way that I knew that I'd fallen asleep was I'd wake up and realize time had passed. I connected that with my obsession about suicide some years before. Because I had this idea that I could escape from life by destroying myself. Since I was an atheist, I thought, "Well, if I destroy my brain, I can't experience anything, which means no more suffering." And I'm sure a lot of people think that way. It's a general way of thinking of death as an escape.

But I realized if I can't experience falling asleep without waking up, then I can't experience death if it's the end of consciousness, because it would mean that I didn't know I had died. It's so logical. It's obvious. I mean, it seems simple, and yet it was profound. And I no longer dwelled on suicide. Instead, I was perplexed by, well, how does reality work then? Neither religious people nor atheists believe this sort of thing or this concept. This led me to a search for what really is going on. That started my spiritual journey. Over the years I came to summarize my insight as, "nonexistence is imperceptible."

To give the full answer to the original question, how I first learned about Iboga. I wasn't really focused on Iboga until I was in college, and it was during my PhD studies in organic chemistry. I was looking for a way that I could contribute my chemistry degree and experience in some helpful way. I couldn't find it. I could go into the main fields my colleagues were looking at, which were pharmaceuticals, pesticides, academia, polymers, stuff like that, which I wasn't interested in or had ethical reservations about. I was still interested in psychoactive drugs. But this was the '90s. It was still the height of the drug war kind of, mostly. And it just wasn't happening.

The way I first learned about Ibogaine was from a fellow graduate student, Dan Bender, who I was living with. He shared with me a brief article in a magazine, *Magical Blende*, where a man in Florida, writing under the name Eric Taub, related a woman's claim that a single experience with Ibogaine was more insightful than all the psychotherapy she had had. I contacted Eric Taub, and he connected me with others working with Ibogaine - Karl Naeher and Howard Lotsof. Howard Lotsof had discovered that Ibogaine could be used for treating addiction, and he put me on an email list that he started. That's where my participation started with the Ibogaine community, where I realized I had a role I could play. So, I think that's the answer.

**Did you feel called to Iboga? Did you feel spiritually called?**
Well, I felt called to psychedelic drugs in general, and finding a way to participate in people's association with them. I've been looking back on this a lot over the years. When I first took morning glory seeds, I was looking to have visions, because I had this weird experience that was with Xanax and desipramine, neither of which are considered psychedelic. And it was like a bait

and switch sort of experience. I went looking for visions and instead had this profound philosophical insight that is what I actually needed at that time. I've experienced the same thing many times since then. Sometimes I'll be hoping to have a specific experience, but I'll get something completely unexpected which turns out to be invaluable.

It has to work that way because if I am going to find these valuable things, I can't be looking for them, because if I knew what I was looking for, I'd already have it. For example, I didn't know there was a problem with my concept of death, so I couldn't know how to seek a correction for it. This pattern of finding wisdom that I need seems to come from beyond myself, from someone who cares for me.

**What was your life like before working with Iboga?**
My (professional) work with Iboga started by asking about and researching everything that was known. It's not so much that I personally discovered something monumental as I learned about Ibogaine. It was more that I found a niche, I found a role I could play that wasn't being filled that would truly help people. Because at the time, there weren't very robust sources for Ibogaine. There were some people trying to extract it from Iboga. There was one company at the time, I think it was Omni-Chem in Belgium, that was producing for Howard and his treatment studies. But it was small scale and expensive.

In the subsequent years the price of Ibogaine got up to $600 a gram. So, there was definitely a need for a good source for it so that people could still get it. I felt like I was needed, finally. I had something I could focus on where I felt like I wasn't wandering anymore. So that was a big change.

**How was your life before consuming Iboga? Is there a marked change in your life before and after consuming Iboga or Ibogaine?**
Well, I know that some people, they take Ibogaine or another psychedelic sort of drug, and they experience profound relief of depression and/or anxiety. They don't know what mechanism it has, it just works. And in fact, things like psilocybin are being proposed as antidepressants for that reason, because they seem like they are much more effective for some people treating their depression than alternative or conventional treatments.

Personally, I haven't experienced anything like that with Ibogaine. There are two profound changes that happened for me regarding Ibogaine. One is what I've already described as far as just finding a role to play, and that's mundane and understandable. I found a job. But the other is, later on, this was in Italy. I was developing the process for my first publication, published in Natural Product Letters in 2002, which was an extraction process for Tabernanthe Iboga.

And during the eight months of my research, I isolated a purified total alkaloid of Iboga, which was mainly Ibogaine. I had two reasons for wanting to take it myself. One is that I wanted to see what it did, and I was interested in having a psychedelic experience, whatever that would mean for me. But the other was an ethical consideration, that since I was putting out a procedure for making this stuff, I felt like I was obliged to show that this would be the right stuff and that it would be as safe as Ibogaine that was known in the literature, because although I didn't propose a specific use, the implication was that this Ibogaine was meant for human consumption.

After watching someone at a treatment provider I visited struggle even from a test dose, I thought "Is it possible to take Ibogaine at smaller doses over a week instead of one big dose in the same amount?" I broke it down into 165 milligrams every day for about a week. A spread-out flood dose. I actually found it rather an intense week. It definitely was not one-tenth of a full dose in terms of effect each day. It was actually difficult to make it through the week. And I didn't experience any profound experiences during the week either.

But I found at the end of the week, I had a couple of life-changing experiences. For the past five years I had been dating a Christian, Dana, while continuing my own spiritual struggle in college. She wanted to get married but was clear that her husband had to be a Christian too, and my study of the Bible only filled me with doubts. Although it had grieved us, we went our separate ways, although I had never been at all sure that I wanted to marry anyone anyway. My week-long trip was many months later. But after the trip ended, I had profound insight into the Bible and was able to suddenly integrate the core Christian ideas and find faith in the loving God. Simultaneously, I had a certainty that marrying Dana was what God wanted me to do, that it was the best thing for me, that I needed to learn to give.

When I told Dana about my revelations, she was incredulous, which is understandable given the enormity of the change and how psychedelic-inspired life changes might be expected to wear off. But this didn't wear off. Dana joined me in Padova, we were engaged in Venice, and we are still happily married, and Christian, 23 years later. I also called my dad, who was an atheist. When I told him what I had realized, he said he might have to disown me. He didn't, and we had many spiritual conversations for the rest of his life.

So obviously, it had a profoundly positive impact on my life.

There have been maybe a dozen times where things were very challenging. They were so bad that I thought, "Am I really sure that I should be married? Maybe I should just run away." Then I keep remembering, the reason I got married is that I was sure that it was God's intention for me to get married. It wasn't because I thought in my own human intelligence, this looks like the best person, or I think things will work out, or I'm going to make some kind of commitment on my own. So, the problem was that if I walked away from the marriage, then I would have to doubt all the other times I was sure I was directed by God, and then I would be lost. I'd also be walking away from my faith. I never received any direction from God that I should leave my wife. That really has been the glue. It's brought us through the hard times. And the problems I was worried about back then, they're over, I don't even remember what I was so upset about.

**Was that the only time you've worked with Ibogaine or Iboga, or have you worked with it other times as well?**
Well, that was just the beginning. I published that research in 2002. And then over subsequent years, I was invited several times to South Africa, to train people to extract Iboga. I helped set up a laboratory at what's called Minds Alive Wellness Center, in Durban. I trained my hosts, and I helped them train other people. I also unintentionally inspired one of the biggest online Ibogaine providers, Iboga World. And it wasn't intentional. My host at the time, Anwar Jeewa, had invited a botanical vendor, Franz, to join us for lunch. He was excited to talk with me about my process, and I was in the habit of sharing what I knew with anyone who would listen and might bring more medicine to the world.

Franz hadn't previously focused on Iboga, and he wasn't trained in chemistry. But after he realized how easy it was to extract Ibogaine, which was very costly at the time, he changed his mind about supplying Iboga for Anwar to extract, and set up a business to produce Ibogaine, which turned out to be a massive competitor to Anwar. Aside from the unexpected competition, Iboga World, which was Franz's company, caused grief in subsequent years due to poor quality control.

As sales of Iboga extracts took off, my worry about the sustainability of Iboga increased. Even from the beginning, in my 2002 paper, I said Iboga needs to be cultivated to prevent it from being over-harvested. That was a problem way back then! It's always been a problem. Over the years, I'd heard people plan to start farms in places like Central or South America or Africa. It made such sense that I didn't really worry about it. I thought, this'll be solved by some enterprising person who will grow as much Iboga as the world needs, and he'll get super rich. Surely this will happen and it just didn't happen...

As the years went on, Anwar told me that there were quality control problems with his own Iboga bark, because the plant was becoming so scarce. Even the people who had been harvesting for him couldn't find the right species anymore. They were sending contaminated bark, containing either immature Iboga, plants looking similar to Iboga or maybe unrelated plants added out of desperation. And so this process was having a problem. He called me all the way back to Durban just to deal with that problem.

So, I realized that the writing was on the wall here. I really needed to find another way for others to produce Ibogaine. I spent much more time developing a production of Ibogaine from Voacanga bark. The complexity of the process is hugely different. Ibogaine is practically two steps from Iboga, while for Voacanga, it takes dozens of steps. Iboga could be extracted in a kitchen, but it's a real factory process for Voacanga. That took a long time to develop. I spent a final year in Durban, on unpaid leave and supported by loans and my church, developing and documenting the process in 2013. And that led to a factory that's still running in Durban, that produces Ibogaine from Voacanga to whatever scale is called for. It has been a perpetual miracle, made possible by faith, to have the four-volume manual and factory come together on a shoestring budget within the limited time we had, with none of the staff trained in chemistry apart from what I taught them.

**How did you prepare for your Iboga ceremonies? And would you prepare differently for subsequent times?**
Well, I wouldn't call them ceremonies so much, because it was just on my own, more self-directed. I didn't really have anyone closely watching over me, though I had help available. That's the way I've normally taken things in general. But as far as preparing, I remember in Padova, that I was doing a lot of praying, a lot of meditating, a lot of reading, to try to make spiritual connections. I was basically living in a guy's apartment while researching the extraction and refinement of Iboga alkaloids. We were buddies. He was a chiropractor that did Ibogaine treatments on the side. So, it was a very informal and friendly situation.

I had a lot of spare time. I had just graduated with my PhD. It was a relaxed situation and I felt like my preparation may have helped make possible the experience I had that was so transformative. It may have put together the pieces for me. What I've read - and experienced - is that people who have transformative breakthroughs tend to have worked towards those without the psychedelic beforehand.

**Were you still taking Xanax and other medications? Before you started working with Ibogaine or Iboga, were you in a relatively good place in life?**
Yes, I was in a far better place, no longer suicidal nor medicated. I had stopped my prescription for those in undergraduate college, because I realized it was bringing my GPA down a point. It was probably the Xanax, which I had started taking as directed. Benzos tend to interfere with memory.

**Did you take any medical precautions to make sure it was a safe experience?**
Well, unfortunately, back in 1998, there wasn't very much known about the medical complications of taking Ibogaine. So no, I didn't have any cardio screening, which would've been the main precaution. So yeah, that was an issue. And a lot of people got in trouble over the subsequent years. Treatment providers learned the hard way about that. Fortunately, there's a lot more resources, particularly safety guidelines, now.

Anyway, when I was a director at GITA (Global Ibogaine Therapy Alliance), we were putting together the "GITA Safety Guidelines." GITA was associated with several conferences, mainly Iboga treatment providers, but also oddballs like myself. We would go and participate, present, collaborate, and treatment providers would share their experiences with how to treat with Ibogaine safely. This consolidated wisdom got put into these guidelines. So, there is a document that can be used to help people administer Iboga safely.

I'll make a note here to get you a link... https://www.Ibogainealliance.org/guidelines/

**What was your intention for consuming Iboga or Ibogaine?**
It was a long time ago, so I don't remember specifically what I prayed for. But in general, my intentions, they've gotten pretty stable. They tend to be the same, where I pray for insight, for wisdom, for healing. But it's become a much more general thing. I don't consider my healing separate from the healing of my family or my friends or my community or my world. So, I tend to have very broadly scoped prayers, to see healing in general come everywhere, and to be able to facilitate that and to get past my own blocks to provide that.

**How did you consume Iboga? What did you take, and where? What was the form and the total dose?**
The times I've taken Ibogaine or the purified Iboga alkaloids, it's usually been in a gel cap. The first time I took it was actually in Paris. I was with a guy named Dennis Morbin in his apartment in Paris. This was the first time when Karl Naeher and I met. I flew to France during a break at my university. The purpose was that he was coming into France with a package of whole Iboga root from Cameroon. He had it powdered at the university there. That university had done most of the research on Ibogaine. Then he gave me the duffle bag, and said, "Good luck!" I stayed at the apartment for a week. That was when I did my very first experiments with extraction of the bark.

One thing that Dennis and I did was make a simple extract of the powdered bark with lemon juice. We made tea out of it. I remember finding it very bitter, but Dennis commented that it was rather pleasant. I thought, "Well, we obviously are tasting this differently." We also had a mild effect from our probably 100 milligrams of Ibogaine in the tea. That was also the place where I actually came up with the first conditions for producing TA (total alkaloid Iboga extract). That's where TA was invented. It was a warm - not hot - vinegar extraction of the bark, followed by precipitation of the TA by ammonia. Which is basically the conditions for making it that I published after going to Italy, with a lot of refinement and additional processing to provide PTA (purified total alkaloid) hydrochloride, a standard used in addiction treatment. Making TA may seem trivial, but I consider it a miracle that it was a stable solid. There was no reason to expect that. Alkaloid extracts are often oils or tars, which is what happens if Iboga is extracted with organic solvent.

**Has your experience always been with purified total alkaloid or purified Ibogaine?**

No, I've tested things like TA. I've also tried things like extracting the TA with acetone to make PTA, and then taking the leftover TA and swallowing that and finding that it does nothing. That shows that the alkaloids did get removed. I've also separated pure Ibogaline, which is the second most abundant alkaloid in Iboga. I consumed that too, the point being to see if it might have properties similar to those of Ibogaine and be a good candidate for use in addiction treatment...

**How was that experience (Ibogaline)?**

It was maybe 2-3 times more potent and seemed longer-lasting than Ibogaine is.

**Do you think that has potential to be a similar compound as Ibogaine? Or is it maybe not commercially viable? What are your thoughts on that?**

Well, other than the experience being similar, I can't say whether it would be more or less promising for addiction treatment. There are other variables that I didn't get to measure, like how it affects withdrawal or the heart. But I do think it's definitely worth more examination. At every conference, I say, "It sure would be great to isolate these other alkaloids and test them out." I just haven't gotten around to it myself, other than that one test. But that seems to be the future is trying all these other alkaloids.

There are a few others like Noribogaine and 18-MC(18-methoxycoronaridine) that have been proposed as alternatives to Ibogaine. But, I think that a lot of the reasons for using them have been misguided. In the case of Noribogaine, the whole point there is to eliminate the visionary aspect of Iboga. The logic was that the visions are not acceptable with the status quo, so we need to get people to go through addiction treatment without having any visions. But since so many people found the visions to facilitate and assist with the addiction treatment, that seems misguided.

The other idea is the 18-MC, which was selected through rat studies to find something that would treat addiction in rats while having fewer side effects than Ibogaine. The problem is that one of the structurally closest alkaloids to Coronaridine is voacangine. That's actually Ibogaine with an ester group attached, the same ester group 18-MC has. Voacangine is the alkaloid in Voacanga that Ibogaine is made from. It's easy to get pure voacangine and try it for treating addiction. The problem is, when people did that, they found, in fact, it just causes severe gastrointestinal problems and isn't psychoactive. So, if voacangine is able to treat addiction in rats like 18-MC can, but voacangine can't treat addiction in people because of its ester group, then the chance that 18-MC can do it in people seems rather remote.

The problem is that these people that are coming up with these patents and these medical trials and stuff, they don't have an ethical way to test these alkaloids on human beings to make sure it'll treat their addictions before they go through the huge process of going through animal studies and clinical trials. So, they don't have the leads. Whereas with Iboga, it's a lead because we know it worked for Bwiti and Howard Lotsof. It was a great head start. But there are ways to do this safely. For example, the other alkaloids in Iboga already have a history of human use because they are present in the bark consumed by the Bwiti and others.

**As a chemist and inventor of TA, what do you see the main differences between someone working with TA versus working the traditional root bark would be? In this book, it's been described as working with TA removes the savageness or the brutality on the body. Do you think that has any scientific basis, or do you think there's any logical reasoning for that?**

Yeah. Plenty of logical reasoning. If you swallow the TA, you don't have to gobble down all that wood that's attached to the TA in the bark. That's entirely a physical thing. You don't have as much inert fluff going down your throat. You don't have to deal with the texture of sharp pieces of wood that you're having to chew on. Maybe part of the process is dealing with that ordeal. But as far as the effect, once it's in your stomach, it shouldn't make any difference.

**So you think the main difference between the TA and the traditional root bark is most likely to be all the wood fiber and the digestion of that?**
I can kind of guarantee that. Because part of my research in Italy was to perform a bunch of optimizations and a bunch of checks to make sure it was efficient. So, for instance, I would extract the bark with acid. And after I no longer saw any more alkaloid come out, then I would swallow the bark to show that it didn't do anything. So, we can be sure that the TA got the goods and what was left in the bark did not have any effect.

**Why did you decide to consume Iboga this way? Why did you pick this method?**
Well, it's kind of a boring answer for me to give. I took gel caps because I didn't want to have to taste the Ibogaine in a cup of water. It'd be intensely bitter. And because it was convenient. It's easy to fit a gram and a half in a couple gel caps. Yeah. I didn't do anything special as far as the way I took Ibogaine.

**What would be your advice to people considering consuming Iboga?**
Gosh. First I should make clear, I'm not that kind of doctor - not a medical doctor, nor have I felt it my place to treat people. There are better qualified people to ask, but I can summarize the consensus I have heard from treatment providers over the years. Well, there's Iboga, and then there's Ibogaine. There are lots of different ways and reasons to take Iboga or Ibogaine. But of course, there's the first concern, which is safety, and make sure that it's not going to cause your heart to stop, which should be done in screening and also monitoring during treatment.

I don't know if there's a way of doing that screening short of getting a cardiogram though. It is important to make sure you're not one of the unlucky 1% that isn't going to wake up. And while lower doses seem to be safer, I don't think there's a threshold, an active dose that is safe without screening. And it's certainly less safe to take Ibogaine in combination with other things like alcohol or methadone or something like that which prolong the QT interval.

Well, one cautionary tale. A treatment provider had been treating probably thousands of people with Ibogaine at his treatment center. But what ended up ruining his program was that he got a client who was needing Ibogaine treatment, but he had been on heavy doses of benzodiazepines, and he did not let him know that. And so he came, and he got into withdrawal from the benzodiazepines, which is kind of like being on a strong stimulant because the benzodiazepine withdrawal is the reverse of the calming effect from them. The problem is that unmanaged benzodiazepine withdrawal by itself can include convulsions, but Ibogaine, being a stimulant, makes convulsions more likely. He ended up dying because he had this combination of effects during withdrawal.

Anyway, obviously, this means that you have to watch out for combinations like that that can cause a fatality. The other thing that causes a lot of fatalities was that Ibogaine eliminates the tolerance to opiates. Somebody might be taking their gram a day of heroin, and they go and they get treated with Ibogaine. They might not feel withdrawal because the Ibogaine mitigated it, but they think, "Oh, I've got to take heroin again, or if I don't, I'll get sick." They take their gram, and then they overdose because now that's too much for them because they don't have the tolerance.

So, everybody in the community kind of knows about those things, but people who haven't heard of Ibogaine before wouldn't be aware of that.

This is why you don't use Ibogaine to treat benzo withdrawal or benzo addiction. It's because the withdrawal would be hazardous with the Ibogaine. So, it's good for treating stimulant withdrawal, because that's the reverse.

**You shouldn't really be treating a benzodiazepine addiction with Iboga or Ibogaine?**

Or other depressants. Although other depressants are usually just alcohol. Someone who's in acute withdrawal from alcohol would definitely have the same problem. Depressant withdrawal is particularly dangerous even on its own as it can include convulsions.

Well, after the acute withdrawal from the alcohol, then it would be safe to treat the cravings for alcohol. That could be treated with Ibogaine, after the withdrawal has passed.

**Is it potentially that the response time from quitting alcohol is perhaps faster versus benzodiazepine, which is much longer?**
For benzos, it can vary. It depends on how it's taken. For instance, fentanyl's a great example. People who are going to the hospital and they're given a pump so that they can treat their breakthrough pain with fentanyl, when they leave the hospital, they might experience withdrawal for a few days or a week, and then it gets better. That tends to be the rule for short-acting opiates like heroin as well.

But when people are given patches with fentanyl, where it's constant, and they're maybe an outpatient, they're treated like this for a long period of time, that withdrawal could be worse than methadone, longer than methadone. And so, it seems to be not just the kind of drug and its half-life, it's more the stability of the activation of the receptor.

**What's the difference between fentanyl and methadone?**
Well, fentanyl metabolizes super-fast, and methadone, super slow. But the receptor doesn't know which is which. It just knows it's being activated. And that's where the withdrawal is - withdrawal is the receptors readjusting to a new lack of stimulation. So, if you make a concentration of fentanyl that's super stable and it's stimulating the receptor in the same way methadone would, then the withdrawal could be like methadone.

So as a rule, long-acting drugs, including benzos, tend to have longer withdrawal. The reason for that is that blood levels at the receptor will fluctuate less if the drug has to remain there longer.

As far as physical hazards, that's one area. But then there's psychological hazards. I've heard of treatment providers, they'll treat people like myself that just lie down and they don't have visions. Whereas others, they may be physically safe, but psychologically, they could be incapacitated, or they can experience extreme anxiety. Since people who haven't taken Ibogaine before don't know where on the spectrum they might be, they have to be prepared for any difficulty.

**What are your thoughts on micro-dosing? Did you ever micro-dose to help integrate or to help your journey or your path?**
Well, I haven't tried micro-dosing very extensively. I don't know if you consider the 165 milligrams a day to be micro-dosing. That's kind of a large micro-dose. It's more like a medium dose.

If I were going to take a micro-dose of Ibogaine for personal growth, I think I would try around 20 milligrams a day. I think micro-dosing in general is a great idea, but I haven't had that much experience with micro-dosing and experiencing healing as a result of that.

I've heard of micro-dosing being used for treatment of craving. Craving for drugs can disappear for weeks or months after Ibogaine treatment, but tends to return eventually. Smaller doses of Ibogaine can be helpful for that without having to take the risk of a full dose.

**Is there anything you wish you knew, before doing Iboga, about the process?**
No. As far as my own experience, I think I knew enough about what sort of thing I could experience before I took it. I was, after all, living with a treatment provider.

**Would you do Iboga again?**
Not unless I had some kind of insight that gave me some confidence that it was a good idea. Because I've taken Ibogaine a few times since Italy, sometimes for testing, and sometimes to see if there might be further insights. I really haven't really gotten anything from it. I got the feeling that "The cheese has moved." It's not that I'm not interested in psychoactive drugs, I definitely am. I'm always looking for what might be helpful. But not only are some drugs much more useful than others for an individual, it seems like useful drugs have a time, and then that time is over, at least for a long rest.

**How has Iboga affected your spirituality?**

Only the one week-long trip that I had in Italy seemed to have any effect, but that was profound, life-changing and permanent. Starting life as an atheist has helped me identify with and understand people who still see things that way. Looking back, the most profound and helpful of experiences from psychedelics have been unexpected and not reproducible. Obviously there would be no point in repeating the same insight or being healed of the same thing, but I mean in terms of general utility, the most useful experiences tend to be unexpected one-offs.

**Was there a memorable moment or particularly profound vision for you? Has this vision come true?**

Well, I'd say definitely. I didn't experience any visuals, auditory effects or anything on Ibogaine except tracers and some distortion of background noise. It was always conceptual. I would have insights. That would be the way I would be communicated with. The insights of "Follow Christ and marry Dana," have certainly come true. I was able to do these things. There was no guarantee that after breaking up with Dana that things would still work out. So, there was another side of this, apart from my simply changing my intention. God had to work things out in the world as they had been in my mind.

**Is there anything else you'd like to add, anything we haven't covered that you'd like to share?**

To summarize, Iboga affected my life by getting me to travel and make lifelong friends, and collaborate with them, and present at conferences, and be part of Global Ibogaine Therapy Alliance board of directors. I tested the Ibogaine on myself, became a Christian, and got married, because of the vision I had.

After years of process development, I led the design and development of the factory still in operation. In developing that, I also got to travel to Ghana and Cameroon and make friends there. I got to do some very pleasant travel.

Also, something I didn't mention is that last summer I did a filming for 'Hamilton's Pharmacopeia'. A recent episode shows me doing the chemistry I developed for the Durban factory. It shows steps of that process. That's probably the most public thing I've done as far as something an average person might see me doing that's related to Ibogaine.

Finally, there have been some researchers like Felix Krengel at the University of Mexico or Ignacio Carrera, a professor in Uruguay, who've done research related to mine. Felix was doing extraction of Tabernaemontana species and comparing my extraction methods with other extraction methods. Ignacio Carrera was looking to enhance the yield of Ibogaine from Voacanga by breaking down Voacamine. Until now, the voacangine in Voacanga has been used to make Ibogaine. But voacangine is part of the Voacamine molecule, which is plentiful in Voacanga bark. So by chopping that one in half, you get additional voacangine for the process. He just published that a few days ago.

And for your other question, broad advice to give to my younger self or others, I was going to say, don't get stuck spending all your time preparing for some day. A lot of people get in a rut where they work at jobs they hate, and they think, "Well, some day, I'll retire." I think that might not be the most effective way to live. Because you won't be the same person by the time you get to your goal. So you have to have something to be glad about in the meantime.

If you can't make a living doing what you love, then keep doing what you love when you can, but pay the bills with something else. That's been my deal with Ibogaine. I've never made any money working with Ibogaine, in fact I consider it a conflict of interest to be avoided personally. It's cost me a lot of money to do all the work I've done with Ibogaine and Iboga, to pay the bills while away in Durban. I've always worked a day job where I feel helpful, even if it doesn't seem ideal. It's technical work where the goal is to protect the environment. But the only time I've felt completely myself is when I was working out Ibogaine chemistry, knowing it is to help free people from their addictions.

And then finally, drugs like Ibogaine have very different visionary effects for different people.

Have you heard of the Rat Park model for drug addiction? The idea being that, it's not that there's something wrong with people when they're getting addicted, it's that there's something wrong with the world that people take drugs to try to cope with. And one of the presenters at an Ibogaine Conference quoted William Burroughs, saying, "Perhaps all pleasure is just relief." That's how he described his first heroin addiction. "Oh, the relief!" But you have to ask, what's the relief from? Why shouldn't we all be afflicted? We all had trauma when we were born, right? Being cast from complete comfort into an unknown world. Imagine the profound experience of being born that we don't remember.

Stanislav Grof, the famous consciousness researcher, the whole concept behind his methods is that our lives have been profoundly shaped by that profound experience of being born that we don't remember. His whole goal is to get us to try to remember or relive that experience of being born so that we can assimilate it. It's just like PTSD. People have these intense, profound, or disturbing experiences, and it cripples them, until they're able to reintegrate that with less fear, from a frame of mind that isn't frightened.

The other is I've come to realize, over the years, that we kind of regard ourselves as healthy or we're fine if we can hold down a job, relationships, and that kind of thing. And I guess it's because I've had insights or experiences where I've seen myself be 'healthier' than I normally am. In other words, sometimes you can have experiences where you're 'super performing', you're doing better than average. They describe this a lot with LSD, that somebody might take LSD, and then suddenly they're doing better than they can do at their best, accomplishing things that seemed impossible before taking it, like mastering the piano.

My concept has changed a lot as far as what it means to be healthy. Normally, we think the average is what mental health is - we call ourselves "fine." But what if we're all actually far below our potential. What if health is something way above our existing state, that we could actually strive toward? Because without thinking it's above where we are, we might not think to strive toward it.

**How hard is Voacanga for the average person to synthesize into Ibogaine? Is it realistic for someone with no knowledge to synthesize? How challenging is it to make?**

Yeah. That's a good question. Because the purpose of my procedure, the intention behind it, was to try to make Ibogaine from it economical by using inexpensive resources. I wanted to make it possible to obtain in countries where high tech or expensive equipment isn't easily available. Also, to make it so that it doesn't require a great deal of training. So, it's kind of self-contained. You don't need an extensive chemical background. Although it does help, if you're doing it, to consult someone like myself to try to clear things up as you're going through it. So, it is possible for someone without much chemical knowledge. In fact, the people that were running the factory in Africa when I left were not chemists. There were no trained chemists on their staff. But they were able to produce Ibogaine without formal chemistry training. I worked with them quite a bit, so they understood the process. So, you might call it more of an apprenticeship.

But the other consideration is that, even though the procedure is designed for a lay audience, it is very lengthy, unlike the extraction of Iboga. If you wanted to do it as an experiment just to show that it could be done, then I think after maybe some months, the average person could work out a few grams of Ibogaine, if they wanted to dedicate all that time. But practically speaking, it doesn't make any sense for an average person to produce small amounts of Ibogaine that way. The only way it would make any sense to do the process, economically or practically, is to dedicate all your time and do it on a large scale so that you can actually compete with the existing businesses that are making it. Because otherwise, you just earn 100 bucks, get a gram, and there you go. There's no real need to go through a month's worth of work to try to make it.

I have to point out - I regularly get contacted by people who want to get Ibogaine because they don't want the hassle and expense to go to a treatment center for addiction treatment. While this can work, like it did for Howard Lotsof, Ibogaine is much more safe and effective when made part of a holistic program.

**How much Voacanga do you need to make one gram?**

Well, when I analyzed Voacanga bark using high pressure liquid chromatography (HPLC), I found that there was 1% to 2% voacangine in the bark. And most of that voacangine weight would turn into Ibogaine if it were converted. So in theory, it would take only about 50 to 100 grams of Voacanga root or trunk bark. But that's if you went through the whole purification process of voacangine without losing any. As far as the practical yield, it's still not really nailed down. Instead of trying to find out what the yield is from the process, because the process has tailings and side products that have to be recycled, what I looked at is, how much voacangine can I detect in things that are going to be thrown away? There aren't that many - depleted bark, water the total alkaloid was filtered from, depleted total alkaloid. And so, by minimizing the amount of voacangine in things thrown away, I figured all the rest in there has to end up in the product. So if you got 50% yield, then it would take 100 or 200 grams of Voacanga bark to make a gram of Ibogaine.

**Are you comfortable sharing the information of how to synthesize it or make it? Or would you prefer not to have that included in the book?**

No, that's fine. Since you ask, I have a website, PuzzlePiece.org, where all my procedures are published. They're open source. Anybody can download the procedure and if they have questions, I'm happy to answer them. But since Ibogaine is a controlled substance in the United States, I trust that anyone asking how to prepare it plans to do so in one of the many reasonable countries where it is not forbidden.

**Author's Note:**

Through Chris's journey we are reminded that when we live in faith and trust, we create space for inspiration and greater clarity to emerge. At an essential moment in Chris's life, Iboga acted as a lighthouse, guiding him to marry his wife and follow Christianity. To me, this illustrates the extremely tailored and unique experience that Iboga facilitates, not every experience necessitates facing traumatic memories or challenging emotions, sometimes the perfect treatment is a supportive hand, inviting someone to follow a particular path.

**Joseph...... Spiritual Exploration and Recovery from Lyme Disease.**

***Bio:*** *Dr Joseph Barsuglia. 33 years old when first working with Iboga, 41 now. 3 grams TA (total alkaloid) plus two scoops of Iboga root bark. Male. USA, living in Europe. Joseph is a former Christian pastor, psychologist, researcher and entrepreneur. He is currently focused on creating centers for excellence for working with psychedelics in naturalistic settings for the purpose of spiritual development. Motivated by "Spiritual exploration and recovery from Lyme disease."*

**Author's Introduction:** With his intelligence and genuine child-like curiosity, Joseph's contribution to the fields of addiction research and plant medicines is gigantic. His interview explores the ideas of interconnectivity and the nature of time. This is also reflected in his research and life path, which weaves together psychology, Christianity, a rigorous scientific background and his own healing, while contributing to the healing of many others.

**Where did you first hear about Iboga?**

I first heard about Iboga, when I had just left a position as a psychologist at the Veterans Hospital. I was working at the Veterans Hospital in Los Angeles, and one of my positions there was working in the addiction treatment center. I was working with a lot of older veterans who had been treated with methadone, an opiate replacement drug, and they were mainly on these drugs stemming all the way back from Vietnam, dealing with opiate addiction, mainly heroin addiction.

I left that position and was connected through a friend, who was working with Dr. Martin Polanco, who was the founder and medical director of Crossroads Treatment Centre in Mexico. He now leads a non-profit group called 'Mission Within' that exclusively treats Veterans with different forms of psychedelic therapy. I had both a clinical and a research background. A friend introduced me to Dr. Martin because he was looking for a psychologist who could do both clinical and research work in the clinic. This was in 2014.

At the time, there was very little published research on Ibogaine or Iboga in terms of larger samples of observational clinical data, and they were also working with 5-MeO-DMT, which had zero human data at the time. He had explained to me about Ibogaine and 5-MeO-DMT, what they were doing at the clinic. I had not heard of either one of those compounds, and when he told me the properties of Ibogaine, what it does, how effective it is for treating opiate addiction, my first response was, "Why the hell haven't I heard about this?! I've been working in addiction treatment and really committed to helping people heal, and there's a natural, plant-based solution that could potentially be this efficacious, why is this not on the front page of everything?!"

That's how I first heard about it, and then I began working in the clinic and seeing what was happening firsthand with these natural psychedelics. We were predominantly treating people from the United States that were primarily addicted to opiates, but also other substances like amphetamines, and alcohol. I began to see firsthand what was happening psychologically and spiritually in these sessions, physiologically with coming through opiate withdrawal, as well as seeing what was happening with 5-MeO-DMT. From that point on, with those two medicines, I really found a sense of my life calling, because having worked recently in the Veterans Hospital, I was quite disheartened by what I saw in terms of options for veterans as well as in the traditional mental health system more broadly.

I've worked in all different sectors of mental healthcare, from adolescents all the way through to end of life in different inpatient/outpatient rehab centers and treatment centers. By the time I was ready to be at the peak of my field, I was feeling like I wanted to leave. I felt like there just weren't truly effective therapies, especially for complex forms of trauma.

I was working with a lot of traumatized veterans and was just not feeling fulfilled with the resources and the options that were available. So, when I found out about Ibogaine, as well as 5-MeO-DMT, to me, it was a very spiritual, personal, revelation of finding my life's calling, what I was to give my life to and what I should be focusing on for the rest of my life's work.

I had gone through these skills in developing academic research, how to publish papers, how to be an effective psychotherapist. When I found out about these new therapies it was like, "This is something I can give all this energy and experience towards and really believe in it and feel that it's going to really impact people's lives in a really effective and powerful way."

To me, this brought together two sides of myself too, that I had a pretty hard wall between, which was before I got into psychology, I was a Christian pastor at a church and was a spiritual director. I led the music and did spiritual counseling. That's what initially drew me into psychology. But, I had abandoned part of that spiritual side of myself personally and also professionally. When I saw the spiritual nature of Iboga and Ibogaine experiences there was this convergence of the spiritual, medical and the clinical therapy. It was the convergence of everything that I had been exposed to in my life, but had been separated in my mind. Iboga found me at the perfect time.

**Did you feel spiritually called to Iboga?**
Yes, I did feel spiritually called because simultaneously I was dealing physically with the symptoms of chronic Lyme disease, at the time I was starting to work with Ibogaine professionally. I felt called to try the therapy to see if it would help my Lyme disease, because Lyme disease had taken a toll on my nervous system. I had a lot of fatigue and neurologic issues and knew about the neuro-regenerative properties of Ibogaine. Also, hearing about Bwiti describe it as being connected to the original source of humanity, the cosmos, and in this spiritual way I was feeling really called to receive the plant. I've been a spiritual seeker most of my life and I was really hungry to have that experience and see what the medicine would show me, on my own path, and about its spiritual intelligence.

**What was your life like before Iboga or Ibogaine?**
Before Ibogaine, I was very much on an academic clinical path. I was working in a hospital at a university and publishing research, and didn't have much awareness outside of just the American dream or the suburban life of having a family and a house and a career. I didn't really have a sense of, number one, knowing the fullness of who I was, and then number two, knowing the fullness of my work, what I'm here to do or to give, and Iboga showed to me both of those things. I always had a connection to God and spirituality, I had moments of divine insight, awareness and connection throughout my life. However, nothing in the universe of what Iboga would show me.

**Building on that, what is your life like now after working, or with working, with Iboga?**

Now I would say I have a much more transcendent view of reality, of the relationship between the material and immaterial world, and the nature of the spiritual and ancestral world. With Iboga, I believe it showed me snapshots of past lives, so I had a direct experiential contact with material that I believe was past life trauma. It was undeniable, and from my rational assessment and those of my colleagues these could not just be pure subjective hallucinations. These experiences shifted my worldview about the nature of the soul.

Through Iboga and subsequent initiations into Bwiti, who are the lineage holders of this sacred gift, I felt like I had this connection between understanding the power of ritual as an ancient and advanced spiritual technology. Through Bwiti ritual and the care around preparation, I have a much more elevated view of the importance of purification, what it means to be initiated and to do the preparatory work. In the West, we do not have robust cultural containers for initiation, and I now see this missing element as one of the most important paths for achieving deeper states of spiritual development and personal growth. There is a likely connection between Bwiti and the initiate rights in ancient Egypt, which involved highly sophisticated rituals designed to purify the physical, emotional, and energetic layers of the body, and ultimately help one reconnect to their ancestors and their own divine nature and spiritual identity.

I feel like now I have a reason for living really. I have something that I feel like it's worthwhile to give my life to until the day I die. I feel like I met one of the greatest gifts in the garden of the planet earth. It can truly help people heal from the most seemingly intractable forms of human suffering like PTSD, addiction, and even neurological conditions. This gift can tap us back to our individual roots and the collective roots of the planet. As a pastor, I was always in service to the divine. In Bwiti, one way Iboga is understood is as God's spirit, or the Holy Spirit. And in my theology now, I believe a primary way that God's spirit communicates to the human psyche is through the plant kingdom, through entheogenic plants.

I trained to be a therapist and a healer, and after Iboga, now I see the depth at which we hold experiences in the psyche and in the body. I had always been taught that trauma is held in the body or the subconscious mind, and I had continuously witnessed this in my practice. However, Iboga showed me the raw, visceral, nature of how we can hold unprocessed suffering, how deep it runs on a cellular level and how early it becomes encoded in the nervous system. I have witnessed Iboga uproot trauma from myself and others in a way that is unparalleled in the healing arts and compared to other psychedelics and plant medicines.

Iboga has shown me the nature of the symbolic mind, which is spoken about a lot in archetypal and transpersonal psychology. Now I see how much of consciousness is held in a visual or a pre-verbal, symbolic, way. I had known theoretically about this, but never had direct experience to that degree as I did with Iboga with the clients and the patients that I've worked with.

**How did Iboga help with your Lyme disease, and do you think it cured you off it? How did it work? What's your understanding of how it worked?**
I would say that coming into my first experiences with the full plant in Costa Rica I had a lot of chronic fatigue and some involuntary tremors in my hands, almost like early Parkinson's. My research specialty was early onset dementia, so I was working with a lot of young individuals that had Parkinson's or Alzheimer's that were in their forties and fifties, and I started having these symptoms and it scared the shit out of me. I was starting to have, not the same symptoms, but similar cluster of issues as the clients and research participants I was working with.

I had a really strong ceremony the first time. I was in bed for 72 hours, and I couldn't walk for three days. After working with Iboga immediately, probably two or three days after, when I was coming out of it, it felt like someone had taken a steam cleaner and cleaned out my nervous system or had buffed and scrubbed out every nook and cranny of my brain. I was able to look at my hand and hold my hand steady and feel strong and connected in a way that I hadn't felt in many years. After 48 hours of traveling through galaxies, dimensions, facing my deepest fears, and lots of physical purging, I felt I was rooted and present in my body in a way that I had never experienced.

It may be bizarre to say that you could feel something working in your brain cells. We don't exactly have tactile receptors in our brain tissue. But, I felt that it was removing damage or debris or residual inflammation that the Lyme disease had caused. These experiences of feeling something akin to a form of brain surgery is frequently reported by people who take Iboga or Ibogaine. I felt a really significant cognitive improvement afterwards. It was like someone had turned the lights on a high beam setting. I remember looking in the mirror three days after the journey, and it was like there was the presence of my soul and my energy in my eyes, it was like someone turned up the volume on it. I felt much more connected in my body.

I had also had a lot of chronic pain for many years, arthritic pain from the Lyme disease, and my pain was gone for about three or four weeks, which was a miracle to me. And I've tried every plant medicine I could since. To me, Iboga was the only one that really rooted me into my body at this depth. I've had so many long-standing challenges from the Lyme disease, other psychedelic medicines like mushrooms and Ayahuasca tended to pull me out of my body, which at times has not been that helpful. But Iboga has been one that has driven me deeper into my physicality in the most potent way.

I remember that day three afterwards, holding my partner, in the hot springs in Costa Rica, we just held each other for four hours, just arm in arm. I felt temporarily cured. It didn't cure my Lyme disease, but it's been one of the most powerful therapies. I think part of the reason it doesn't cure Lyme disease is because Lyme disease replicates quickly in the body, so you'd have to be doing flood doses every week, or something, to knock it down. It's just not logistically possible on a number of levels. But I think it does help over in the long run. It's definitely helped with fatigue, energy, stamina, physical strength, cognition and cognitive abilities. It does feel like it did some repair work on my nervous system.

Iboga has neurotrophic factors called GDNF, and it is able to stimulate brain cell growth. I am excited about it as a potential for Lyme sufferers as well as neurodegenerative diseases. For many of them, we don't really have any good cures at this point, like Parkinson's and Alzheimer's. There’s a lot of fighters (martial artists and veterans) now, too, that are turning to psychedelics. One of the programs that spawned out of Crossroads was called 'The Mission Within'. It is exclusively to treat veterans that had traumatic brain injury from combat, and they're having pronounced brain neurologic benefits as well. Iboga alkaloids are being advanced for many neurologic diseases.

**How did you prepare and would you prepare differently a second time?**
For the first ceremony I did a lot of reading. I worked as a psychedelic researcher and psychologist, so I had a lot of firsthand experience seeing people go through working with the medicine. I really got clear on my 'why'. Why was I doing it at that time? I attempted to strengthen my body as much as I could through working out. And I was told because I'm very thin, to bulk up a bit, which was very helpful information because my first experience was very deep. I didn't eat for a long time.

I tried to purify my diet and abstain from all substances, alcohol, and try to eat mainly a plant-based diet. I really just prayed a lot. I just prayed to the medicine to show me what I needed to see, and just stayed really open. I did have a bit of fear going into it and really just trying to work with that fear and come more into trust.

Even before I worked with the medicine, I was talking to the medicine just like another person in the weeks leading up to it, just communicating to the consciousness of the spirit of Iboga. I saw things showing up in my daily life that were synchronistic and undoubtedly connected to the preparatory phase. And I read a lot, but I felt like in some ways I read more than I needed to. I'm a researcher, so that's what I do, but I read a lot and I think in some ways it was helpful, in other ways it was limiting the experience. Iboga is infinite, and while it's helpful to have navigational coaching, it's such a variable experience, I've found people get expectations which are not consistent from person to person.

Then what would I do now, I would say I would do even more physical preparation to be really strong, healthy, and deeper physical purification, I think. In Gabon, "vomitivos" and ritual bathing are used in the week beforehand. In the months leading up, doing some fasting, not right before, but in the months leading up. I think doing other psychedelic work, other plant medicine work, before could be helpful, like going through a series maybe with psilocybin or Ayahuasca to shed layers of density prior to coming to Iboga.

I think working with other medicines to prepare or pre-initiate someone before doing any Iboga is useful. I think you can make it smoother and easier to carry less density, whether that's trauma or unprocessed emotions. I think physical preparation, trying things like acupuncture, massage, really deep body work movement practices, and spending a lot of time in nature beforehand, I think all set someone up in a better way for the work.

**What medical precautions did you take to make sure it was a safe experience?**
I had a full metabolic blood panel. I had an EKG, and I just made sure I was physically strong at the time, because I had lost weight due to the Lyme disease, so I was attempting to bulk up. I was taking some medications that I stopped because they were contraindicated for the medicine. I had a good three month window off the contraindicated medications.

**As a psychologist, are there any medications that you would say are the most contraindicated or ones people should really avoid?**
For sure amphetamines. Many people take amphetamines for ADHD issues, which can compromise the heart, and then most psychiatric drugs will interact with the Iboga, so many anti-psychotics, antidepressants, hypnotic drugs, sleep medications, will be contraindicated. And Ibogaine and Iboga have such a broad, complex pharmacology. They interact with the vast majority of medications that are used in psychiatry, so it's almost an exception to find a psychotropic medication that doesn't interact with Iboga.

**Interviewer: That's a good point. I think it's really important to talk to your facilitator or talk to the person holding space for you about the medications people are using. It's more of a rarity, what doesn't affect Iboga rather than what does affect Iboga.**

That's very true. And the only person that's going to know that is a pharmacist or a psychiatrist who has an understanding of Iboga and can read the literature on Iboga. Even in the world of pharmacology, what Iboga and Ibogaine do in the brain is on the deep end, so an expert like Dr. Kenneth Alper, who is a psychiatrist and has studied Ibogaine for decades, even he says we don't even fully know what Ibogaine is doing. So, you do need to talk with a specialized pharmacist or an MD or someone that's in the medical profession that knows all the known contraindications with medications and Ibogaine.

**Interviewer: I think it's a really useful, but broad blanket rule, is that "presume it's going to affect it unless you are certain otherwise."**
I think that's a really good metric.

**What was your intention with working with Iboga?**
My intention was to understand the medicine because I was working in a clinic with it. I feel that anyone who's serving this medicine or working clinically needs to have the experience with it, and many especially on the medical side do not. I really wanted to know firsthand what it was like, just from an experiential perspective. I was calling in physical healing to my body and then I also wanted to understand the spiritual nature of reality, because I've always been a seeker and I wanted to know what Iboga could show me about the spirit world, basically.

**How did it go about achieving that third part of your intention? Do you feel like it answered a lot or explained much to you?**
In a massive way. My first Iboga experience was one for the books. I mean, it completely blew my mind on every level. Because of the Lyme I've done an obscene number of flood doses, I've done probably 40 flood doses of Iboga, and the first time was uncanny in comparison to subsequent journeys. It was like it took me on a guided tour of the dawn of civilization and through a visual tour of the cosmos and star systems and planets, and then zoomed into the earth. It showed me what appeared to be the dawn of human civilization and showed me that it was Africa, and it showed me... It was also incredibly humorous. I asked, show me the first humans and it showed me this visual picture of a map of Africa spinning and disco lights, really funny neon flashing lights. This is it. This is the birthplace. I don't know if that's historically accurate, but that's what the medicine showed me through my own mind.

It took me through different snapshot images that were so crystal clear and so cinematic, but it was through the eyes of a witness or a person. It was like a person looking out through a set of eyes at different scenes from different timelines in human civilization, and all I could fathom was that it was maybe past lives or it was collective consciousness. It was just showing me human experience through different sets of eyes throughout history.

There were different historical eras. Some were in China. A really vivid one was I was looking down at my body and I was in a military suit, it looked like World War I or World War II, some kind of battle scenes. But it was like I was looking out through the eyes of the person that was in those memories.

Then it took me through what appeared to be like if someone took you on an elevator from third dimensional consciousness, all the way up to unitive source consciousness, it was like starting on the earth plane and then going up the pyramid into higher dimensional realities all the way into formlessness, and I said, I want to keep going, take me all the way into the heart of God. I want to keep going.

It was going higher, higher and higher, and then there was this ceiling and there were these hieroglyphs, geometric patterns, and there were closed doors. It was like an alien circular vault, like what you'd see on the front of a bank vault or something. But it was vertically above me. And the message was "None shall pass (like through the vault). This is the end of the line buddy. This is as high as you can go."

It showed me a vision of Heaven, or a perfected reality. That could have been from my programming being raised in the Christian theology, but it showed me what seemed to be some form of the afterlife of heaven, everything was perfect. It was just celebration, bliss, no suffering, pure love, beings were interacting from a place of psychic communication, and it was pure peace and harmony and coexistence, and it seemed to be a higher-level dimension than earth.

I asked Iboga to show me the darkness that's on the earth. Show me what's messed up on the earth. It depicted a really funny, humorous, visualization of corporate greed. The funniest image that I saw was on the lower half of the screen there was a rainforest, the beautiful lush vegetation of the planet, and then there was a box on top of that and it was all these men in business suits. They were double fisting, eating fried chicken, and they had no pants on and they were pooping on the earth, pooping on the lower frame of the planet. It was like a board meeting happening with guys and they're half dressed, eating junk food, and then just dropping waste on the planet.

It showed me the beauty of nature. It felt like a David Attenborough tour through African topography; the savannas, the jungle and the forest. Beautiful scenic landscapes. That was by far, 100 times more vivid than any subsequent journeys I've had, which have been all over the map.

**How does the first couple of ceremonies, compare to where you are now, 35+? Are there any big differences between doing it so many times?**
I would say I really trust the medicine now. But, it always brings up some fear. Now I trust that it feels like strapping into a rocket ship or something when I cross over into the spirit world. I trust this technology and I'm just going to let it do me, let it take me. And it's physically easier now, still challenging, but I celebrate the purges. It's easier to allow my body to release when it's clearing something. I also find it now much more present moment focused and direct, sharing with me personal insights into my life and direction and really a mirror, an accountability, a bit less like a cosmic tour.

The medicine shows me where I'm getting in my own way. Also, relationally, how I'm treating others, and who I may be neglecting. It shows me my blind spots consistently. It feels more personal actually, now, than it does cosmic. And it continues to bring me back to presence and quiet the mind.

**How did you consume Iboga? What did you take and where, what was the form and the total dose?**
For my first journey there were two heaping spoonfuls of root bark and then two grams of total alkaloid extract. And I'm a small guy, so for me, I was horizontal for about 72 hours. And subsequently after that I did an Ibogaine journey, which was 1100 milligrams of pure Ibogaine HCL. I found that to be much shorter acting. I came out of it much faster the day after, and it was not as

therapeutic, both psychologically or physiologically in the nervous system, Ibogaine compared to the full plant.

Now, current journeys for myself, what I typically do is one to two spoonfuls of root bark and about a gram of TA. That's a strong dose where I have someone sitting for me and I'm laid out for a day, and then it's a day recovery and about 48 hours back to baseline. I find the TA to be my favourite means of consuming it. I like root bark for regular use or for micro-dosing, and I like the physical scrubbing that comes from the root bark. However, to do a root bark only flood dose, I think it's good and in line with Bwiti. That's how it's done traditionally, but I find it to be harder on my body than TA when consuming large amounts.

**What would be your general advice to people considering Iboga?**
Start with other psychedelics first, and I would look at Iboga across the landscape of psychedelics, in a way like graduate school, because of the intensity, because of the duration, because of the depth. If you look at the human body and energetic system as an onion, we all hold different levels of density from trauma, generational patterns, toxic substances in our environment or our foods. It's good to think about approaching Iboga like a stepwise progression of self-purification, both physically, mentally, psychologically, prior to coming to it. In contrast to using Iboga as the thing that's going to solve your current problem. Try everything you can on your issue or problem before you get to Iboga.

However, I would make a caveat for someone that's in a life-threatening situation. It could be their mental health, whether it's depression, suicidality, or addiction. Iboga can be a very effective starting place if they're in a desperate place. It's one of the big tools in the toolkit in terms of healing. If someone is in a place where they've been resistant to other forms of treatment, I would say Iboga could be a lifesaver in certain cases. But from the psychological standpoint, in a perfect world, someone should have a number of lower intensity psychedelic experiences under their belt before they go to Iboga, because it can be psychologically destabilizing and require a very long time to integrate.

**I think if you're working for psycho-spiritual growth, it should be not a last resort, but like a post-graduate school, and then if you're working with Iboga for emergency reasons, when you feel the call or when it's appropriate, I think then it's a good early option.**

Agreed. I think for medical issues, most medical issues could probably be treated with somewhere like a moderate dosage or micro-dosing. I actually don't recommend people, like myself, with Lyme disease, do a lot of flood doses. Many people with chronic illness may be too medically frail. Many people that have medical issues that may want to try this for treatment reasons, it may be too much on the body to do what would be equivalent to a flood dose. There's a place for gentle, consistent micro-dosing, or intermittent mid-level dosing for things like multiple sclerosis or chronic fatigue or Parkinson's or HIV related issues. I think the flood dose may be overkill in terms of the intensity that's required.

**Do you think micro-dosing is useful for integration, for integrating the flood doses? Do you have any other thoughts on micro-dosing?**

I think micro-dosing is profound and it's consumed pretty regularly in traditional ceremonies and at lower dosages. Micro-dosing can be helpful for integration and maintaining the levels of NorIbogaine (an Ibogaine metabolite) in the system after a flood dose, which can help the positive and healing effects continue like reducing cravings and the positive psychological effects. I think the current world of micro-dosing can be a little bit too focused on biohacking or performance enhancement. I don't think that's a high enough ideal or reason for using Iboga.

If you are thinking of micro-dosing Iboga, I don't think it's a valid enough reason right now to justify the current harvesting of plants to use it just to boost your energy or creativity. There is an overharvesting and poaching of the plant. It can be useful for this, but there's a long way to go to plant enough Iboga for it to be a sustainable resource. The sustainability issue in Gabon needs to be addressed first. For ongoing long-term use and the reasons that most people are micro-dosing like for mood, focus, energy, creativity, compounds that are easier to grow, more sustainable, or less endangered should be used, like San Pedro, psilocybin or LSD.

If we start to think about Iboga as one of the most precious resources on the earth, and Bwiti as a beautiful ancestral spiritual tradition, then what would be a virtuous way to approach this medicine and tradition and the topic of micro-dosing this "holy wood" as it is called in Bwiti?

**Author: It wouldn't be mass consumption. It wouldn't be widespread micro-dosing for corporate efficiency. That's for sure.**

**Is there anything you wish you knew before doing Iboga about the process?** Just how varied experiences can be and that there is no stereotypical Iboga experience. There's no common Iboga experience. I guess I wish I would've known in my experience the beauty of the full plant in contrast to Ibogaine, because I feel like there's bias in both contexts, medical or spiritual, depending on what people are more familiar with. I didn't realize how different the two sources would be, Ibogaine versus a full plant experience. Iboga can last much longer and be more physically challenging.

I also didn't really appreciate the depth and the sophistication of Bwiti and the beauty in all the symbolism and how much is there. I thought it was a more simplistic Indigenous tradition, but it's really high level, developed ritual practices and deep spiritual technology. It contains rich stories, healing techniques, history and symbolism, sacred protocols, and cosmology.

One of my Bwiti teachers refers to the techniques as 'psycho-magic' rituals. Beautiful rituals that create symbol and form for the initiate, and also safety and spiritual protection with the ceremonial use of the medicine. Maintaining inclusion of the traditional or ancestral Bwiti knowledge is essential. Iboga is like a spiritual surgical tool, and in my opinion requires as much training as a surgeon. From what I have heard and seen, the chief Nemas in Bwiti train for a minimum of 10 years. The Bwiti tradition has hundreds or thousands of years of development and rituals. I think we need to respect and learn from it. It's not just something you can just start playing with or doing on your own. Some people do Iboga on their own and can have meaningful experiences, but it's not the highest way or the most respectful way it can be. We don't know what we don't know, so there's a lot to learn. I realized regarding the process I had vastly underestimated how rich and sophisticated Bwiti truly is.

**Was there a memorable moment or particularly profound vision you had? Has this vision come true?**

There was something really remarkable that happened to me in my life. When I was 18 years old, I was suicidally depressed from, what I didn't know at the time was, Lyme disease. I asked the universe to show me a reason to live, and I put my head down to pray on my floor. What came to me was the vision of this cosmic tree that was spread over the planet.

I was 18 years old at that time. Then when I first did Iboga, I was 33. I didn't know what that tree was at the time when I was 18. I had no idea. But it was really profound and vivid, so I was like, this is a sign that I'm getting that I need to not kill myself and hang in there.

What I saw on Iboga, I became really tearful several days after, because I realized on some level, I think this was the tree that was shown to me, this cosmic tree that was enveloping the earth. I saw almost exactly the same vision in my first Iboga journey as I saw when I was 18.

This tree, its roots were holding the entire earth and were wrapped around the earth. It was lifting the earth and all the people on it up into a higher state of being. It was drawing this planetary ball into its highest expression, and that included healing nature, healing the water of the earth, healing the people of the earth, healing the trauma in the people of the earth. It completed a full circle for me and that's how I knew it was my life mission. This plant had probably saved my life a decade and a half before I actually took it.

That vision was so beautiful, because I saw Iboga as a planetary technology and a gift. Its consciousness encompasses high-level planetary wisdom and wisdom from the immaterial planes. To some extent, it feels like it's something from a foreign dimension. It's something that's elevating us to a higher level of existence.

In Bwiti, it is thought that the tree is the tree of knowledge from the original Garden of Eden. I've had this thought that to get back, if we want to make this planet like the Garden of Eden, to get back to the Garden of Eden, we have to eat the root. You got to eat the garden to get back to it. It's only through the garden that we can get ourselves back to it.

**Why would someone want to combine 5-MeO-DMT with their Ibogaine experience?**

I want to make a really important distinction from the get-go, is that the way it's been used so far in combination has only been after Ibogaine, not after Iboga. The difference is because with Iboga there are many other alkaloids and it lasts significantly longer in the body, with a longer metabolism. So, combining 5-MeO-DMT after Iboga is not the same thing as combining it after Ibogaine. Ibogaine has a much shorter half-life than the other alkaloids that still have to be determined, but experientially, we know Ibogaine, people are back to their baseline much sooner than the Iboga full plant.

Because I know there's a lot of psychonauts, if you read online, you can see that this may be a good combination, but if you don't make that distinction, it could be potentially fatal. Another safety caveat around this was that the excretions of the Sonoran desert toad, contain a number of different tryptamines and one is bufotenin, and that can place an additional burden on the heart. There's some cardio-toxicity to it and it is a vasoconstrictor, so it increases blood pressure and heart rate. That can be a safety risk in combining these things. So screening is even more central if someone's going to work with these. That said, from a cardiac perspective, it's safer to work with synthetic than the bufo toad extract or the 'natural' bufo secretions.

I can talk about it in a couple of different domains. So, on the pharmacological side, why it's interesting is Ibogaine works on a plethora of neurotransmitters, but it actually doesn't work that strongly at the classical psychedelic receptors, which are the serotonin 1A and 2A receptors that psilocybin and LSD work on, that are associated with a mystical or unitive experience.

So, in a way, 5-MeO-DMT is like a jigsaw puzzle with Ibogaine in the brain. It's complimenting what Ibogaine does not do, in some ways, from an experiential perspective. Because typically when people do Ibogaine, they're not having euphoric, unitive experiences outside of time and space. Usually, you can orient yourself to where you are. Whereas with 5-MeO-DMT, time and space are dissolving. It tends to be pretty euphoric. And, it tends to be very unitive and mystical. So, from an experiential perspective, they're very distinct, very unique, and each have their own healing potentials.

I would say in regards to working in addiction with Ibogaine and then 5-MeO-DMT. Ibogaine is very heavy, very purgative, it's detoxifying the body. It can be very confrontational with someone's subconscious mind or traumas. It can be very dark. It can really psychologically shake someone. In some cases, people feel a bit broken afterwards or shattered and require a lot of integration.

The 5-MeO-DMT experience people have described it as being like a cleansing or release of a lot of the density or the heaviness that was brought up by the Ibogaine experience. So, it can soften and bring in some grace and release. On Ibogaine, oftentimes people are not having emotional catharsis because your body is anesthetized, and so that can happen in the days after Ibogaine though, people are much more connected to their body, and 5-MeO can really help catalyze emotional releases, catharsis, be very heart opening. It can help complete the process of Ibogaine, of what was stirred up.

Often with 5-MeO, after Ibogaine, people have really deep releases of grief, primal screaming, anger or just really repressed emotions.

I think from an addiction perspective, and also from what we know about the psychedelic scientific research, the mystical experience, that experience of unitive consciousness or oneness, that experience tends to be what is driving some essential aspect of the healing. Whether it's looking at psilocybin for end-of-life anxiety or LSD for alcoholism, or even some of the research with ketamine and cocaine addiction. Across these different psychedelics it seems to be this unitive experience that is driving the efficacy in terms of having positive outcomes afterwards.

In the addiction setting, and also the mental health setting, it seems very complementary to the Ibogaine experience to have someone cleanse and purify themselves with Ibogaine. It helps them to have that internal reset, that deep, deep physical and neurologic reset. The 5-MeO-DMT allows them to tap into a more unitive, expansive, experience. Also, a lot of times people are connected to just feelings of love and positivity and which can be really helpful after some of the heaviness or the shadow work of Iboga or Ibogaine.

I found when people did 5-MeO-DMT after Ibogaine versus just doing it without Ibogaine, the heavy lifting of the Ibogaine set someone up in a way that they were energetically rooted. They could surrender easier to the 5-MeO experience, and they were more open. I think, in some ways, they were more grounded too, because Ibogaine really draws you into yourself. Ibogaine helps them to be able to be grounded in the 5-MeO experience.

As an aside, the Ibogaine alkaloids potentiate 5-MeO-DMT, so it makes the 5-MeO stronger because Ibogaine works on something called the serotonin transporter, which influences how long serotonin hangs out in the receptors. 5-MeO-DMT is a serotonergic substance, so it turns up the volume on 5-MeO-DMT, so you require 20-30% less 5-MeO-DMT to have a breakthrough experience with it. So that's also important from a safety perspective.

**Is there anything else people should be wary of?**

I would say this was something that we pioneered at Crossroads and some Ibogaine clinics are doing it, and people have talked about it like the root and the crown. The root of the tree of healing and the crown, 5-MeO-DMT being like the light at the top in the sense of bridging people to the unity of awareness. But without the roots, you don't excavate and go deep and really unearth what the core of the issues are. So, I think 5-MeO-DMT on its own can be a bit superficial, because people are blasting into unitive consciousness for a really brief period, but they're not able to do the characterological work or the inner transformational sludging through the muck of their own issues to purify and evolve.

I think the medicines really complement each other in an important way. I think we're just now at the point in history where we're approving single molecules, psychedelic molecules, for different conditions. But I think in the future we're going to look at how to sequence these medicines together in series and how to combine them in the best and most responsible way.

To me, as a healer, as a psychologist, and a researcher, I haven't found two more potent healing medicines than those two. I think in some way they represent some of the tools that can cause the greatest shifts in people that otherwise have been very stuck or unable to heal. I think there's space for every plant medicine in the spectrum, but these two in particular, in terms of their potency, I think are at the top of the scale. Thus, they require the most thoughtful and sophisticated preparation, integration, guidance, parameters and education. They're really NOT to be taken lightly.

I think in the future, once these individual medicines come through safety approvals, I think they'll be very complementary in the future of addiction treatment. I wrote an academic paper on the topic of why sequencing 5-MeO-DMT and Ibogaine in the treatment of alcoholism holds promise in the future, both the pharmacology of it and the psychology of it.

**I have all of my published scientific papers available for download on my personal website (Author's note: links to Dr. Barsuglia's work can be found in the appendix).**

**Author's note.**

I was personally very intrigued by Joseph's long, timeless journey. Joseph's evolution of being a suicidal teenager and seeing the tree of life (possibly Iboga) to then working with Iboga extensively in his adult life, really made me question the "linear nature of time." Was Iboga working with him and guiding him from his teenage years? Was he fated to meet a tree of life at some point? Often the synchronicities and miraculous manifestations of visions play an important role on the healing journey. How we talk to ourselves and unpack our personal stories is vital to the healing process.

Although Joseph treated and mitigated Lyme disease with Iboga, it is not something I or he would recommend to others at this time. He has a lifetime of training and a professional background in alternative medicines and is uniquely placed to work with Iboga. From the outside, his treatment of Lyme disease appears to have helped build a deep relationship and profound understanding of Iboga. I am grateful for his pioneering work and hope that in the future more targeted treatments of Lyme disease can be tailored so others don't have to go through the ordeals he has courageously gone through.

**Anthony...... Healing Childhood Trauma, Connection to Source, and Standing in his Power.**

***Bio:*** *Anthony Esposito. 38 years old when first working with Iboga, (May 2013 was first experience with Iboga). Male. USA. Root bark and Total Alkaloid extract (20-25 grams for each of my first two ceremonies). Anthony is the co-founder of Awaken Your Soul Iboga Retreats in Costa Rica and the Iboga provider for the retreat. He lives and works in the jungle with his wife Amber and daughter Luna. He is committed to spreading the healing and wisdom of Iboga in a safe and sacred environment. Basse! Motivated to work with Iboga for "Healing childhood trauma, deepening connection to source, and to stand in his power."*

**Author's Introduction:** When I interviewed Anthony on the phone, I immediately felt I was talking to an embodiment of the 'divine masculine'. Anthony was professional, direct, authentic, open and extremely helpful. As the founder of 'Awaken your soul' in Costa Rica, Anthony has guided many people to new, awakened lives with Iboga. He brings a wealth of knowledge that comes from witnessing the transformation of countless people.

**Where did you first hear about Iboga?**

I first heard about Iboga, when I was in Peru in 2010-2011, working with Ayahuasca, someone brought Iboga up. My initial reaction was "Woah, that sounds really strong!"

In 2013, we were back in the USA for about a year and a half and my Angel and brother Peter called me and asked if I had ever heard of Iboga. I told him I had. He invited me to join him, if I felt the call to it. Two seconds before he asked me, the decision was made. I was going. It was clear.

**How were you called to Iboga?**

I felt spiritually called to Iboga. The medicine called me in a very deep way. So deep, that since May of 2013, after my first 7 night, 2 Iboga ceremony experience, I have been working with Iboga ever since. I returned to Costa Rica a month later to work and train with it. I haven't done anything apart from work with Iboga, serve the spirit of the medicine and build bridges for people to come and experience it.

I felt the call in my whole being. In my body. For example, when I was on the plane coming to Costa Rica the medicine was already working. I started noticing some things that had been lying dormant for some time. It was so strong, before the ceremony had begun, I was already trying to figure out how to get Iboga back to my house in Miami. I hadn't even taken it yet. It was strong on a cellular level. I could feel something shifting within me. I was noticing things change before I even took the physical medicine.

**What was your life like before Iboga?**
I was pretty messy. I was suffering from a lot of anxiety, I was not feeling a connection to myself, to earth. I had suffered a lot with depression. I had a lot of childhood trauma. I was running at 10/10, very high octane. But I was running from life because I was afraid. There was a lot of self-destructive behavior, I was never physically addicted to anything. Still, I was traumatized and afraid to know who I was and be who I am. I didn't know who I was, I had no idea.

**What is your life like after Iboga?**
It has been 8 years this May (2021), my life has shifted and transformed in ways I could never have imagined. I feel very grounded, I feel in my body. I am rooted to the earth. I'm connected to nature. We opened a retreat in Costa Rica in 2018. I live and work in Costa Rica.

Iboga has helped to heal, on a physical level, my brain and the chemistry within my brain. My neural pathways have been improved and my brain feels better connected. There's definitely been some deep, deep work on my central nervous system. Maybe a year after I started working with Iboga I realized that I'm not anxious like I was. I felt very comfortable being in my body, learning more about my being and how I get on with the world. I get along much better with myself.

I feel much sharper. Very sharp. My brain operates at a very high level. I have also been able to understand the importance of getting rest. The medicine has taught me how to take care of myself and get rest. Serving the medicine, I am always giving. But there has to be times where I am receiving and resting as well.

**How did you prepare? Would you prepare differently a second time?**
I didn't prepare at all. I watched one video of a Gabonese Bwiti Shaman and that was it. I had already made the decision to go. I got on a plane and went. I did no research. I looked at no testimonials and no reviews. I felt the medicine calling.

Now that I have more experience, I always invite people to try not to look at everything that's out there on the internet. Eat healthy, drink lots of water, get rest, put your intentions out to the universe. Trust that if you are being called to come and work with this medicine, then follow that. You'll get the soul call and then the mind and ego will try and get in the way and disrupt it. The mind will create doubt as to why you shouldn't go. The decision was already made from within you, from your intuition. Follow that and trust that you will receive what you need.

**What precautions did you take to make sure it was a safe experience?**
When I first went, I don't think I even did an EKG. Now, I require everyone to have an EKG at their home base and then I have a trusted doctor review it. For people coming to my center, they can have an EKG done here with our doctors or you can get your exam at home. If people have had trouble with their liver, I require them to get a liver panel test.

Iboga is very safe for the right individual. A lot of the information on the internet and the complications at Ibogaine clinics have been when people are detoxing from heavy drugs. I have assisted with detoxes early on, as I was training in an environment where there were detoxes going on, but I haven't done detoxes myself. The detoxes weren't done at my facility. For the last 6 years, I haven't facilitated any detoxes and I have never had ANY complications whatsoever. I probably worked with 800-900 people over this time.

**What was your intention?**
Initially, To heal. I was looking to heal the trauma that was in my body. To begin to release that congestion that was within me. I wanted to heal my anxiety. I

didn't want to feel nervous energy anymore. I was really hyper aware of everything. I was stuck in a fight or flight mentality. I wanted to ground and release energy that wasn't serving me. I wanted clarity and direction.

Now, in subsequent ceremonies, I look to deepen my connection with Source. Iboga has taught me that there are no mistakes in anything. There are no mistakes, there are no wrong turns. Everything that has happened to me is exactly as it was supposed to be. I continue to work with the medicine, to deepen my connection to source and trust the divine plan of the universe.

**How did you consume Iboga? What did you take and where? What form? Total dose?**
The first time I took it was Root Bark and then TA. I would say each ceremony was about 30 grams. It was a good amount.

Now as a practitioner I work with root-bark and TA. I make my own extractions just with vinegar, no ammonia. I would say on average people are getting around 15-25g through this method. I've noticed over time that a little medicine goes a long way, with many people. You have to be really tuned in to study their tolerance, their energy fields to know how much to give them.

The nice thing about TA, is that for us westerners it is really tough to get the necessary bark down. TA can help. For people that have higher tolerances, I introduce TA for that 3rd or 4th dose. To get them what they need.

**Why did you decide to do it this way? Why did you pick this center?**
The structure of the 7 night 2 ceremonies, with the first ceremony on night 2 and the second ceremony on night 5 and day 4 the spiritual shower in the river, was the layout that they had at Iboga House when I went there in 2013. When I started working in different retreat environments, we followed that program.

When my wife Amber and I decided to open up "Awaken Your Soul," we wanted to have that layout of 7 nights, 2 ceremonies and a spiritual shower, but we wanted to add yoga, breathwork, art therapy, integration circles and amazing high vibrational food. We wanted a holistic experience. We knew people were coming for Iboga of course, but we wanted to provide a well-rounded experience. That way, people can take this practice home with them.

**What would be your advice to people considering Iboga?**
My best advice is "Is the medicine calling you or do you feel a call on a cellular level?" Are you hearing this call, when you check in with your body? If you put your mind aside and sit quietly for a period of time, and keep doing this for a few weeks, a month, is it there? If you keep feeling that call to go, GO!

The other piece is truly understanding, that we are all unique. When this medicine goes into your body, it aligns with your spirit, your intuition and intention. Together, the spirit of Iboga and your spirit design a treatment plan that is for you. There are a lot of commonalities that people experience, but the journey to how you get there is going to be unique to you. Do the best to embrace what you are receiving. Not what you're not receiving. Stay away from what you didn't get. You will receive a lot. If you look at what you didn't get you are missing the wisdom and healing you did receive.

**What are your thoughts on micro-dosing? Did you micro-dose after a flood dose for integration?**
Yes. I micro-dosed after my flood dose and I started training right away. For the person that's coming to do the retreat and then returning back home, I think you have to be mindful and conscious around Iboga. This is not a recreational thing. If you really feel that connection to Iboga after the retreat, I think micro-dosing can be good. It's not a daily thing. You should only do it, when you feel called to do it. You need to have a very clear intention as to why you are putting this medicine into your body on a given morning. What are you looking for? What are you wanting to release? What are you wanting to invite into your life? If someone is present, in their body and has reverence for Iboga, I think micro-dosing can be beautiful.

**Is there anything you wish you knew before doing Iboga about the process?**
Everything was perfectly designed for me. I know a lot of people like to really prepare and "get ready" for the experience. For me, it happened just the way it was supposed to be. We are our own healers. Iboga is a tool, yoga, breathwork, Ayahuasca are all tools too. But they don't do it for us. We do it, we have to do

the work. They help us get to that place and to shed, become more aware and more present. But they don't do the work for us. I noticed that in my integration, once I was feeling great, I thought I could sit back and just live. But then Iboga was like "HELLO!" You need to integrate, there is more to do!

I would say come with an open mind, come with an open heart. Come with the desire to look within and get to know yourself.

**Would you do Iboga again?**
Yes.

**Was there a memorable moment or particularly profound vision you had? Has it come true?**
There were definitely multiple visions. There was one where my wife Amber was leaving the relationship. She found another man. At the time, I didn't understand why I was seeing this. It was really comical because I was actually at her wedding in this vision. What I came to realize was I needed to get myself grounded and realign, in order to have this amazing woman in my life. There were times over the last eight years, where things were going a little sideways and I would think "Man, if I don't realign, this can possibly come true." It was very, very clear what I needed to do. That vision was very helpful.

**Has Iboga affected your spirituality?**
It has heightened my spirituality to levels I can't describe. It has enhanced my whole being. In terms of my spirit, I understand there's a physical world we all live in, and there's also a spirit world. Where, we can't see it, but we can feel it. It exists, all the time and everywhere. Iboga has really helped me understand both the physical and the spiritual. My practice is to walk one foot in each world.

**Anything else you'd like to add**
Waking up to yourself and to life, is not the easiest experience. But it is the most freeing experience, once you really are able to embody and accept who you are on every level. There is a process that happens, some people it happens quicker than others. If you have the desire, and really want to work out how to live a life connected to source, then these medicines, specifically Iboga can really help people with that connection and clarity.

**Author's Note.**

Anthony's journey highlights the non-linear and mysterious ways Iboga can work. For Anthony, he noticed that Iboga was already re-arranging and changing his life before he physically consumed the medicine. Many practitioners note that the medicine starts working when someone commits to Iboga. Often, this is when they return the medical form or book their flights. It's good advice to be very mindful and observant of how your life begins to shift, from the time Iboga is on your radar and when you commit to work with the medicine.

Anthony's experience embodies the lesson of connecting with an Iboga facilitator who is settled in their life, doing 'the work' themselves and totally focused on helping others. Another lesson we are reminded of in Anthony's interview is the practice of receptivity, really listening and tuning into the call or pull to work with Iboga. How can people know that it is the right medicine and time for them? For many, it is a deep, cellular knowledge that this is the right medicine for me, now. Or an intense curiosity or intrigue towards it. For many it seems as if Iboga is singing to them, seducing and enticing them to come. When that song becomes so loud and you can feel it in your heart, it might be the time to work with Iboga.

If that paragraph was mumbo-jumbo to you, it is probably not time to work with Iboga yet. ;)

**Amber...... Spiritual Curiosity and Growth.**

***Bio**: Amber Antonelli, 37 when first working with Iboga 45 now. Female. USA born but living in Costa Rica. Various doses of Iboga root bark and Total Alkaloid (TA). Amber began working with Iboga and other plant medicines out of spiritual curiosity, and later discovered the depth of her childhood trauma, finding deeper levels of needed healing. Amber worked as a professional chef for 24 years and is now co-owner and an Iboga provider at 'Awaken Your Soul'. Motivated to work with Iboga for spiritual curiosity and growth.*

**Author's Introduction**: As the chief of 'Awaken your soul' and counterpart to Anthony, it was natural that I felt that I was talking to the 'divine feminine' while interviewing Amber. Empathetic and compassionate, Amber gracefully shared her wisdom and authentic experience.

**Where did you first hear about Iboga?**

In 2010 while living in Thailand, my husband Anthony and I were fortunate enough to encounter a beautiful Peruvian Ayahuasca facilitator in Thailand. This retreat was our first Ayahuasca experience and marked our 'breaking open'. It was the beginning of our awakening. A couple weeks later, we were having dinner at a friend's house. There was a woman there who had just finished an Iboga experience with a group somewhere in Thailand. She was incredibly "war torn" for lack of a better term. I don't know if it was specifically the facilitators that did not hold an impeccable space, or if she just had a lot of darkness. I don't know that they were specifically mal-intended but that was the vibration that she put out, she indicated that they were very out of alignment. However, this can be hard to determine because when people's deepest and darkest comes out, sometimes it gets projected onto whoever's around them.

I remember hearing about her story and thinking there is absolutely no way I would ever do that medicine!

There was also another young man in our Ayahuasca group and he and Anthony were talking about an Iboga Shaman in Costa Rica. These encounters were the planting of the seeds. Fast forward, probably 2-3 years and we were living in Miami. A friend of ours invited Anthony to an Iboga retreat in Costa Rica. He came home a changed man and returned to this same retreat two weeks later to work and has never done anything ever since. Anthony's passion essentially paved the way for me to experience the medicine. It found me organically.

I would definitely say that my relationship with my partner has been the catalyst for my awakening. Both in essence of him seeking this medicine for his own healing for some pretty complex trauma. I came to Iboga because he was working with it. Initially, it was not for my own particular healing. So, I'm pretty unique in that way, not that I didn't have healing to do. I absolutely did and still do of course. I just wasn't seeking Iboga out directly (knowingly anyway!).

**Did you feel spiritually called to Iboga?**

My first retreat was good, it was definitely of another dimension. I came to the medicine more because Anthony was working with it, not with my own specific intentions. Because of this it was not one of the deep transformative experiences that we see all the time, for people that come to do this work.

However, in the week after, when I went home, my life was completely reorganized. It felt like my whole life fell apart. Then it was reorganized. Because of the medicine, I felt very stable, grounded and capable in that time of change. It was a dark night of the soul for sure. Anthony and I split up, for the first time ever. It was the first and only time in our whole relationship that we have broken up.

I don't know if I was fully aware of the presence of this medicine. My story is not a classic encounter of Iboga since I didn't seek it directly. I am a perfect example of total transformation, with this medicine, little by little, by little. You don't have to have one of these complete reorganizations of your life, your psyche and reality within one week in order to receive the massive benefit. A lot of people have that. But it doesn't work that way for everyone. For me it was slow and steady.

My deeper calling came in 2017, when I went to work with Anthony at 'Iboga Wellness'. I was initially working in the kitchen, because I had been a chef for most of my career. I thought that I didn't have a draw to other aspects of the retreat. The medicine changed that VERY quickly. A few months later I was helping in the ceremonies. Then I was being drawn to helping more in the ceremonies than the kitchen. It started to feel like "Oh my gosh, this might be part of my path!" It started clicking. Six months into that, it felt like it was time to go to Africa. Two years before I had said "You couldn't pay me $100,000 to go and take the strongest psychedelic on the planet in some dirt hut in the middle of Africa!" Going there for this type of work was terrifying. Hahaha, it still is terrifying! It's a big deal.

**What was your life like before Iboga?**

My life before the beginning of my awakening, which was before Ayahuasca (and Iboga), was free spirited. But I was still enchained by codependency and smaller traumas as a kid. I did not really connect to aspects of my childhood being traumatic, until I started doing more deep work. Slowly, I began to realize "Oh my gosh, that was totally inappropriate!" You become conditioned to think that these traumatic experiences are normal. My difficult experiences as a child, really gained a lot of clarity as I did the work, and ultimately Iboga helped with this. My life before my awakening was free spirited but very one dimensional. I didn't have a whole lot of connection to the divine. I didn't really understand the nature of reality, I didn't have trust in the process, I didn't have faith in the Universe. I meet people now who have no plant medicine experience and are very far down their path. They've had a lot of "awakening" already. I didn't have any of that. For me it was a very clear before and after moment with Ayahuasca.

Moving into Iboga, this medicine is so deep. It is profound. When you commit to working with it as a facilitator, you are called to do the deepest work you could ever imagine. It doesn't end! Every moment is another level. I have moved so much energy and learned so much, grown so much. I have so much faith and trust in this process. I know I still have so much work to do. I'm getting into aspects of my childhood recently, especially with this pandemic, that I thought I had definitely healed. But, I hadn't.

I wouldn't trade any of my traumas and challenges, for the life that I had before I understood the nature of reality, before I cultivated real heart centered beliefs and connected to what we are here to do. Previously, I looked at adversity as being really arduous, painful, unnecessary and to be avoided at all costs. But now, I don't say "Bring it on!" because I don't need anymore, I have enough going on, hahaha! But I'm very quick to surrender these days, and I'm grateful for that.

You gain the freedom of not having to believe that things are happening against you. They are happening *for* you. Adversity is not a torturous experience to be resisted and avoided, at all costs. Not at all. It's to be leaned into, relished and invited. It's an opportunity to level up your experience. It helps to open up to love and compassion. Every level of our own personal work makes us more capable of holding space for people. I feel really grateful for that, because the world needs it! So badly!

**What is your life like after Iboga?**
One of the things that we feel passionate about is that, "We do our own work." I've experienced other space holders that believe they are the healer and it's not their job to heal themselves, they think they are only there to heal others. Anthony and I don't believe that we are healing other people, the work starts with us. In that commitment is a constant "Ringing of that bell" if you will, of "This is not in alignment." You really need to look at it. In all of my experience and surrender there are still untouched parts of myself. There is still resistance to really being fully vulnerable and being at fault. I still have my stuff. I'm not a completely different person, but different in my understanding of it all. That's one of the things that my life with Iboga has taught me is "Accept all of me, love all of myself." That doesn't mean I like myself all of the time. It doesn't mean I don't have things I constantly want to shift and fine tune. I also accept the parts of myself that would be considered the "Shadow side." I know why those programs are installed. I know how I became who I am. In that process, I am able to have a lot more compassion for the world around me.

There is a lot of freedom and liberation. There is a lot of ass-kicking (getting my ass kicked). This medicine will kick your ass six ways to Sunday, especially if you are not listening. Especially if you are not showing up for the work. There are times where I don't show up for "The work." There are times where I want to blame and turn the pointer outwards. It doesn't tend to work well! But it happens, I am human.

I would say I feel way more tuned in after working with Iboga. I feel exponentially more emotionally intelligent. I feel more intelligent in relationship to seeing and understanding other humans, which I don't think there is enough importance placed on. I feel uber, uber aware as to how broken our system is. I'm aware of what we pass down to our kids and what the system tells us: that we don't need to know how to be in relation to each other, how to cook, how to grow food, build things. These fundamental tools. I can live without knowing about calculus and the mayflower. I'm pretty sure I'll survive. Hahaha! Will I be able to survive without knowing how to be in relationships with other humans? Without knowing how to cook and grow food? In terms of intelligence, there is a fine-tuned awareness that is part of my everyday experience.

There is this feeling of a lot of people that come to work with us, that they are failing. That's not fair to them, when really, they never had a leg to stand on. They never had a foundation built for them to be successful in important areas like self-love, how to be in relationships and working with the ego. It is heartbreaking. That is the kind of intelligence that this medicine teaches. How to relate with and understand others. It wants us to be more aligned with nature in every way. In every breath. A lot of people are connecting to that. It teaches emotional wisdom.

The more I learn, the more I realize I know nothing, about anything. I do feel wise. I feel very in tune, I feel connected. I feel connected to what is happening within me. That's a very important distinction. I really know nothing at all, but I try to follow my own inner compass and it usually leads me in the right direction.

**How did you prepare and would you prepare differently a second time?**
First of all, I don't really believe in mistakes. I think looking back I would have liked to be very clear on what my intentions were. I was doing it as an exploration because my husband was working with the medicine. That's not how people come to find this, typically. It's a very, very powerful process. There are not many people seeking Iboga for the fun of it, or "by accident." Having really clear intentions is essential.

I would have also liked to have done some preparations with a coach, or some sort of other healing modalities. This would help to access and refine those intentions. The medicine is going to do, what it's going to do. There's no wrong way to do it, provided you're doing it with a good facilitator. Every journey is different. If we asked 500 people about their experiences, they would all be different, and each subsequent journey for each 500 people would be different again. If you're not prepared, you're still going to get what you need. It will blast through the layers that it can get through. But maybe it won't get everything. There's no wrong way to show up, in the right environment, in a safe container.

This is ABSOLUTELY not the medicine to do by yourself or with a friend. You can take a few grams of psilocybin and go to the beach or go hiking. Iboga is not like that. It is the next level. You need to be safe energetically and physically when these types of portals are opened.

In terms of preparing mentally and emotionally, if you show up blocked, the medicine will get through what it can get through, in that space. You will still receive healing, but you will get so much more if you can get really to the essence of what you are looking to work on in advance. If you show up and are just thinking "I don't feel all that great. I know that I'm unhappy, I don't have any idea of what is going on." You will only get so far. For me to have gotten more out of my first experience, having more intention and clarity would have been very helpful.

I also believe that having an integration coach set up for afterwards is vital. We have a preparation workbook that we give to all of our guests, it goes pretty deep. Often people have a hard time finishing it, it excavates a lot. Again, you are left with yourself. It is good to work with someone, in this space, afterwards who understands how much therapy you can receive in such a short period of time with this medicine. It is really profound. Having this support can take the healing to a whole new level. Although I use many different modalities, I would not be where I am without the coach that we use. Her reflection, nurturing and pushing me into spaces I don't feel comfortable or capable of navigating on my own has been incredibly useful.

Most people get a full reorganization of their sense of reality. Weaving that into your everyday life is very complex. If you really want the whole process to be as effective, if you really want your financial, emotional, spiritual resources to be used as effectively as possible, the integration coach is essential. To make this medicine as effective as it has the potential to be, integration support is vital.

I love the ceremonies, the guided journeys and watching people have these transformative experiences, it's very nourishing, humbling and profound. I can't stress enough how important it is to continue that process. To use a western medicine analogy, like going to the doctor to get treated for cancer. Because essentially, the state of our mental, emotional and spiritual health is akin to cancer. If we are broken and battered and really seeking the help of Iboga, which is a total reorganization of your reality, we can effectively consider it to be a cancer that is attacking our wellbeing. You have to do follow ups with your doctor. You keep checking in. You don't just get treated and then disappear. You need to continue to dig and make sure that you are getting to everything.

**What precautions did you take to make sure it was a safe experience?**
The EKG is absolutely non-negotiable, you have to have it. The liver panel, is typically only encouraged if someone has a history of drinking or they have a history of having liver problems. Although, some people are very, very thorough in that way, you could absolutely get a liver panel, just to feel safe.

You absolutely do not want to be on any pharmaceutical medications. There are a few that are not contraindicated, for some benign things. You don't want to be on any antidepressants, anti-anxiety medication or things of that nature. We offer safe tapering protocols and suggestions.

In terms of mental, spiritual, physical, emotional safety, really try to connect with the providers and have a conversation. Ask them about themselves, ask them about how they set up their center? How do they work in terms of holding space for people? You will learn a lot just in that conversation. Do the facilitators do their own work? Do they think that they're the ones doing the healing or do they get out of the way and allow the medicine and the participants to do it? Do they hold your hand and give you hug, if you need it, or do they just leave you in a room to figure it out?

That's kind of what they do in Africa and that works for them, it's beautiful. That's not how we do it. We also don't coddle people but we do provide some help navigating through the process. We provide a lot of compassion and nurturing and reflective truth when needed. We also provide a lot of freedom and space for people to discover their own truth.

Getting a sense of whether or not you connect with the provider is important. Whoever it is, wherever they are, how they're serving the medicine. I think that's really, really important. And you know, are they someone who is going to force medicine down your throat if you're not really ready and willing to take more? The Indigenous approach is a different process in that regard. Although I do believe that you should never be forced to have medicine, no matter where you're taking it. We should always have our own agency, no matter what.

We give people a lot of different options. People should have a conversation with both the facilitator and integration coaches and see if they resonate with you. Don't just pick a center, based on how good they look on the internet. Talk to the people!

**How did you consume Iboga? What was the form and the total dose?**
I have absolutely no recollection of my experience the first time in that regard. I know I took TA capsules after some root bark, but I'm not sure how much. I think a medium scoop (5-10 grams total) and then half a capsule of TA.

Now, as I've worked with the medicine over the last 7 years my tolerance is so much lower. With plant medicines, you need less. Whereas with pharmaceuticals and alcohol you need more and more, to take you where you want to go. Now, because I am super open, I don't have the same walls I used to. Overall, energetically I'm far more open. I take very, very little medicine to have a full experience.

In Gabon, for my initiation I think I took 3 spoons. It was fresh bark. I got very violently ill, very quickly. After the third spoon I was throwing up harder than I have ever thrown up in my life. Harder than many ceremonies combined. There was no spiritual experience for my initiation, it was all physical cleansing. I really came to understand what happened in the months afterwards. It took me a long time to understand what I received. It was not nearly the type of initiation dose that I was expecting. But it did what it needed to do. I also discovered a week later that I was almost a month pregnant! I felt amazing throughout the entire pregnancy, and was easily able to facilitate ceremonies up until the ninth month. We are blessed with an amazing daughter. She's very vibrant and connected and the heartbeat of our space. We believe that there was a lot of energy and space cleared for her, by the medicine I took in my initiation and during my whole pregnancy.

I take a lot less medicine now, than I ever did. It's not about the quantity per say. It doesn't go by body weight, but by how open you are, for the most part.

**Why did you decide to do it this way? Why did you pick this Center or method?**

When I first started working with this medicine as a practitioner, it was a very masculine environment. I received a message, working with Ayahuasca, where she said "Honey, if you're going to do this work, you have to bring the femininity." I've struggled balancing my masculine and feminine a lot of my life, I'm a pretty powerful woman. I worked in professional kitchens for 25 years. In and of itself, that requires you to be very strong. From the age of 17, when I started working in professional kitchens, that is how I was molded. I'm sure it was already within me but I got to really ground that type of behavior into my programming. When Ayahuasca told me that I needed to "bring the femininity," I knew she was speaking not only for the experience of the guests but also for my own healing.

The Bwiti tradition is something that we weave in, as well as a lot of our own wisdom from the medicine and life in general. We've added other supportive modalities, like Yoga, breathwork, Reiki, art therapy and integration circles. We've emphasized that nurturing component. The land itself is breathtaking. The space is well decorated, we have flowers everywhere and beautiful plants, the retreat has a feminine vibration. We felt drawn to blend different modalities. We've come up with our own flair and really, we allow our medicine to speak through Iboga.

Iboga is a very adaptable plant. I believe it to be the perfect blend between the masculine and feminine. A lot of people see it as a masculine spirit, I see it as both. I think in developing the way we hold space, it was important to find a balance between the masculine and feminine. We are always learning, tweaking and growing. Our practice is so much stronger than when we first opened. It continues to grow and change. Bwiti is the foundation, but Anthony and I bring our own individual medicine to the experience.

**What would be your general advice to people considering Iboga?**
I think if you're considering Iboga, it's because it's calling you. This medicine is not for everyone. But typically, if it's come across your field and it's pulling you, there's a reason. You have a date with destiny, so to speak.

My advicc is to listen to the call. You might not be ready the moment you hear about it. For some people it takes 10 years for them to put the medicine in their body. And that's okay. Some people hear about it and three weeks later, they're on a plane. If you're feeling the call, then answer it. Understand that this medicine has a reputation of being really strong and it has the capability of being REALLY strong and intense. What I feel is the *true* intensity of the medicine is in its deep and transformational power... Most of the time it's not a 72 hours psychedelic experience that completely plasters you to the mattress like some think. Hahaha!

A lot of the testimonials are done by people that are healing from addiction. Their bodies are going through a lot. It's a whole different process for addiction than it is for psycho-spiritual ceremonies. That's not to say that it can never be intense like that, it can be but that's not the norm. So, understand that the medicine can be very gentle, nurturing and loving. It does not have to be an ass-kicker. You also don't have to take heroic doses in order to get what you need. If Iboga is in your field, it's because it wants to meet you. It's time for that transformation to happen.

It's normal to come with fear, anxiety and anticipation. I even have anticipation and a little anxiety when I do a personal ceremony for myself. You never know what you are going to get. You can always trust however that this medicine doesn't want to do anything but return you back to wholeness. It does not want to hurt you, ever. Never ever, ever.

**What are your thoughts on micro-dosing? Did you micro-dose after a flood dose for integration?**
In the beginning no, but now, yes. Absolutely. We micro-dose often. I think micro-dosing is amazing, I don't know if it is for everyone. I think micro-dosing is something that needs to be done by someone who's done a pretty significant amount of work. If you're really new and unfamiliar with diving into the depths of yourself, I don't think micro-dosing with Iboga is necessarily the first step. If that is something that calls you, micro-dose with psilocybin. I would absolutely encourage someone to do more integration work after a flood dose, if they are really new to this process, before they look at micro-dosing.

Micro-dosing should really not be done when you are "tasking." It should be done when you can spend time in nature. You can spend time with yourself. When you can spend time with loved ones, just being, not when you have a bunch of stuff to do. Especially not when you are out in the world, your energies are really open and you're really sensitive. So that's not to say I've never done it. I do obviously have a significant amount of practice.

The whole point of the experience (micro-dosing) is to make you feel more centered and grounded in what you've already learned. There's no need to go out and take on the world when you are micro-dosing. It's the opposite of the intention.

**Is there anything you wish you knew before doing Iboga about the process?**
I really do wish I had both the preparation support and the integration support. Our coach that we work with now, I had not found at that time. This was 7 years ago.

Iboga is a manifesting machine. If you are not in alignment and things in your life need to go, and you're not looking, Iboga will make them leave. It will shake your world to the core. I didn't know that and I didn't have the proper support. I figured it out, but I would have landed so much more softly, if I had someone to help guide me. We cannot stress this enough and we stress this ALL the time. I want to scream it to the world! Hahaha!

I think there is way too much plant medicine being served out there and not nearly enough integration support. It's coming, there's lots of people joining and beginning to offer the support. But there's not nearly enough given the amount of medicine that is being served. To really give these medicines the type of reputation they deserve, the integration is vital. Where you make the impact in the transformation, is through the integration. It's not really in the ceremony. Yes, some things can fall away, thought patterns, behaviors and perceptions can magically disappear, the smaller stuff. You might notice "I don't want to watch horror movies, I want to eat better" but the real deep, excavating work and implementing that into your life doesn't happen in the ceremony. It happens after. If you don't have support doing it, it's harder to really capture the breadth of the power that comes out of the medicine experience. INTEGRATION, INTEGRATION, INTEGRATION!

**Was there a memorable moment or particularly profound Vision you have and has this Vision come true?**

My first experience was not particularly impactful in terms of the actual ceremony or what I learned directly from the medicine then. For me, integration has always been where the rubber meets the road. I think that is how it is for everyone. That's where the profound shifts are happening for me, but I did receive the teaching to "completely trust the process, always." I tattooed “trust” on my arm, just days after and I don't even think I really understood the depth of what it meant at that time.

For me the two most powerful teachings from this medicine in my life and what I see as a common thread are to "Trust the process explicitly." Not only with the medicine but in life in general "Trust the Universe" and the second one is to "Love Yourself."

That self-love piece is really the key to everything. It all starts with love and trust. With these two things you can make it through anything. I didn't have the self-love in the first ceremonies, but the trust piece came through really, really clearly. The self-love has come in over and over again. In every shape, fashion and form, with myself and also the people we work with.

People come here (to Iboga) broken, and hating themselves. That's not something they (society) feels is important to teach, how to love ourselves and how to forgive ourselves. That, I think, is Iboga's true mission. That is our natural state, to be our own little child who loves themself. Iboga wants to return us to that natural state of self-love. As a child you are born in trust too, until you learn otherwise. You have trust that the sun will rise, trust that food will come to your table, trust that someone is going to love you. You don't think otherwise, you just receive it. I see that with our daughter, she has everything she needs, in the love department, so she just trusts! She knows everything is coming her way. She hasn't been conditioned to believe otherwise. Iboga shows us how to return to that state.

**Has Iboga affected your spirituality?**

Totally. I'm not going to say that Iboga is solely responsible for my transformation and all of my spirituality. I've worked with a lot of other modalities. The light switch going on, to what I believe is the true nature of reality, and this human experience has come forth in a lot of different ways. I can't say that Iboga is the only vehicle for that. But, I'm an extremely spiritual person, and I have learned a lot of this path through medicine.

I'm also not a believer in the idea of 'the more medicine the better'. I'm not someone who is taking medicine all day, every day. I'm not seeking out the next journey. I like to integrate what I learn. I don't need the medicine, but I do use it for profound teachings, but very infrequently. I do maybe two journeys a year.

I'm an incredibly spiritual being, but I'm also very grounded. I like this three-dimensional world. I don't like to bypass 'stuff', I encourage people to feel their pain, don't just understand that there's a higher purpose to it. You have to feel it, for me that's real. That's the three dimensional, that's part of this human experience. Then there's another layer of divinity happening, all the time, in and around everything at every moment. Sometimes we just need to be human, it's about balancing the two.

Another thing I love about Iboga is that it is very grounding. It's very present in the body, it's very present in your personal experience. It shows you the way. It is very clear and applicable to human life. Whatever this incarnation is, as Amber Antonelli, it is very applicable to that. Whereas Ayahuasca is a bit more ethereal and esoteric. Ayahuasca is a beautiful medicine, and I love her. But Iboga is very grounded. Iboga is about YOU. How can you be in Ego whilst also maintaining your connection to the divine? It teaches you to be present in this life.

**Is there anything else you'd like to add?**
I would really like to encourage people to look below the stigma of Iboga for addiction. It is SO much more than that. If anything, that (addiction) is an afterthought. The ability that this medicine has to raise our awareness, help our love for ourselves and each other, move ancestral energy, constructs, pain, trauma and conditioning is amazing.

Its ability to detox the physical body is just one of many alkaloids. People come to Iboga because they have so much emotional pain. We all have emotional pain, some more than others. This medicine is so committed to helping us feel the love that is present within us. It has so much more to offer than just the detox. It is a very cheeky and comical spirit as well. It is not all the intensity that it is cracked up to be. I encourage people to open their hearts and open their minds. If you are reading this book, chances are this medicine is calling you and there is a reason.

I often like to say, it takes a lifetime to get to where we are with our emotional pain and suffering, it does not take nearly that amount of time to undo it. 24 hours of intensity is worth the 10 years of therapy that you get in the end. No question. Maybe 20 years of therapy, or even a lifetime of therapy can come from a ceremony with integration.

You don't need to take that much medicine and go that deep to receive profound wisdom and healing. This medicine is a miracle and incredible gift from this beautiful planet, it is here for us to connect and heal.

**Author's note.**

The marriage of Amber as the divine feminine and Anthony as the divine masculine is inspirational symbolism. Their story highlights the power of Iboga to magnetize people, bringing themselves into union with their best self and others in support of the higher good. Amber also mentions that "Iboga is a manifesting machine." Things that are for us, can be called in. But often, things that are no longer serving us are rapidly pushed out.

Amber's journey took her through a "baptism of fire," working in professional kitchens, places that are traditionally observed as "toxic" and hyper-masculine. As an observer, her expression of "bringing the feminine" to her life, practice and healing center, is quite healing. Amber's story reminds us that in the healing journey we all must embody both the divine masculine and divine feminine. Only when we have explored, healed and supported each expression, can we freely express the archetype which we feel most aligned too. Thank you Amber, for showing many how to do it with your embodied example!

**Joren...... Curiosity and Spiritual Insights.**

***Bio:** Joren De Smet. 27 when he first worked with Iboga 31 now. Male. Belgium. Banana filled with Iboga and some additional spoons of Iboga. Joren is currently traveling and exploring the world, he will commence studies in philosophy soon. Joren was motivated to work with Iboga through curiosity and spiritual insights.*

**Author's Introduction**: I met Joren in Gabon in 2018, while we were both living at Tatayo's compound. He had just undergone a very intense traditional initiation in Gabon. Despite being 'burst open' following his initiation, he was joyful, kind and a delight to be around. His traditional initiation was more physically intense than the initiation style many underwent with Tatayo, involving less sleep and physically pushing his body to the limit.

**Where did you first hear about Iboga?**

I remember watching a documentary when I was around 18-20 years old. I pretty much forgot about it until I started traveling in Africa a decade later. My friend mentioned Iboga and images of spiritual journeys and beautiful ceremonies came back to life.

**How were you called to Iboga?**

While traveling through The Congo, my interest started growing. All the music, dancing and energetic vibrations made me curious for more. I followed that curiosity to Gabon.

**Did you feel spiritually called to Iboga?**

Yes. I bought a painting that really resonated with me after the ceremony. Every time I saw it, I was taken back to Bwiti. It was a really hard time for me, but it doesn't mean it's not beautiful. I visited the depths of my existence, and I don't think that's a bad thing. It opened up a lot.

**What was your life like before Iboga?**

I always felt blessed in life, I experienced ups and downs yet it seemed that I had received the opportunities to live my dreams.

I feel that something was guiding me already. I was already following my heart, not thinking about what would happen next or the future. I was already on a different kind of path. Iboga didn't change that direction or anything, but it made the progression stronger. If life goes in waves, Iboga makes the waves go higher, and lower. I don't mind sitting on those waves, if they are higher or lower. I can see them and enjoy the rides. If I fall down, I can enjoy the fall, I can enjoy the butterflies in my stomach. If I go up, I can enjoy the beauty of life. It gave me something extra, the experience of life is different.

It's hard to say exactly, I traveled a lot and learnt many things along the road. Along the way, many things happened to me. It's hard to point to any one thing and say "That is what made the change." I feel like it's the same with Iboga. The path in life involves the birth and then the transformation into who we need to become. If I look at my life, from the past to the present, Iboga is something that fits exactly into my life. It's not that it changed something, it flowed with the current. It's not that there was a waterfall (or major event) and suddenly something changed, it was a big curve and I enjoyed it.

**What is your life like after Iboga?**

Life still unfolds in beautiful ways for me. However, the way I perceive it changed, it cleared some of the fog. It took me quite some time to integrate the visions Iboga gave me. I'm still a work in progress, but at least now I experienced some deeper insights that still guide me today.

Iboga opened me up a lot, it made me a much more gentle person both to myself and to other people. It's not that I am more gentle, but I try to be. I'm still in the process, I'm continually trying to become more gentle. Iboga made me more spiritual, that's for sure.

**How did you prepare?**

I didn't really prepare for the experience. Curiosity was the main reason for me, I pretty much stepped into the unknown. I was working with myself for a while and I had the feeling that some Bwiti magic would serve me well.

**Would you prepare differently a second time?**
I definitely would, yet I'm not sure how. I feel that If Iboga finds me again someday it will become more clear.

**What precautions did you take to make sure it was a safe experience?**
I trusted the people who guided me through the experience. My shaman had my confidence and I surrendered, something that wasn't easy for me and a big part of the journey.

**How did you consume Iboga?**
It was given to me in small wood chips with a little bit of water to ease it down my throat. Also I ate a banana filled with a honey and Iboga mix, something that wasn't pleasant to swallow.

**What did you take and where?**
The Root Bark in natural form during ceremonies.

**What form? Total dosage?**
I haven't a clear idea of the amount that I consumed, especially because the ceremony lasted a very long time and Iboga was given to me during this time. At times a spoonful or just a little bit to get me connected with the spirit. The second night I was given a banana filled with Iboga and honey and some spoons.

**Why did you decide to do it this way?**
I wanted to close my African adventure with a special experience, a last chapter to end a book in beauty. I agreed with whatever that came my way as I was living by the motto "In life, I trust." What I received turned out to be something unforgettable.

**What would be your advice to people considering Iboga?**
Be humble and treat it with respect. Be with people you trust and in a safe environment so you can enjoy its magic.

**What are your thoughts on micro-dosing? Did you micro-dose after your flood dose for integration?**
I didn't micro-dose and haven't really thought about the benefits it could offer.

**Is there anything you wish you knew before doing Iboga about the process?**
I wouldn't change my experience in any way, in my case ignorance was bliss. It blew me away and I truly lived it.

**Would you do Iboga again?**
The answer to this question changed over time. For a while I couldn't imagine another experience like this ever again. Now, two years later, I embraced the idea again. I won't go and search for it just yet but my heart is open to receive the medicine a second time. Iboga and Bwiti are part of who I am today and it would be amazing to reconnect with these powerful guides.

**Was there a memorable moment or particularly profound vision you had?**
I had two that changed me in incredible ways and still affect my way of life today.
One, embraced my being with love. I went back to one of my first moments on earth. Both of my parents were looking at me with so much admiration that I felt adored. The love I perceived in their eyes was the blessing of my life. A soul is pure when it comes to life and in this moment my parents embraced my soul with unconditional love that is still trapped inside this body. Because of this vision, I see more of the romance in life.

Another vision appeared one night when the lack of sleep influenced the effects of Iboga. My body was tired and weak, disorientated. I found my way out of the temple. I had a hard time vomiting whatever was left inside my stomach. It felt like the biggest cleansing I ever experienced. All the negativity that was left inside found its way out. Exhausted, I laid myself down on the floor and went into a dreamlike state different from the previous visions.

Previous visions were about my past, this was a visualization of a state in between life and death. I had to let go of all attachments with life. I had to let go of everything so I could pass on and feel peace. I struggled for a while because of my desire to live. When I finally gave in, I couldn't pass on to the afterlife and went back to the ceremony. I never felt fear of dying and in a way felt that I already died. Because of this vision I accepted death.

**Has Iboga affected your spirituality?**
Iboga amplified my spirituality in certain ways. I feel that the art of self-reflection is painted differently after taking Iboga. As if there is less blaming of others and more taking responsibility for my own actions.

**What did Iboga teach or give you?**
I think it taught me that it's okay to be a vulnerable person. It is not a bad thing to show others that you are not perfect. It's okay to have downfalls and accept those downfalls. Iboga stripped me back and showed me most raw, vulnerable and authentic state. It shows a lot of love. For me, it was in a harsh way, but in the end it showed me love. It made me a stronger person too.

Iboga lives in us, it lives in me. It has strong lessons. The more time that passes by, I have a feeling that one experience is enough to see but not enough to really understand what happens. The wood, the Bwiti, is calling me again. Slowly. It took me a couple of years to integrate the lessons, but at one point I will need to go back, just to see it again and feel it again.

With Iboga, it's not just eating the plant, but you are stepping into the Bwiti as well, if you go to Gabon. The Bwiti can be very intense. It's not only the plant that gives you something, but the whole culture that takes care of you and teaches you as well.

When I went to Gabon, I wasn't expecting what I received. I came there with no expectations, other than wanting to see what it was about, what kind of magic there was. It slapped me in the face, it woke me up in a way. If I were to go back, I would experience it in a completely different way. It allowed me to see through the eyes of the jungle, a little bit. Now, from time to time, I can go into nature and see with those eyes. I don't think I had that before, when I go back, I would really try to take in all the ceremonies and effects on the body.

I think it would be a completely different experience a second time. It's going to happen. It's one of the few places I know I need to go back, see it again and stay for a longer time. If it wasn't so expensive to get to Gabon, maybe I would have gone back already. It's not that I need to go back right now, there are other things on my path.

Immediately after the ceremony I thought "Never again. Never again!" But, the more I look back to it, it's a part of me and an experience I really like. It changed me in a really beautiful way. It's something I like about myself now.

**Anything else you'd like to add?**
Bassé!

**Author's Note.**

Over the years, Joren has studied with different teachers and continued living a magical life of adventure. The major themes of this interview were self-reflection, softening to one's self and the world, love, and vulnerability. Although the Iboga experience can be intense and is commonly described as masculine and sometimes brutal, it also has a gentle, softening and sweet side. Sometimes, the brutality and somewhat relentless beatings can have a beautiful long-term effect. Similar to the beating of a fruit, it can make us sweeter and more enjoyable for all.

## ADDICTION (EMERGENCY-PURPOSES) INTERVIEWS.

**Juliana…… Healing Opioid Dependence**

***Bio:*** *Juliana Mulligan. 27 when first working with Ibogaine, 38 now (10 years doing Ibogaine related work). Female. USA. 40mg per kilo of Ibogaine HCL (far beyond the safe amount!). Juliana is a former opioid dependent and formerly incarcerated Ibogaine specialist, she offers preparation and integration sessions to people undergoing ibogaine treatment, consultation for those running ibogaine clinics, is currently completing an MSW at NYU, and is working on projects related to the topics of ethics and accountability in the psychedelic therapy space. In Juliana's words, "Iboga is an exceptional tool which offers a plethora of benefits that are severely lacking in traditional western mental health and drug treatment models." Juliana's motivation for working with Iboga herself was "treating opioid dependence."*

**Author's Introduction:** Juliana and I met in 2018 whilst she was traveling through Gabon, visiting different communities working with Iboga. She radiates softness, generosity, kindness and patience, in a way that only someone who has been through as much as she has could. She is a force of nature, dedicating her life to helping people work with Ibogaine, healing, and advocating for Ibogaine safety.

**Where did you first hear about Iboga/Ibogaine?**

I heard about it maybe 3-4 years before I actually did it, from a friend of mine who was very nerdy about psychedelics. She had come across it online. I wanted to go and do it, but didn't have the resources to do it at the time. It was always in the back of my head from there, because I was an opioid dependent person. I really wanted to try it, and it ended up being the final thing that I tried, and it worked for me!

**How were you called to Iboga/Ibogaine?**

I was called through my destructive patterns with opioids. I spent 7 years using heroin and other opioids before I did Ibogaine. I went through all of the typical things: rehabs, 12 step programs, county jail, overdoses. It was back-to-back disastrous things. Occasionally I would have some time away from opioids, but would then relapse, because none of the mainstream treatments address the neurochemical imbalances that occur from prolonged opioid use. Ibogaine was the one thing that I hadn't tried and that's how I ended up looking for a clinic.

**Did you feel a spiritual calling to Ibogaine?**
For me, everything is spiritual. I don't separate my spirituality from how I exist on a daily basis. It's interwoven into every single thing we all do and in every interaction we have. In that, yes, it spiritually called me. Especially because it was a calling about something that is so life changing - getting out of a substance dependence.

**What was your life like before Iboga?**
It was back to back disasters. There was a lot of instability and bad relationships, it was pretty rough. The typical stories of someone with substance use issues.

**What is your life like after Iboga?**
Afterwards, my life completely shifted. When I came out of my experience, I felt like a million pounds had been lifted off my shoulders. The biggest thing that Ibogaine did for me, was that it showed me that all of my years of struggling were actually my training for the work I am called to do.

I knew right away that I wanted to work in some capacity with Ibogaine after my treatment, but also that I wanted to do everything I could to change the terrible drug treatment system in the US and the corresponding faulty philosophies supporting it. Literally, all in a moment, I had all of these realizations about my purpose. Then I was off and running, working towards my goals. I knew I would be working with Ibogaine but also that I would be working to change the narrative around what substance use is about.

It is a completely different world, my life before and my life after working with Ibogaine. It does not even feel like I'm on the same planet.

**How did you prepare? Would you prepare differently a second time?**
Hahaha! I didn't really prepare. I was just like, get me there and let's get this done! This is the dangerous part: people who are coming to Ibogaine with substance dependencies are often feeling very anxious and very urgent. They feel like if they don't do this right away, then they are going to die. People end up

picking clinics that aren't safe, because they choose the clinics that will take them the soonest. They also often don't follow the preparation instructions, because they don't realise how important they are. I was one of those people.

They told me to stop using fentanyl as soon as possible and switch to another opioid, which I didn't. I didn't listen to them and I kept using it until I left. The clinic was also not operating safely overall since they weren't following proper clinical safety protocols. They didn't have me do the proper preparation nor did they stabilize me properly.

The appropriate preparation depends on what substance you are coming off of and what your intention is. It really differs. But across the board getting an ECG and liver panel blood test are the basic preparation essentials. But first of all, you need to be really thorough in choosing a clinic. I wrote a guide on how to choose a clinic, and it's a list of questions that mostly weed out the unsafe people. I always send this to people, and it's on my website.

**Author's note: Juliana's guide can be found in the appendix section**

You really have to be thorough in who you are choosing, because honestly 90-95% of people working with Ibogaine are not working safely. I co-founded a women and gender queer-led collective of people working in Ibogaine, and we take grievance reports from people who have had bad experiences. We constantly get nightmare stories and these stories sometimes even come out of clinics that are highly regarded. Honestly, I have about 4 clinics that I would ever feel safe sending anybody to right now. It's a tricky thing to find and recommend clinics currently.

Ibogaine tends to attract people who are working on the biggest traumas and many feel called to work with this medicine immediately after their own treatments. Sometimes, people haven't taken the time to work on themselves before working in clinics, and their unresolved issues can manifest in abusive or harmful behavior towards clients. Unregulated Ibogaine treatment offers the perfect environment for dangerous or untrained individuals to thrive; an unmonitored and unsupervised community in which you can get praise for being a healer and also make money off of it.

In terms of dietary preparation, I would advise people to stop eating processed sugars before Ibogaine. This isn't a standard ask, but it's my personal recommendation, because sugar affects dopamine and serotonin production. I think it's good to have your brain chemistry as balanced as possible before you do Ibogaine, because then the Ibogaine (or Iboga) can do its best work. I would recommend typical healthy behaviors, like eating fruits and veggies, drinking a lot of water and coconut water (electrolytes), doing some kind of physical activity, spending time in nature, start journaling beforehand and start working with a therapist or coach.

I would say that it's essential to have a therapist that you are already working with beforehand - That's one of the things I offer, sessions preparing people for their experience and helping them integrate it afterwards. I work with people from a few different clinics, but I think that one of the biggest gaps around Ibogaine clinic treatment protocol is clients not having enough support beforehand and afterwards. People seeking treatment often rely too heavily on the medicine itself, as if it is going to do the work for you. This process takes a lot of preparation. The people I've seen be the most successful are those who are already working with a therapist and who are implementing healthy daily practices beforehand.

(Juliana's website and contact details can be found in the appendix and at InnervisionIbogaine.com)

The final thing I'll say is to start scheduling time every week to do something that is just fun. This doesn't have to be productive, and it's not about "making progress" necessarily, it should just be something enjoyable. Because most of us have been raised in this capitalist world, people are hyper focused on production and being productive. Having fun or relaxing is looked at like an afterthought. After years of associating having fun with using substances, one of the hardest things to do when leaving a substance dependence behind is to relearn how to have fun. If you can start practicing this ahead of time, if you figure out which things you actually enjoy doing, it can give you a really good head start for afterwards.

**What precautions did you take to make sure it was a safe experience?**
Haha!...I didn't really. I think you already know the story of my treatment and why it went wrong, but I can tell it here....

I picked the guy that I first went with because we had what felt like a good interpersonal connection. This guy seemed to have a good heart, but he was just kind of a mad scientist, cowboy type who followed his own rules. This can be very dangerous when it comes to Ibogaine because you can't have an ego that gets in the way of being meticulously safe.

I arrived at the clinic on a Friday night, and they started dosing me on Saturday with almost no stabilization time whatsoever. Usually, if someone is arriving who has been regularly doing fentanyl and has a high tolerance, you want to monitor them and do multiple ECGs (EKGs) over the course of 5 days to a week, maybe longer if necessary. They also need to test negative for fentanyl on a drug test before ingesting any Ibogaine. They didn't do any of that and started dosing me 24 hours after I arrived. They said I had the highest opioid tolerance they had ever treated, despite me being small and extremely underweight. My withdrawals weren't going away with the initial doses of Ibogaine like they normally do, so they kept giving me more and more.

Later on, I found out that the amount of Ibogaine they gave me (somewhere around 40 mg per kilogram) was around twice the amount that you should ever give someone. They also gave me a lot of Valium, because I wasn't able to calm down and lay still. I don't really remember almost anything, and I think it's because of this. So I ended up having 6 cardiac arrests because the cardio-toxic effect of Ibogaine is that it slows down your heart rhythm (bradycardia) and it prolongs the QT interval, which is the interval in between your heart beats, basically. If you prolong that for too long, you go into a deadly rhythm called 'Torsades de Pointes'. Torsades looks like a bunch of squiggly lines on an ECG, and untreated it will eventually lead to cardiac arrest and death. This is what I had and it caused 6 cardiac arrests that I had to be revived out of.

Finally, they put in an external pacemaker, which they did not actually have in the hospital. The doctor from the clinic had to call his cardiologist friends in Guatemala City, and he had to assemble a team from outside of the hospital to come and treat me, because they didn't have the proper support for this situation. I ended up on an external pacemaker for almost two weeks. They eventually turned it off and I was fine. There was no "damage" since the cardiac side effects go away once the level of Noribogaine in your system decreases. I'm not the first person that the pacemaker thing has happened to, I've heard of 3 other pacemaker stories as well.

I didn't have any pre-existing heart conditions. This happened because they didn't stabilize me and they gave me an insane amount of Ibogaine. If you give anyone that amount of Ibogaine, then they are probably going to die or end up in a hospital. That's what happened to me, that's why I've become hyper focused on safety and why I only have about 4 recommended clinics currently. I have seen adverse events happen in clinics because people cut corners on one little thing, which they didn't think was a big deal in the preparation phase. You have to be super diligent about following proper safety protocols no matter what, it is essential. Even if someone is a doctor, if they are not experienced with Ibogaine, they won't be able to do it properly. You need someone that's really experienced and trained with ibogaine.

I did an ECG and a liver panel before I worked with this clinic, and like I said before this is the bare minimum in treatment preparation. But even if you have an ECG this doesn't necessarily cover all the bases.

The essential preparation is an ECG, liver panel, full medical evaluation and history, and close communication with the provider you are going to work with about your substance use. It's important to get to know them, and that they get to know you. The best providers I know speak to their clients for 2-3 months before they even come down to work with Iboga. That way they get to know what their substance use is like and what their emotional state is like. Don't go with any clinic that is rushing you to get down there or is offering you a cheap deal to come sooner. That's unethical, unsafe, and it's a red flag.

Do whatever the providers tell you to do, in terms of the preparation. Take it seriously and be super honest about what substances you have been taking. I've heard about a lot of dangerous incidents happening because of people not telling the provider exactly what substances and medications they have been taking. It is crucial that you are transparent.

**What was your intention?**

I wanted to get out of the trap of opioid dependence and depression. I left that behind with that first treatment.

Also, I wouldn't call what I did a "ceremony", it was a very clinical setting. There wasn't even music playing.

The second treatment I did was at the clinic I trained at in South Africa. I was going through a tough breakup and I was having a hard time dealing with it. The person running the clinic offered me a free treatment. It was actually a harder experience emotionally than the first, partially because I had absolutely no one to talk to afterwards about what I was experiencing. They had no therapist on staff, which is also a red flag!

**How did you consume Iboga? What did you take and where? What form? Total dose?**

For my first treatment I took Ibogaine HCL in capsules and the total dose was around 40mg per kilogram of body weight. Which is EXTREMELY dangerous and about double what is even a safe dose.

The second time I had something called PTA (purified total alkaloid), which is mostly pure Ibogaine and a small percentage of the other alkaloids present in Iboga. I'm pretty sure it was under 20mg per kilogram of body weight.

**Why did you decide to do it this way? Why did you pick this center?**

(Answered previously) I had a good connection with the facilitator and I was in a hurry.

**What would be your advice to people considering Iboga?**

Write down a list of your intentions to get clear on what's important to you. I would also recommend you to really get in touch with what *you* want, not what your society or your family wants, which is usually total abstinence from drugs. It might be that you are not ready for total abstinence or maybe that isn't even the right path for you. People need to be honest about that. Maybe people want to stop doing heroin, but want to keep doing other drugs, and that's totally okay too.

The goals of a person should be completely up to them. If there is pressure from a spouse or family member to do this treatment (and the person doesn't want to or isn't sure), then they shouldn't do it yet. They have to do it for themselves only. That's the most important thing. Coerced treatment very rarely works out well and is often dangerous. I would also recommend to start working with a therapist, start journaling about intentions, and start writing about what you would like your dream life to be like. Start getting a picture of what you value and what you want, what is important to you.

Sometimes I advise people to try Ayahuasca first. Ibogaine and Iboga are very intense, they can really beat you up, hard. You have to be prepared to do the work. Most of us have been raised to believe that we can buy our way out of anything, or we just wait for something external to do the work for us, or we maybe take another drug to do it for us. Ibogaine (and Iboga) do not work like that. You have to work through your stuff, you have to confront your stuff, you have to be honest with yourself and be willing to be present with discomfort and do things that are hard.

It is important to know that although Ibogaine is an amazing door opener, it is not the be all and end all, it is not the answer. It is a tool that acts as a door opener to a new path. After the treatment, the hard work comes on a daily basis. I'm still uncovering and integrating things 11 years later. There's an overemphasis on Ibogaine being this magical thing, or a cure, which is really dangerous to tell people and sets them up for disappointment. I really advise people to listen to this and check in with themselves if they are really ready to do this work.

I also think it's important to start building community, rather than just relying on a significant other or a family member as a singular support. It's so important to have a good supportive community around you. The hardest thing is sending someone home from a clinic to the environment that they were living in beforehand, where they don't have any friends, where they have no community.

That's just setting people up for relapse. If you're planning to go for treatment, start working on building healthy community in advance. If you're running a clinic, don't treat people if they will be returning to an unsafe or unsupportive environment afterwards.

**What are your thoughts on micro-dosing? Did you micro-dose after a flood dose for integration?**
I didn't micro-dose directly afterwards, I actually didn't touch any substances for 2 and a half years, because I was still partially brainwashed by the 12 step program to think that micro-dosing or working with any other medicines would be breaking my "clean time". I realized eventually that that was bullshit. Eventually, I started micro-dosing Iboga occasionally and that has been really helpful. But also, I do think it was helpful for me to take a 100% break from mind altering substances for that beginning period. What works is going to be different for everyone.

I didn't start micro-dosing with Iboga until I was working with clinics (professionally) 3 years later or so, and I still micro-dose with TA occasionally. It helps me with working through old patterns and difficult programming, it is really helpful. There is something about Ibogaine where you are able to step outside of yourself, and outside of the messaging in your head, where you can see it from an unbiased perspective. Suddenly you see, I don't have to be that blueprint, I can step above it. Even in really small amounts I have noticed that happening, and often I can just step out of my mental loops pretty easily.

**Is there anything you wish you knew before doing Iboga about the process?**
Yeh, I wish I knew what the safety protocols were! I wish there would have been somewhere to look them up! I wish I knew that many of the people working in Ibogaine (professionally) are/were so unbalanced and dangerous. There really are a lot of scary characters working in this space, who actually have no business working with other human beings. Ibogaine attracts people who are in need of really deep healing. It is like a magnet for people who have a lot of unaddressed trauma, but also for people who are not willing or ready to self-reflect, take responsibility for their behaviors, and do work on themselves. I wish I had known about that, and I would have been more selective in finding a clinic.

The psychedelic world, because it is unregulated and unmonitored, often attracts people who have a lot of unresolved issues. Sometimes, they are looking for a way to have power over other people or they want to be highly revered. It often attracts people who have this shaman complex, and it's the perfect breeding ground for that because you can declare yourself a shaman, which plenty of people do, and then everyone is looking up and bowing down to you. There's nobody to check it. It's the perfect breeding ground for sociopaths and untreated personality disorders.

**Author's note: For more in depth advice on safety from Juliana see the appendix**

**Would you do Iboga again?**

I do want to do a Bwiti initiation in Gabon. I thought I was going to do it this past summer, but obviously because of the pandemic that didn't happen. I'm hoping to do it in the next few years and I want to get initiated in a woman-led ceremony. Myself and some other women from the community are hoping to go together.

**Was there a memorable moment or particularly profound vision you had? Has it come true?**

I didn't really remember anything because they had given me so much Valium. It was more like I felt the changes as soon as I came out of the experience and I knew it had worked. I felt the sensation that a lot of work had been done.

Three months later I remembered a little snippet of a vision, but it wasn't something that was going to come true per say. For me the experience was more about realizing that everything I had been through was my training for the work I was supposed to do. And that has come true!

**Has Iboga affected your spirituality?**

As I said before, for me, everything is spiritual. Spirituality does not happen in a vacuum, it affects every single thing we do. Before Ibogaine, for my whole life, I already had a strong spiritual connection. So, it's not like I needed Iboga to awaken that spirituality because my issue was never a question of a spiritual connection. My family and I are followers of Avatar Meher Baba and I grew up going to India to visit his Samadhi and the center that's there. Iboga doesn't change that, but it's definitely helped me on my path in other ways and it's reminded me of how close I am to Meher Baba.

**Anything else you'd like to add**

In terms of conservation, I think all Ibogaine clinics should only be working with Voacanga sourced Ibogaine, unless their Iboga comes from a verified plantation. This is one of the most crucial things for conservation and Iboga. Voacanga is a tree that grows super plentifully all-over West Africa and its main alkaloid, voacangine, can easily be converted into Ibogaine. Because it grows so quickly, and in more locations than Iboga, it is the most sustainable way of obtaining Ibogaine. If all clinics switched to using this, we would be able to give iboga a chance to be replenished. Iboga has to be 5 or more years old before it can be harvested for medicine (and it is very hard to grow and only grows in a particular climate). There are many villages now in Gabon that don't have access to Iboga because people are stealing it out of the protected forests and selling it to people in the West online. Switching to Voacanga Ibogaine is a really important step to help with this issue. Even if only half the clinics switched to using Voacanga Ibogaine, it would make a huge difference.

There is a debate in which some people say "Well the spirit of Iboga doesn't come with the Voacanga Ibogaine," and that's just bullshit in my opinion. The spirit of Iboga does not operate on the science that we operate on and it knows when it is called no matter what. Regardless of where the Ibogaine comes from, the experience is not different. I have taken both and it's the exact same thing. The website for my collective can be found at Ibogainecollective.com

Right now, we take complaints and grievances from people that have had bad experiences at clinics or retreats. In the future, we would love to facilitate mediation between clients and clinics and offer training to help them to work in a safer manner. We also eventually hope to offer a training course for people wanting to work with Ibogaine, so that they can be certified to be safe to offer treatment.

**Author's note.**

Juliana's profound personal transformation is reflected in her passion and dedication to her professional work. Despite having one of the most intense and dangerous Ibogaine experiences ever, she transmuted her challenges into lessons and education she could share to help improve safety for others. Now, as both an acclaimed speaker and voice for Ibogaine and Iboga safety, she helps ensure that people can work with Iboga in the most safe way possible. This ranges from helping people find centers, screening unscrupulous providers, conflict resolution and reviewing of facilitators, providing preparation and integration services and generally being an Ibogaine angel.

Juliana and I I met whilst she was traveling through Gabon, visiting different communities that were working with Iboga in 2018. Juliana was extremely helpful in writing this book, she provided many contacts and soft introductions to many people who were interviewed. Juliana's work, contact and useful resources can be found in the appendix section.

**Yann...... PTSD and Cocaine Addiction.**

**Bio:** Yann *Guignon. 30 years old when first working with Iboga, 48 now. Male. French/Gabonese. Iboga root bark, type "Baillon / Mayuba." Yann is a consultant in intercultural mediation and sustainable development. Founder of the NGO "Blessings of the Forest," which is dedicated to the conservation of the cultural and natural heritage of the Peoples of Gabon. Yann's motivation for working with Iboga initially was for "Healing PTSD, childhood trauma and cocaine addiction."*

**Author's Introduction:** To me, Yann is a titan, spearheading the movement ensuring Iboga's longevity and protection. Although he is now supported by a great team, for a long time he was a one-man army, on a great mission to help Iboga. In a way, the combination of his traumatic background and the deep work he has done with Iboga has made him the perfect and unique person, to stand up with Iboga and change the world. He is a warrior, and for me, the best embodiment of the masculine spirit of Iboga in a human form– strong, relentless, aggressive, but ultimately a powerful force for good, who gives his all to help others.

**Where did you first hear about Iboga?**

In 2004, I was the business manager for the department of "French speaking Sub-saharan Africa" for a large listed French company. I was working on a project for the 'computerisation' of the national education system with the Gabonese government. We had recruited a Gabonese Technical Director, Aristide Nguema, who was also initiated to Bwiti and president of the French association E-Boga dedicated to the uptake of the use of Iboga in psychotherapy. One day in February 2004, while we were on our way to a professional meeting in Paris, Aristide confided to me that he had noticed that I was taking cocaine before every important appointment! He then spoke to me about Iboga, he told me this plant was a "Pygmy cocaine," giving me as much energy and self-confidence but without side effects and much cheaper! He invited me to discover this medicine one weekend in Normandy. It was in a ritual setting that he had developed for this purpose and in the presence of a doctor and a nurse. I had no idea what was waiting for me. It totally changed my life. It made me permanently disgusted with cocaine. It also taught me a lot about the reasons that had pushed me to use all sorts of drugs in the first place.

**How were you called to Iboga?**

As I explained, I was introduced to Iboga by a Gabonese work colleague. I didn't hesitate for a second to go and meet this plant because I was very open to all sorts of experiences of modified states of consciousness. Also, working with Gabon, I was curious to see what pygmies had been working with since the dawn of time!

Afterwards, I can obviously say that Iboga was a key step on my path. Aristide explained to me that Iboga had ordered him to find people like me to defend it... Nowadays, he has left France. He continues to say that he thinks that his mission in this country was only to bring me to Gabon to lead the fight that we now lead together for the benefit of the Iboga and the traditions linked to it!

**What was your life like before Iboga?**

My life before my encounter with Iboga was an unbalanced life: intoxicated, motivated by material power and revenge on a childhood that haunted me in vain.

Indeed, I had a very difficult childhood with a mother with severe psychiatric problems and an alcoholic father who was either very physically and psychologically violent or totally absent.

I did not know my parents' love and fled their home very early on, going through life on the streets, then the army and then military prison. Given the powerlessness of modern medicine to deal with my mother's problems, I didn't want to be helped by a psychologist. I then, like many people, chose drugs to escape reality and to give myself the courage to move forward. However, I was hard-working and thirsty for material success in order to prove to my father that I wasn't the piece of shit he said I was. So there I was, living in a mixture of deep sorrow and a desire for revenge, regularly going to extremes, living on the edge...

**What is your life like after Iboga?**

I could not speak about a life "After Iboga" because I am always a practitioner of the "Bwitist" tradition. I am intimately linked to Iboga, it is part of my daily job, moreover I am an active defender of it. I specify that I rarely consume Iboga and when it is the case it is in small or very small quantity. Indeed, I became very sensitive to this plant to which it is sometimes enough for me to think about it to feel its energy.

It is difficult for me to dissociate the benefits obtained in my life only due to the Iboga, from the cultural adventure that I have experienced living around this sacred plant in Gabon for 17 years, here is a summary of what I have observed as results concerning me: I have eliminated from my life an astronomical quantity of bad habits, that were physically and psychologically toxic. I think I perfectly understand the logic of my path, who I am, where I am and what I am supposed to achieve in my life. I have faith in the perfection of the universe and all its manifestations; I have cured many internal and external conflicts; I learned to measure the energy in all things and to balance them, to feel what is good for me or not; Iboga taught me to look at the world differently and to anticipate the future, to feel the invisible in the daily life in all its dimensions, to read the life with a spirit much more flexible than I could have imagined. I came from an environment that was very distant from my current philosophy of existence.

I feel rooted and connected! But I still do not feel perfect of course!!! Iboga is always improving me...

**How did you prepare? Would you prepare differently a second time?**
The first time I took Iboga in France, as told earlier, I had very little preparation. It went very quickly. My Gabonese friend, who guided me through this extraordinary experience, had been watching me for several months without saying a word to me. He had simply asked me not to take drugs at least 72 hours before the Friday evening when I ate the root and ideally to be fasted from the morning. He had also advised me not to have sex the week before.

I am ashamed to confess, but I have to, that I did not respect any of his advice and bitterly regret it.

I was very ill and the experience was extremely intense for me. Luckily, I was very athletic and healthy by nature, with an innate fighting spirit, but also the guide was very professional and caring. I was very scared and I wouldn't advise anyone to do the same. I really thought I was going to die. I saw myself die.

Since then, I can hardly tell you how many times I have used Iboga, most of the time during Bwiti ceremonies in Gabon and a few rare times for therapeutic work targeted at myself.

What is certain is that my preparation improves with each time I take the sacred wood. I respect the dietary restrictions that are imposed for at least 3 days if not much more before the occasion: no red meat, no spices, as little sugar and salt as possible, no acidic foods, no dairy products, no food that is heavy on the digestion.... Also, if need be, I do concoctions of certain plants to clean my blood, my kidneys, all my digestive organs, my eyes and my sinuses.

To prepare, I abstain from sex, rest as well as possible, exercise, sweat, take meditative baths in which I put certain plants or other elements according to the objectives of taking Iboga that time.

Of course, I am very careful about the environmental and human factors surrounding the use of Iboga. I don't consume it just anywhere with anyone. I am also very attentive to the weather and the energy of the places where the Iboga will be used. I take care to employ the precious tools which were taught to me by my Masters in Gabon or revealed during my experiments. The most important basic tools are fire, water, some key organic elements and music. The quality of the Iboga (especially its exact provenance) and good intentions are naturally central and equally important.

**What was your intention?**
The first time was just to show my Gabonese friend that I was not scared of this drug. Hahaha! If there was a chance that I might feel better afterwards, I thought I would take my chances. I didn't know what to expect.

After that, each intention was for healing, to heal myself. I also wanted to understand myself and life "What am I meant to do?"

**How did you consume Iboga? What did you take and where? What form? Total dose?**
The first time I took Iboga, in 2004 in France, it was in the form of root bark from Gabon. I took 3 teaspoons of it, about 6 grams.

For 2 years, I accompanied my Gabonese friend to about ten weekends of Iboga treatment in small groups. Generally, I took between 8 to 10 grams of Iboga in 2 nights.

When I was introduced to Bwiti in Gabon in 2006 I ate about 50 grams of fresh Iboga, which I had uprooted, took the flesh from the root and crushed it myself. The Iboga was mixed with other plants belonging to the initiatory secret. It was extremely strong but incomparable in terms of energies with what I had experienced in France.

I have been practicing Bwiti in Gabon since 2006... and I have participated in many ceremonies in more than thirty different villages, where the way of doing and consuming Iboga, of mixing it with other plants, is very different. Some people make a drink with Iboga, others put it in a green banana with honey, others mix it with leaves... I consumed it in many different ways.

Otherwise, I sometimes take a “micro-dose" of very fine crushed Iboga, put in capsules of 0.33 grams each. I take 1 to 3 of them a day, in the morning, following a special diet, for a maximum of 10 days 1 to 2 times a year. I do it especially when I spend the winter in Europe, when I come out of a bout of malaria or when I have a bad flu.

**Why did you decide to do it this way? Why did you pick this center?**
The first time I did a treatment based on Iboga, I didn't know anything about it. I just responded favorably to the invitation of a friend/professional collaborator. I followed him because I trusted him and I was curious. All in all, it was a challenge. I hadn't done any research on the internet.

Then I was so impressed by the results that I asked to accompany him for a few more weekends that he was organizing in France.

I was then directed to my first initiator and father in Bwiti in Gabon (Master Atom Ribenga). Again, I knew nothing about him or how it was going to happen.

There was very little information on the subject on the internet at the time and I just followed the lead that I was told to take. I was not at all disappointed and made several initiatory steps in this faith. But I had some difficulties with the syncretism of this branch of Bwiti practiced by the Fang people of Gabon. So, I tried to gradually go back to the roots of this multi-millennial tradition. I went to meet several dozen traditionalist villages throughout Gabon.

It was through these encounters that I continued my initiatory journey with Bwiti and Iboga, right up to the Babongo pygmies. I couldn't recommend all the places I went to. My choices were motivated by the feeling, the opportunities, the amount of money requested, the resonance of the consultations carried out, and the positive signs observed in general. I was never in a hurry to do things. I really try to avoid gurus, charlatans, swindlers, people trying to hustle for much more than they initially proposed. I have a rather innate talent for not falling into certain traps. Unfortunately, I see far too many people fall into these traps, especially Westerners, who are too hurried and too trusting blindly, too naive or too uninformed.

**What would be your advice to people considering Iboga?**

If you wish to consume Iboga, I think that the first question to ask yourself is if it is good for you physically and psychologically? We know many pathologies and conditions that are not indicated (allowed) with Iboga, especially cardiac, gastro-enteritis, renal but also mental conditions, for example; bipolarity, schizophrenia or certain forms of autism.

Then it is necessary to ask if the facilitator is really competent and clear about its interests. Also, I can of course only recommend checking the precise origin of the Iboga that you are about to consume. If these preliminary questions are not answered with certainty, then I advise you to ask yourself the question if the Iboga is the only solution to your problem.

There is a "fashion" effect around Iboga as there are many other entheogenic plants. This has many consequences, in particular the ecological and sustainability ones. I think it is fundamental to question with sincerity if there is not a more adapted solution in your immediate environment. For example, in Europe there are other plants specific to the local environmental and cultural conditions, such as mushrooms, but also a whole host of other plants, bark, minerals, techniques, etc. It would be a good idea to dig into the ancient practices of our own origins. Personally, I am doing this by learning a lot from the Druidic and Celtic traditions.

Iboga is not and should not be the answer to everything. If we think of it this way, it would certainly condemn it. Iboga also asks for a solid social framework, an appropriate accompaniment over the long term. For example, when you use Iboga you become hyper aware (sensitive) and that can entail major changes in your relations with the others, with your environment. It is necessary to be able to integrate all that Iboga will reveal to you but to remain tolerant and open minded. The gap between what you could see during your experience with the plant and the daily carnal reality can sometimes generate phases of "decompensation." That can be rather brutal psychologically. A kind of feeling of inability to realize one's "dream" and a feeling of extreme isolation. Iboga calls for a lot of discipline and patience.

Also, the deep changes that the Iboga generates within you can disturb the relations with your friends and family. You could change “too quickly” in the eyes of your close relations. Sometimes the distance can be so large between you and your loved ones that you are incompatible. You may even have to totally cut the link which unites you.

It is not uncommon to see candidates where the experience totally changes their life days, weeks or months later, for the better but also sometimes for the worse. If you rush the process, which is common with the western mentality, it can be deleterious.

In short, Iboga is neither a miracle solution for everyone nor easy to integrate, especially if one is socially isolated.

**Is there anything you wish you knew before doing Iboga about the process?**
Before the therapeutic process with Iboga, I would have liked to know how to prepare myself physically, psychologically and socially. I would have liked to understand the importance of not speaking too quickly about my experience to others. I would have liked to understand that visions are timeless, multi-

dimensional and symbolic. Therefore, they are very difficult to interpret through the prism of a basic cultural perception.

I would have liked to understand that one should not entrust the interpretation of one's experience to others either (don't share your visions). What is shown to you belongs to you and to you alone, or else to a competent master in this delicate art. I would have liked to know exactly where the Iboga that healed me came from. But well... with hindsight one can always say to oneself that nothing is to be regretted and that this is the way that presented itself to me. Let's just say that I wouldn't advise my own children to do as I did.

Preparation, supervision and follow-up are really the 3 fundamental pillars for an optimal experience without major risks.

**Would you do Iboga again?**

When I present with certain symptoms such as; flu, a weakness of the immune system or fatigue, a state of depression, unanswered questions, then I can on rare occasions consume 1 gram of Iboga.

It also happens to me, once in the year, most often if I spend the winter in Europe, to make a treatment in micro-dosing going from 0.33mg to 1g per day for a maximum duration of 10 days. I maintain the appropriate conditions and of course the adequate, general discipline.

Apart from that, I am still practicing Bwiti in Gabon and I take part in ceremonies from time to time where I can consume 1 to 6 grams of Iboga.

Finally, at the initiation level, which is always specific to Bwiti, I still have a few steps to go through for which I have been preparing for years. I am not in a hurry. It will probably happen in the next 2 to 3 years if all the conditions are met. I have no idea at this stage how much I should ingest but I am fortunate to be very sensitive to this medicine. I have already experienced the full psychoactive effects of the "Sacred Wood" several times before I even ingested it, simply through the ritual prior to taking it.

I specify that I have never felt the slightest compulsive need to take Iboga. I can very well go months without taking any. Taking it is always an ordeal and very rarely recreational. Iboga is a mirror in which it is not always comfortable to look at oneself. It is a double-edged knife, as they say in Gabon. To consume Iboga, it is necessary to have the desire to look the truth in the face and this one is sometimes very difficult to integrate. Most Gabonese people are afraid to consume Iboga because they know that what they will get out of it is not always comfortable. Besides, the bitterness in taste holds a very strong symbolism in many traditions all over the world, especially in the West... One does not cross (work with) it without courage.

**Was there a memorable moment or particularly profound vision you had? Has it come true?**

Of course, I had tons of memorable moments or visions, some of which came true but not always in the exact way I was shown. It is explained in the Bwiti that what is important is not so much the vision as the related energy felt through it.

For example, you can forgive in spirit someone with whom you have a conflict, but this does not mean that you will do so physically or even that you will reconcile with that person. It can simply be about removing a weight, a blockage in your life.

So, it is the energy released by this vision, your understanding of it, its impact on your psyche that will have positive effects on your life.

It is not healthy at all to be too hasty in interpreting your visions.

You need to be patient, open and flexible to grasp the essence of your visions. Of course, it can happen that you see something that is exactly what is about to be materialized, as happened to me with my NGO logo for example. The Iboga showed me how to draw it and I did it immediately. The name of my NGO too... etc... I also saw places and people I met afterwards.

But, I would like to explain a little something to you by telling you about a particular vision: in 2007 I passed a new initiatory stage with the Master Atome

Ribenga who is called "Mimbara." It is a step that is meant to prepare you for a fight that you know you have to fight. You go through this stage when you already know yourself well but that an ordeal in your life presents itself and that you are in search of strategic information.

During this initiation where I ingested approximately 20 grams of Iboga, I saw myself in tears on the tomb of my son. Then I saw myself in prison, all this was in vision. It deeply upset me because I had no idea how to interpret this. Was my son, who was then 5 years old, going to die? Why would I go to prison? It was extremely frightening. My master then explained some things to me about the visions, in particular by telling me about the biblical story of Abraham. He had been commanded in a vision to kill his son in order to test his faith.... My son is still alive to this day but this vision made me realize how important he was in my life. My relationship with him has totally changed. Also in 2012, 5 years later, I had legal problems in France because my son's mother used the fact that I was using Iboga when it was forbidden in France to have me withdraw from my parental authority. I didn't see my son for 2 years. But the fruit of this 2007 vision helped me fight to have my rights restored after 2 years of proceedings. I always told myself "Your son is not dead, there is hope, you can see him again, fight for him."

I didn't go to prison either! Moreover, my vision really pushed me during these years to be very careful about the possible consequences of my activist engagement in favor of Iboga and Bwiti. I learned to be very careful.

But in 2015, a friend called me to ask me if I wanted to assist in prisons to lead workshops on “Deconstructing Racist Prejudices” with prisoners incarcerated for radical Islamist terrorist activities. I accepted right away because I said to myself "If I have to go to prison one day, I prefer it to be of my own choice and even better if I can earn a living by helping my fellow man!” It was when I first entered the prison, walked through the corridors and stood in front of the inmates I was supposed to help that I understood the meaning of my vision during my initiation to "Mimbara" in 2007 in Gabon.

I could tell you a lot of visions that have materialized and others that are still waiting to be interpreted. I stress that it is very delicate and potentially damaging to become too attached to visions. It makes some people rather disturbed... with deep egotistical delusions.

Also, the visions are not systematic or guaranteed. Many people consuming Iboga don't have visions and that doesn't mean that nothing happened or that they failed. Of course, it can mean that the Iboga was not good... or that you were not ready physically or psychologically. But everything can have been prepared very well for you and you don't see anything. Sometimes what you have to see is right in front of you. Iboga simply shows you your reality through a different prism. It is useless to wait until Iboga shows you extraordinary things. Some clumsy people spread stories of their experiences. Besides, in Gabon it is forbidden to talk about one's visions and even more to make them public. Unless you can explain without hesitation what the visions have shown you and led you to.

Everybody seems to be attached only to the "visionary" properties of Iboga. That can lead the initiates or candidates to error or even to their total disappointment.

**Has Iboga affected your spirituality?**

Yes, definitely. Before Iboga my understanding of spirituality was conceptual. My first master used to say "We don't ask you to believe in god, we ask you to experience god." Before I believed in spirituality, I had done a lot of research. Even with the books I read, I didn't feel very much. As a kid, entering church, it was just fear, cold and boredom. After my first experience with Iboga, I was no longer looking for something, I had experienced it myself. I continue to experience and feel it deeply. It has totally changed my life, to have faith in the rules of the universe, that are totally perfect. In a way, Iboga is a great clue in understanding the equation. To really see in the largest way.

We used to say that drug addicts are people who are looking for God.

My spirituality now is no longer conceptual but practical. It is materialized in my daily life. I think I have captured how to connect to the "world of the spirit" rather easily and have the privilege of affirming that I have been touched many, many times by divine inner feelings. Hence the categorization of Iboga as a plant called "entheogenic."

**Anything else you'd like to add**

Please make a donation to our organization "Blessings Of The Forest." If you can't show your gratitude directly to the people who have revealed Iboga to the world, please help us to do so.

Do not participate in the destruction of the Iboga and the destruction of ancestral traditions linked to this heritage of humanity. Do not buy Iboga on the internet from unscrupulous sellers who do not respect the elementary rules of transparency, fairness and sustainability. As much as 95% of the Iboga that circulates in the world is looted in the public and private domain in Gabon. This is totally illegal and very damaging to the resource but also to the people, animals and insects that depend on it locally. Don't believe blindly, because it suits your compulsive desire or your conscience, what the Iboga sellers on the internet tell you, especially those who assure you to have a plantation.

Almost all the Iboga that leaves Gabon is plundered by Cameroonian poachers who do what most Gabonese people are afraid to do: sell the Iboga. These poachers are very often linked to a lot of other trafficking such as the trafficking of ivory, pangolins, great apes, panther skins, but they are also sometimes associated with the trafficking of gold, organs, drugs and human beings. Sometimes Iboga is stolen from around temples, or near traditional villages that depended on them for their spiritual practice. It also happens that the Iboga is planted on someone's grave and that it is carrying a particular spirit to be used by someone in particular. In short, do not consume the Iboga of which you do not know the exact origin.

Have gratitude and respect for the Pygmy and Bantu peoples of Gabon who have shared the knowledge of Iboga with the world. We can't do to Iboga what others have done with tobacco or Coca, or with a host of other natural resources sacred to Indigenous peoples around the world. Don't think that you will be totally healed by selfishly participating in a consumerist destruction of this heritage. If you want to honor this medicine, seek to get closer to its guardians or cultivators rather than to its private promoters.

**Author's note.**

Yann is relentless in his work, helping to protect and support Iboga across many different domains. From working with politicians to change laws regarding Iboga, to establishing Blessings of the Forest, his tireless work tracking poachers and extensive research into the global market and world of Iboga continues to be essential for the protection and livelihood of Iboga.

The comments Yann shares about his life rapidly changing after Iboga, are very prescient of one of the many ways Iboga can work. Following his initiation, a lot of his life was re-arranged. This period following working with Iboga can be both beautiful and challenging, as many old patterns, relationships and beliefs are let go. Often, if something is not working for you, Iboga may help it leave. Quickly.

Yann is one of the elders who I sought permission from to write this book. In addition to this, he has been a friend and teacher to me over the years, helping me to understand Iboga and life on the spiritual path. Thank you Yann.

**S...... Healing Opiate Addiction.**

***Bio:*** *Name and details redacted for privacy, Female, living between USA, Costa Rica, and Southeast Asia. Initially motivated to work with Iboga to treat opiate dependence.*

**Author's Introduction**: This interview was recorded when S was in a good place, working as an Ibogaine facilitator and having been free from opiates for many years. I was given her details by a mutual friend. After the interview, S's life took a turn. She approved this interview whilst still healthy, but was not contactable at time of publication.

**Where did you first hear about Iboga?**

I had seen it on online forums. For a long time, I had seen the word, I didn't know how to pronounce it, I didn't know what it was. I was an opiate user and I could not get off opiates. I had googled how to get off opiates so many times and a lot of forums would mention the word "Ibogaine." I had seen that word for a long time and assumed it was an herb, like valerian root or something. It seemed too good to be true.

I got put on suboxone, I was able to kick short acting opiates pretty often and easily. I was then put on methadone and I kicked that cold turkey. And then I was put on Suboxone, and that was the first thing I couldn't get off. It stays in your system for a long time, the withdrawal was so rough and lasted so long. I couldn't get off it.

I had a partner at the time who said "We have to get you some Ibogaine." My response was "What!? That works?" He had done Ibogaine before. He had contacts and he said "Let me call Eric T***." We were in NYC, Brooklyn at the time. He met us for tea in lower Manhattan the very next day. He said "Let's get you off to Guatemala and get you off suboxone. I'm going to send you to this guy Lex, I think you'll like him..." and he sort of cackled and made a comment that he had tattoos. It was strange and didn't make sense until I met Lex.

A month later I flew down to Guatemala and a few weeks after that, I did Ibogaine.

**How were you called to Iboga?**

At the time, I wasn't thinking about being called to anything. I just wanted to be free of opiates. It wasn't until that (Ibogaine) alkaloid entered my body that I felt like I was re-meeting an old friend. I felt a really deep connection to it (Ibogaine). After my experience with it, I could not stop thinking about it. I was obsessed. I had to do it again. I did it again maybe 10-11 months later. It was then, that I thought "This is what I'm supposed to be working with. This is what I am supposed to be doing. I want to be completely immersed with this plant."

When I did it, it was this clear feeling of "This is an old friend, that I haven't talked to in a while. This is something that has to be in my life." It really was like meeting an old friend, but it was a plant. I felt the calling afterwards. Before working with Ibogaine I was too clouded. I wasn't feeling anything, just opiates. There was just the desire to get off. My partner at the time told me it worked and someone else I trusted told me it worked, so I believed it.

I didn't feel the call initially, but the second it entered my body, I knew. I want this plant to be around me all the time.

**What was your life like before Iboga?**

Before, I was a high fashion model. I was traveling all the time, 3 months in one place, 5 months in another place. I was traveling all over the world. I would say it was very hedonistic, very nihilistic. I was out all the time. I was partying all the time. It wasn't just opiates, it was alcohol, cigarettes and amphetamines.

Some things were the same: I was adventurous, I wanted to try new things, I liked yoga. I had interests such as yoga, hiking and Buddhism that were healthy. I had brief periods of clarity where I got into these things I enjoyed. My life was very fast paced, very impulsive and extreme. I was either studying with monks in a temple in Taiwan or I was injecting heroin backstage at some rock and roll venue in Brooklyn. It was dancing with opposites. I didn't believe in anything. I felt the world was very black and white. I felt invincible in a lot of ways, it was probably selfish and narcissistic in some ways. But, I wasn't thinking about the future. I was very in the moment and very impulsive. But I think a lot of that was a mask for extreme trauma, sadness, and loneliness, and a complete blowback for a sense of belonging.

**What is your life like after Iboga?**
It completely changed my life around. Completely.

Afterwards, as part of the integration, I signed up for anything I was remotely interested in. The biggest thing was "How do I fill up my time if I'm not looking for and using drugs?" I got really into yoga, hiking, and I got back into drawing. I did free diving lessons. Anything that interested me I went full on into.

The main thing that I noticed was that I got smarter. I had a brain that was always there, that previously I just wasn't utilizing. Afterwards, I was really using my brain a lot. It allowed me to spend time with people who were smart, and I was writing again, which was something I hadn't done in a long time. The writing was a lot better than when I was on drugs. I was creating again. The main thing I noticed was that I was interested and passionate about so many things. I had the time to really delve into so many different subjects. I got to really know a lot of things I was interested in, from Ashtanga yoga to free diving with sharks. Travel became a lot better, because I didn't have to worry about sickness and withdrawal when I arrived. Travelling became a much more exciting and fun thing. Relations with my family were better, my relationships in general were much better.

The biggest thing is about a year or so after my first experience, I started working with this medicine (Ibogaine), I was surrounded by it. That completely changed my world. I went from being a high fashion model, getting high all the time - hanging out in dive bars in Brooklyn- to being in Costa Rica and Thailand and working with the medicine.

I definitely transformed. Even modeling sober was a totally different thing. No wonder I was on drugs! It is a really horrific industry, it's miserable. It's not fun at all. What was I thinking!? It was really hard to do my job after Ibogaine, I thought "I don't like this, I'm not having a good time doing this, I don't want to do this, it's a very weird thing to do when all of your senses are working." That only lasted for about another year. I did an 8 month contract in Hong Kong and a 3 month contract in Bangkok and then I thought "I can't do this anymore." I ended up apprenticing with someone to learn how to prepare Ibogaine.

**How did you prepare? Would you prepare differently a second time?**
My first time doing Ibogaine, I didn't prepare at all. I did everything wrong. I was on suboxone, the provider told me I should switch to a short acting opiate for 90 days before. I didn't. Again, I was very arrogant, I thought "There's no way it's going to take that long to get out of my system." The whole reason I was doing Ibogaine is because the withdrawal (from suboxone) lasted so long, it's almost never ending. So, I switched to heroin and then I went to Guatemala and the doctor at the center prescribed me oxycontin for a couple of weeks. I ended up being off Suboxone for 5 and a half weeks total.

I had a contract in Japan that I was trying to get to, which was my excuse as to why I couldn't do the full 90 days (12+ weeks). I was dehydrated, my colon function was terrible. I had opiate induced constipation, every X factor in the book - which as a provider I now understand was like "Wow! I'm really lucky that nothing bad happened!."

The person who treated me told me that if I had come to him several years later, he wouldn't have worked with me. I was smoking a lot of cigarettes right up to it as well. I didn't prepare at all. I didn't understand it. I didn't know how powerful it was, that it is a medicine. I didn't understand the weight that it carried. I didn't understand how vast and nebulous Iboga is. I didn't prepare at all and as a result I was in withdrawal for 6 weeks (after). The provider had warned me that it might happen. I came out and felt great for 2 maybe 3 days and then the withdrawal hit me. You feel good initially, because Ibogaine takes care of the receptor withdrawal but you still have **noephrine** in your fat cells. As it slowly metabolizes out of that, you have withdrawal issues.

I didn't make it to Japan either way. I did make it to my parents basement at the age of 25. I was really sick. I had to extend my stay in Guatemala. There was no way I could get on a plane. I ended up staying in my parents' basement until I could get back on my feet. I booster dosed for 6 weeks. It did take a full 90 days before I was doing well, 5.5 weeks before and 6 weeks after.

I didn't prepare at all and I suffered the consequences for it. It was rough. The only reason I can say these things about it, is the process and transformations I went through afterwards were profound. The rewards were so great once I started feeling better. I went through absolute hell. It was the hardest thing I've ever done. It really was. It was so worth it. It changed my life around.

Subsequent times, as I've kept doing it, almost a decade later, preparation is just as important as the experience itself. Going into it now, I want to do a full flood dose. I will prepare for a full 30 days beforehand. Electrolyte hydration, setting an intention, having a plan for afterwards are all really important. Having supportive people around, having a supportive environment, eating really well. Just doing things that are in line with the medicine. Now I understand it's a lot of work, that integration is really important. I want to be in a good environment afterwards. I want to really, really have my intentions at the forefront, do it at a time where I'm feeling great. Have all the necessary tests done. EKGs are important. What you do before and after a session is just as important as the session itself. It's all connected.

People look at the Ibogaine (or Iboga) flood as a singular event. It is a process. People look at it like flicking a switch, a singular peak experience. I think the process is just beginning once you get through the flood. Calls I get from clients normally come 3 weeks later. The day after, people often feel terrible.

**What precautions did you take to make sure it was a safe experience?**
I got an EKG and that was it. The provider asked for an EKG and that's what I got. I have a really low resting heart rate. Looking back, I should have definitely had a liver panel done, I probably needed a safe colon cleanse in the weeks beforehand (to combat opiate induced constipation), and then electrolytes to replenish from the colon cleanse.

**What was your intention?**
The first time my intention was just getting off suboxone. All I wanted was to be done with it. I just wanted to get off. It was very surface level, it didn't go deeper than that.

The second time I wanted to process the breakup from the partner I had, when I first did Ibogaine. We were engaged. I had a really hard time with that breakup. I didn't know why I was in this cycle of really toxic relationships. The pattern was always the same. I wanted to look at my relationships, which were a dependency in themselves. We can be dependent on relationships and humans, just like drugs.

Other times, I've done it to process trauma. I've had sexual trauma, I've had different intentions each time, peeling off layers, as I go. I feel that I've targeted different traumas now, I'm planning on doing it again and wanting closure on some deaths that have happened. I want to get better at processing grief and also want to work on my anger. Those are my intentions moving forward.

**How did you consume Iboga? What did you take and where? What form? Total dose?**
It was HCL from Tabernanthe Iboga. I do not know the total dose. My first facilitator was known for dosing heavy. I would guess that I was in the 24mg/kg range. Definitely over 20mg/kg. I didn't think I could handle more, so I actually turned down some doses. The Ibogaine HCL was powdered and came in a capsule.

I've worked with both HCL and TA. I've had really profound experiences with TA. The second time I did it, I know I did 20mg/Kg of TA.

I've also worked with PTA, which is "precipitated total alkaloid." It's three of the alkaloids from the root. It's 85% Ibogaine, Ibogamine and Ibogaline. I think it breaks down to 10% of one and 5% of the other. It tends to be pretty chaotic, pretty harsh, people seem to really like it or not like it at all. I do think it is a little bit unpredictable working with clients. Some clients request it, there is something unique about it.

As I've gone on, I've become really sensitive to the medicine. I can do 8-9mg/kg and I can really get "there." Recently I did 15mg/kg which would normally be a small dose, but it really floored me.

**Why did you decide to do it this way? Why did you pick this center?**
The first time I did it, that was with someone my partner trusted and had worked with before. He recommended that I should go down to a specific center in Guatemala. So, that's where I went. I trusted my partner and I liked the recommended facilitator. I didn't think about it, I only reached out to one other

person, and he didn't get back to me. He got back to me almost 9 years later and he said "Hey I just saw this message do you still need to get of Suboxone?" but I'm glad he wrote to me, because he's become a friend and mentor since.

I didn't do any research and I just went. I just needed to get off opiates. I was desperate.

**What would be your advice to people considering Iboga?**
My advice is not to rush it. I see people get really desperate and just go to a center that will take them or the center that costs the least. My experience is, if we let someone rush right in, it doesn't mean it will be bad but we don't see as vibrant of an outcome. This is compared to people who really take the time to prepare.

My advice is to take your time. Do you research and find a safe and reputable place to go. I've written an entire essay on finding a center, a guide to red flags, and probably at least 15 other articles on Ibogaine and maybe more, ranging from safety, to this new Era of opiate use we are in, to why buying Ibogaine online is a bad idea. My advice is to research. Start with that easy checklist of finding a center and then read everything you can on Ibogaine, but make sure the authors, websites, or people quoted are credible. Make sure that the place not only meets that checklist of requirements but is also someone who you really resonate with.

You want someone you can be open, honest and resonate with. You want to find someone who you can be completely 100% yourself. I want people when they work with me to be themselves, to feel free to work through whatever comes up. If that's yelling, crying, throwing something, I want them to feel safe and know that there is no judgment. You have to be with someone where you can let your guard down and be vulnerable and know that you are safe; emotionally and physiologically.

My main advice is to take time and do your research. I think it's a disservice to Ibogaine the way it is labeled as a "cure." People need to really realize what they are getting into. It is probably going to be the hardest thing they have ever done. Look at it as a minimum 3-month process. Ideally, put a plan in for 30 days before and 3 months after. Know how you are going to prepare and integrate it.

If you put no work into it, you probably won't have that huge experience. For me, if I didn't go into that 6 week withdrawal, it wouldn't have worked for me. But because I was forced into this hellish experience, it helped me get to know the medicine. It gave me time to change my approach to it. If I had just had the flood, and nothing else, I probably would have gone back to using. Being so sick forced me into not going back to New York and totally changed my experience.

Know that you're going to have to do the work, and start putting the work in as early as you can. It's a really big thing to do. Iboga is the hardest thing I've ever done. It requires so much work before and after.

The people with a lot of Ayahuasca experience have some of the hardest times. I've seen it over and over again. The "gray day" is really hard for them. They are normally very good at handling their acute visionary experience, but not how challenging it gets the day after. Sometimes there is no sleeping for days, it just keeps going and going. Lots of Ayahuasca people are not prepared for that. They've come into it as an Ayahuasca ceremony, but they are VERY different. People who come from a spiritual background and have been working with Ayahuasca often have a harder experience than people that have just been using heroin. Heroin users are used to being miserable. They know how to get through the suffering.

We've also noticed that if we can educate people from Ayahuasca backgrounds and they realize what a big task this is, they can have great experiences. They have built themselves for these big experiences.

The "Gray day" is something a lot of people don't know about.

**What is a "Gray day"?**

A gray day is an industry term and it typically means the day after your flood dose. It's confusing for some people, because it can arise at different times. For some people it is 2 days after, for others it's immediately afterwards. What we typically see is after the visionary state, the reflection state, when you're at a stage where you haven't slept yet. You're over the 24 hour mark, approaching the 36 hour mark with no deep sleep. My teacher had a person that lasted for 6 days, I've had someone last 72 hours. It gets rough. Very manic.

Essentially what the gray day is, is the period after taking Iboga (or Ibogaine) where the restarting process of the brain hasn't really been felt or happened yet. What I have noticed is a wide range of emotions will come up. For some people, it is total grief and maybe crying for 12 hours. For other people it may be anger, they might throw a shoe at me or slam something against a wall. For some people it is total numbness, they don't want anything to do with anything. They just want to sit and be. Other people may feel high anxiety, super anxious ruminating thoughts. Insecurity is another one. I tend to get really sad and insecure. I feel like I am everything, I hope I'm not, I am that times 100! I get really sad about it. A lot of things come up and you need to process it. It ranges from really heavy to minor, where people may be "snappy." It can happen on low wave doses too, but on a much lesser scale.

I fully believe the gray day is the most important part of the journey. Sitting through that, is where the healing happens. A lot of centers give people Benzos or Cannabis, whatever's around to help them get through it, without too much discomfort. Often, it's when people haven't slept and they start to get very frustrated and restless, they think they are going to lose their minds. I think it is really important to sit through that. If you block it out with drugs, you're not going to learn as much. UV rays and walking tend to help. Usually, when someone finally gets 5-6 hours sleep, they feel amazing or at least a little better.

Whatever comes up on a gray day is what people need to be liberated from. If anger comes up, that's what you need to be liberated from. The insecurity I have felt on gray days, is something I needed to overcome and be liberated from. You have to sit through it.

**Was there a memorable moment or particularly profound vision you had? Has it come true?**

Yes. In my first experience, I saw a man I was with. I was standing in front of a white house in a very green area. I did not know this man. My first flood was mainly old memories. I haven't had a flood like that since. But this was definitely not a memory. I had no idea what it was.

Fast forward 6 years and it's the person I am with now. It's my partner. It was absolutely him. We live in a white house right now, in a sub-tropical environment. It's green everywhere. I definitely believe, I know in my mind that he was the person I was standing next to in that vision. I think he's my person and the person I'm going to be with. We were standing there, it was a brief image but it really stuck with me. I thought "Who is that? Why is it so clear?" A lot of the images I saw in my first flood were in cartoon form. This one was not, it was a really clear image. I could tell I was happy. It was a really breezy vignette.

Then he came into my life!

I also saw Covid a few years ago. I saw the entire Covid thing play out. I didn't know it was a pandemic. I saw the events. I saw air travel stop. I saw the propaganda change. I saw staying at home. I took that to be about me traveling for so long, I saw that as Iboga telling me that I needed to get in touch with my roots and stay in one place. In the vision, I was stuck on an Island, but I wasn't living on an island. When covid started, the news and the graphs started happening just like Iboga had told me and here I was on an island, two weeks away from heading back to Costa Rica, but very much stuck as the travel bans set in.

**Has Iboga affected your spirituality?**

Yes it has. I grew up Mormon. My family is not Mormon anymore. They left the church after I did. I was not at all religious or spiritual when I went into my first Iboga experience. For me, after my first experience, I thought there was no way everything I saw came just from myself.

I knew part of it had come from me. It was very clear Iboga was interacting with my brain. It also seemed Iboga was sentient. There was a spirit there. There was a third component I couldn't put my finger on. I saw it with open eye visuals. Some of it was demon-like figures trying to steal my memories. There was something else there and I questioned if it was always there, but we just can't see it. No doubt, Iboga is sentient and has its own place during an experience, but you, yourself, are part of it too, and then there is this third component...I don't know what that is yet.

The open eye visuals were distinct. It wasn't me and it wasn't the Iboga. It felt like things that are usually there but I can't see with my eyes. I'm not normally in a state of awareness to see it. I asked the provider "What is that!?" He responded with "That is the question!!" I will say that the world is not black and white. It has changed my perspective of the world a lot. What was a very strict and scientific view of the world has been changed a lot. It has given me something to believe in. I do believe in Iboga. It challenges my views on everything, from past lives through to ancestors. I don't have an answer as to what I believe in, but it has opened up some space for some spirituality to exist, where that wasn't the case before.

**Author's Note:**

This is a heart breaking author's note to write. When I spoke to S, she was in a great place. She was living by the beach with her partner and working hard to facilitate treatments and share medicine with other people. On the phone, S was really cool: someone who had lived a wild, rich, and adventurous life. From being a high fashion model, dealing with abuse, and facing her own shadows, to living a life of service for the Iboga and plant medicine community. All seemed well and idyllic.

However, life takes twists and turns. I couldn't get back in contact with S and heard from a trusted friend that she had relapsed recently and was uncontactable. I don't know the full story and only wish S well, hoping that there is deeper healing and some lessons to integrate for her when she is ready. It goes to show that Iboga is not a "one time forever miracle solution." Even Iboga experts, who appear to live dream-like lives, can face issues that challenge their sobriety. I pray that S can find her way back home soon, with deeper understanding and healing to share with the world in her own perfect time.

**Levi....... Detox from Opiates and Psycho-spiritual Experiences.**

***Bio:*** *Levi Barker. 31 when first working with Iboga, 44 now. Male. USA. Initial treatment was 25-30 grams of ground Iboga root bark. Levi is a Bwiti initiate and has been studying himself and life thanks to Iboga. 8 years ago Levi started serving the medicine full time at Iboga Wellness Centre in Costa Rica. Iboga Wellness Centre was started by Levi's mentor and dear friend Gary Cook. Motivated to work with Iboga to "Detox from opiates and subsequently psycho-spiritual experiences."*

**Author's Introduction:** There was a wave of calmness, kindness and patience that shone through Levi in his interview. He was extremely generous with his time and the consummate professional. I cold contacted him, through messaging his website and he was nothing short of a gentleman, agreeing to help with this project without personally knowing me. His passion and dedication towards working with and helping Iboga was obvious. Levi studied with Moghenda, a 10th generation Bwiti shaman and by many accounts does a terrific job at holding the tradition, whilst also ensuring it is accessible/manageable for people seeking treatment.

**Where did you first hear about Iboga?**

I came to live in Nicaragua in 2009, where I met my now wife. I had a really dear friend, who knew more about plant medicines than anyone I know and I asked him "Is there anything that can help, that can get someone through withdrawals and help with addiction?" he said "Yes, Iboga. I have some, I'll send it to you." He sent it to me in California and I brought it down with me to Nicaragua.

**How were you called to Iboga?**

For me, that process was a long one. My first Iboga detox finished 11.5 years ago, then I started working with Iboga for spiritual reasons about a year after that. I had wanted to work with the medicine, but I wasn't in a place to do it for a long time. The medicine will show you the steps to take. It will give you the guidance and a push. But you have to work hard to get there. It's not something that can be rushed or pushed. Iboga is a very patient plant. It takes a long time to grow in the physical realm, and on one's spiritual path.

**What was your life like before Iboga?**

I was an opiate addict throughout my 20s. I was part of the first generation of heavy opiate users, that started coming out of the US in the 1990s. I broke my wrist snowboarding and got prescribed percocet to manage it. But even before that, my grandfather was a heroin addict too, for all of his life. When I got opiates, I felt like I finally understood where he was coming from. That led to stronger opiates. It was a gradual progression of trying harder ones.

One day, when I didn't have them, I realized I was sick. I never planned on that happening. That went on for a good 10 years, going to harder opiates, eventually ending up with heroin. I got it together for a few years with vicodin. During this time I was pretty productive. But then things would get bad and something would happen and my life would crumble down. I would have to come back and build it back again.

I did the opposite of what you want to do. I did a home detox, at my house in Nicaragua. It was pretty gruelling. It is a very different experience, detoxing, verse going in for spiritual discovery. Going in for psycho spiritual reasons is a very different experience compared to a detox experience... It was really dark. I saw very dark energy moving through me. I was seeing myself being cleansed but during the time I was in it, I just saw myself in a very dark place.

*** His dog Howls***

I came out the other end and wasn't physically addicted anymore. It was miraculous. I knew from then I wanted to work with this medicine. But that didn't happen straight away. I went on living my life, free from being physically addicted, but still struggling a lot. I had to learn how to live again. Iboga very much breaks you down to build you back up. When you are being built back up it is a very raw experience where every emotion hits you twice as hard, but you have a new way of looking at and managing that emotion.

From there It was really about relearning how to do everything again. 11 years of opiate use, trying to mask all of my emotions. Then afterwards I had to face them. Everything. I learnt how to face those emotions that I had been hiding from.

About a year or so later the same friend that sent me the Iboga in the first place invited me to help out at Iboga House, with Moughenda Mikala who is a 10th generation Bwiti Shaman. I started working for him, as I owned an internet marketing company. I had my first ceremonies with Mougenda which were very helpful in bringing my life together quicker. I started training with Moughenda on how to hold and serve the medicine.

**What is your life like after Iboga?**
I don't know where I'd be if I didn't find Iboga. It has given me everything. My health. Being able to manage my mind, it gave me my spirituality. I can't imagine being in a better spot in life, and the medicine has been a huge help in that. It has kept me focused. It has kept me real. It has shown me what's important in life. In the West we are taught to be hard on ourselves and to be down on ourselves if we don't do something right. I've kicked that programming out of my system. I'm motivated to work hard and get the things I want, but I'm not going to beat myself up anymore if things don't work out how I had planned.

At some level in life we all want to be happy. I am happy now. Life was really rough before. Detoxing was hard. I felt like the biggest piece of crap that ever existed, having to go chase drugs down. It's a beautiful 180 from that!

I've been full time at Iboga wellness center for 6 years now and on the path for 12. I've never gone back to opiates.

In my practice Bwiti we say a prayer every morning of gratitude for another day of life, I'm really appreciative of every day. No matter how in tune we are, life's challenges still come up, but overall I'm in a good spot. I appreciate what I have.

**How did you prepare? Would you prepare differently a second time?**
That's a funny question. When I first had Iboga for the home detox, my friend sent me 50 grams. The only instruction I had from my friend was "Down it and try not to move your head." I worked my way through about half of it and I thought "I think I have enough." Back then, the information on the internet was even more unreliable and harder to find.

I didn't do a good job at preparing or being careful. I got the root bark from my friend and a couple weeks later, I did it. Thankfully, everything turned out okay. It is super important to be careful and prepare correctly. We don't work with detox patients anymore at Iboga Wellness. It's risky. Especially with fentanyl, people really need to be careful. You don't want a fatal accident to happen.

With that said, there's only so much you can do before you "Get in there" and actually experience it. I would definitely recommend people to work with facilitators who know how to work with the medicine. Good facilitators know what to do when really challenging things come up, whether that's physically, mentally or spiritually. If you don't know how to deal with the things that come up, and you're doing it at home, people can get stuck in a 36-48 hour very dark space.

My advice would be to definitely do it with a facilitator and also someone who cares! It is important to work with someone who loves the medicine and has done it themselves. Be careful... Even the most experienced Psychonauts can be hammered. It can just hammer you. But those deep, challenging experiences are important because that's how things get moved out. There are a lot of things in people's minds that they don't want to look at, but the medicine works to allow you to release those things. You NEED someone around who knows the space and knows how to guide you. Rather than leaving yourself stuck in a psychotic break.

**What precautions did you take to make sure it was a safe experience?**
Avoiding medications is a big one. A lot of people need to get off SSRIs. People need to know about any existing heart issues. If someone is healthy, there are no heart problems and no medications (or drug usage) they should be fine. We've had people from age 14-75 that have gone through the healing experience. Obviously, these people have to lay off the large dose of the medicine. They had the gifts and healing of Iboga. If you are working with someone who knows how to work with it, they will give you good guidance on how to prepare. You won't get that with the solo home route, or the friend whose read about Iboga sitting for you.

We make everybody that comes to us take a heart scan before they get to us.

People with schizophrenia should not take Iboga. Perhaps if they were working in Gabon it might be workable. In general it is a no... But schizophrenia is very different to extreme anxiety, heavy depression or PTSD. For people that go into psychotic breaks or have schizophrenia, Iboga is probably not the medicine for them at that point in their life.

**What was your intention?**
For the first time it was to get clean and to get rid of addiction. For my body. The mental part takes time. Getting physically clean was my first intention.

For subsequent ceremonies, it was definitely learning to love myself and figuring out who I was. It's important to know who we are and what we want. Really knowing who we are, how to interpret our past, what our thoughts mean. It all goes into learning to appreciate the gift of life. Really learning to value my life, step by step. Learning to make the right decisions at each step. Learning to love oneself is the important one. If love for oneself doesn't happen then success in other areas of your life aren't going to make you whole. If you love yourself, you're always going to be whole.

**How did you consume Iboga? What did you take and where? What form? Total dose?**
I took root bark the first time, for the detox which is a little unusual. Normally it's Ibogaine or Total Alkaloid (TA) for a detox.

Subsequent times were always with (Iboga) root bark or total alkaloid extract.

I've never had Ibogaine. I've heard from a lot of people that the Root Bark or the Total Alkaloid is a fuller experience. Doing Ibogaine may strip the spirit out of the plant. Within the plant, within nature, there's different keys and codes. We don't want to mess with nature.

**Why did you decide to do it this way? Why did you pick this center?**
The root bark was the only thing I had at that time. I was pretty desperate. I had no other options. Subsequent times, I was working with a teacher who used root bark.

In my experience, the root bark is more grounding, whereas the TA goes a bit more into the mind. Root bark seems to move through a bit quicker and people recover quicker. TA stays a bit longer.

You can get everything you want from the medicine with just root bark. A lot of times, people from the west report not feeling anything with root bark... TA can be really valuable for really breaking through to people. Even so, Iboga is such a different medicine it really grounds people, especially if they've never been grounded before. You can try and fight it but you're not going to win.

**What would be your advice to people considering Iboga?**
Make sure that this is what you want. It's not going to change your will. Sometimes people come to us because their spouse or family wants them to do it, this is not a good motivation.

Make sure it is something you really want.

Find the right practitioner for you. Different people come to different providers for different things. Going to an Ibogaine provider for detox is different to going to Gabon. Make sure you've done the heart scan.

Let go of any expectations or anything you've read. That can really get in the way. Focus on surrendering. It's important for people to know that if you come in open, with clear intentions, the medicine works in mysterious ways but it will show you. It will keep teaching you.

**What are your thoughts on micro-dosing? Did you Micro-dose after a flood dose for integration?**
I didn't micro-dose after that first detox at home. I got down as many spoons as I could, until I couldn't take anymore. I had my fill of Iboga.

Micro-dosing can be super valuable, but I do believe that people need a big experience first. This helps people get the momentum behind them, then they can micro-dose. I imagine you could get a lot of benefits from micro-dosing, but if you are looking to solve a serious problem, something you've carried around for a long time, then it's important to have a big dose.

Micro-dosing can be very powerful, but people need to be careful. Iboga stays in you a lot longer than anything else. Once you ingest the root bark it stays in you longer than any other medicine known to man. It goes deep and releases gradually, depending on the person's physiology and how they treat themselves. It can start stacking in your system. With micro-dosing, you want to take less as time goes on.  Iboga has a reverse tolerance to it. You need less of it the more you work with it. It continues to clear things out of you, your mind and body, you don't need as much.

**Would you do Iboga again?**
Yes. I work with it all the time (Levi is a facilitator and founder of Iboga Wellness Centre).

**Was there memorable moment or particularly profound vision you had? Has it come true?**
Iboga visions are very different from other plant medicines. They can be anything, from geometric visions to the famous "movie of your life."

A lot of that, people see faces, we see so many faces throughout our life. In Iboga we can release or make room for our subconscious.

There are also the big visions. Beautiful things happen. There was not one vision that I had that was super significant. I went at life in a place of fear for a long time, always putting that fear into the future. I created a horror story of how things were going to turn out. It never got as bad as the energy that I sent out, but it definitely didn't help in my life.

During one Iboga ceremony, I was sitting cross legged and I started having drops of gold liquid start dripping on my head. It slowly encased my whole body. Once it got to my feet, my whole body was covered in gold. I then lit up like a star.  It was one of the most beautiful moments of my life.

When that vision happened, I knew I didn't have to be scared anymore. It was giving me my own spiritual protection. I didn't have to live in a place of fear anymore. And that's happened. I haven't had to fear, not serious fear. I'm not creating useless anxiety for myself. There is a time to be careful and cautious, but not the useless fear from the mind that we create.

**Has Iboga affected your spirituality?**

Absolutely. Before Iboga I didn't believe in a creator. I was pretty agnostic on things. Now, I'm not going to say I know what the creator is, who it is, or what it looks like. But everything is given to us through nature. Everything that we will ever have in life: our food, clothes, loved ones all come to us through nature. It's too perfect not to have been planned. It definitely wasn't an accident.

Working with the Bwiti tradition, which is passed down as an oral tradition. It provides lessons on how to live life, and the things we have to deal with as humans. I've really ingrained those lessons in. It took a long time. There's a difference between knowing those lessons, understanding them and practicing them and living them.

It has changed everything about spirituality and what I thought was possible. My whole way of being has shifted thanks to this medicine. Everything that is taught in our bwiti comes from the medicine. We go to Iboga, to answer questions or receive guidance, we don't seek the answers from a human teacher. We can understand something told to us, but we have to experience it to fully know something.

We encourage people to ask questions and to frame them to their experience here on earth. On all the big questions, people tend to get the same answers. Iboga gives us the truth on things. We want the truth, so we know what we have to do. Where are we lying to ourselves? Iboga teaches you, how to teach yourself. It really digs it in deep to you and continues teaching.

**"How did Iboga change your relationship to Opiates? What did it show or teach you?" Let me know if the below works. Thank you.**

Iboga showed me opiates were a symptom of deeper problems. Most people get into and like opiates initially as it allows them to get away from their mind and be. When they can shut off their mind and leave behind their problems, they think opiates are great. Eventually things go downhill quickly though.

Iboga in the end makes you take a hard look at yourself and also shows and gives you the willpower inside to make shifts in your life. The shifts can take some time, but we know in our tradition that the spirit of the medicine stays with us for the rest of our life, if we don't expel it through substances. Iboga can leave a blueprint and list out the changes that need to happen for people to heal and continue on living. Our job on this planet is to live and experience the wonder of being alive. It doesn't get much better than being alive as far as our senses tell us. Maybe the afterlife is there and better or maybe not, but we don't know as we are here now, so in the Bwiti we focus on this life.

**Anything else you'd like to add?**

I hope more people start growing Iboga. If as many people are going to come to this medicine as I anticipate we are going to need more people sustainably growing Iboga.

**Author's Note:**

Personally, it was really interesting for me to see someone who has worked so hard to heal intergenerational trauma and addiction with opiates. I wondered did Levi's soul choose this family to heal the intergenerational poppy addiction? Was it the fastest way for his soul to meet Iboga? Nonetheless, it highlights the power of Iboga to heal intergenerational trauma and "hit the blindspot" that many other medicines and modalities cannot get to.

Levi's interview also highlights some of the dangers of working with Iboga by oneself. This is the only interview in the book, where someone did an initial flood dose by themselves, unsupervised. It was included because of the firm warning Levi provided and his advice on the importance of preparation. In my opinion, Levi was lucky that nothing bad happened. This was also before there was as much information available about Iboga and the dangers of doing it alone were not widely known.

**Agnes…… Healing Opiate Dependency and Trauma.**

***Bio:** Agnes Bos. Female, Ibogaine, Motivated to work with Iboga for "Opiate dependency and trauma."*

**Author's Introduction:** Agnes is a pioneer in safety and education for Ibogaine treatments. A truly compassionate nurse, who is driven by helping people and ensuring they are safe. Her kindness and gentleness shone through in this interview. Her own personal journey with the poppy softened my stance on opiates and made me realize that they are an ancient medicine that can save lives, but unfortunately are commonly misused.

**Where did you first hear about Iboga?**

I did my own research, I was an opiate addict for most of my life. I started on opiates when I was 13 and was given escalating doses over the years. Eventually, I was taking quantities that were in excess of what someone with a terminal cancer diagnosis would be prescribed. It got to the point where I was desperate to get off them, but I was struggling so badly with the withdrawals. When I tried to, I was also unable to taper on my own. I started doing some research and I happened across it (Ibogaine) online somewhere. This was in 2006. It was still quite new then. There were only a few official clinics, and most were in Mexico. I did my research and figured I'd give it a shot.

I was treated in 2007. I can't say that it was a successful treatment. It was not in the way that I was hoping. I was still in withdrawal when I left the center. So much so that I had to use a wheelchair at the airport because I was so sick and weak. It was not a successful detox but I was given a glimpse of the power of Ibogaine. It helped me resolve a very significant trauma that I had. For me, that alone was worth what I went through.

I still had residual withdrawals for over a month afterwards. Looking back with much more knowledge and experience, I now know that the reason I was left in this state after the flood is because I was on pharmaceutical fentanyl. Even though it is a super short acting opiate, it takes a long time for it to clear out of your system. Iboga doesn't clear synthetic opiates very well. I was taking a combination of synthetic opioids, long-acting hydromorphone, Dilaudid and

Fentanyl. We now know that you should be off Fentanyl for a minimum of one week prior to a flood and that long-acting opioids should also be switched to short acting opioids. It is no surprise to me now that I was in such bad shape physically after my first flood.

I also went to a place where they did a very standard dose by weight and was only there only for 3 days, from start to finish. I received a dose on the low end of what was recommended and this was not nearly enough to fully reset my opiate receptors.

That being said, I caught a glimpse of the power of Ibogaine. I knew I needed to explore it further. I started going into full research mode, knowing that I wanted to have another experience. I did end up doing it (another flood dose) again in 2015. That was a really powerful experience for me. It was very different. I wasn't doing it for opiate dependence, so it really peeled away more layers.

I started working with the medicine and doing treatments (for other people) in 2009. I didn't want to work with it until I felt comfortable and understood the medicine really well. I am a medical professional so I was very cognizant of the dangers of Ibogaine. I devoured medical journals, spoke with providers and gathered the necessary medical equipment before I ventured into treating other individuals. I also personally worked with the medicine to develop a relationship with it. I took varying doses, sometimes they were micro-doses and other times booster doses which are always less than a flood dose but much higher than a micro-dose.

**Did you feel called to Iboga?**

It's hard to say. When you are coming to it as an addict, your only motivation at that time is to get clean. Honestly, I didn't expect it to be a life changing experience. I had my doubts that it would do anything like that for me. I knew that it had been shown to almost eliminate withdrawals. That was enough for me. I was happy with that.

The second time I did it, it was more of a calling. I again suffered a serious life altering trauma and I knew it was time for me to flood again.

**What was your life like before working with Iboga?**
I was a broken shell of a person. I felt only pain and it was unbearable. I'm honestly grateful for my addiction because I truly believe it saved my life. If I had not had opioids available to me then I don't think I would still be on this earth. They made living tolerable.

I had a lot of trauma. I still have that trauma, but I have a different perspective and it no longer consumes me. I think the most important lesson I learned from Iboga was to love myself, my flawed self and to be kind to myself. I learned to extend the same kindness that I gave to others to myself. To break the loop of negative self-talk. There is a lot of shame and guilt surrounding addiction. I carried that for a very long time. After my second flood, a lot of that was lifted and I am still actively working on it to this day.

**What is your life like now after working with Iboga?**
For me, it has peeled away so many layers. It has exposed issues that I wasn't able to recognize even with the help of a therapist. It unearthed the root causes of my addiction and helped me understand that my past behaviors were a response to my traumas.

When I was ready to face things and make changes, when I was strong enough to do that, Iboga helped me start off in the right direction. It doesn't do the work for you, but it opens the door and gives you a fresh and healthy perspective.

After my second flood, I worked extensively with the medicine at home afterwards. For several months afterwards I was taking booster doses of PTA (purified total alkaloid or precipitated total alkaloid) Ibogaine weekly. Every week I took a booster, sometimes two in a week. The amount of work that I was able to do on myself over that year, the healing that occurred was unbelievable. It far exceeded any benefits I had from a single flood. It completely changed the way I look at things. It brought insight on such a deep level and the revelations were so huge and so flagrant that I was incredulous to how I had never been aware of them before.

All of a sudden, everything started falling into place. Iboga allowed me to find that one critical puzzle piece that I needed in order to put the puzzle together and I could finally see the whole picture. It was painful, but a beautiful experience. The Ibogaine gave me a clarity that I had never had before. It showed me the source of my deepest pain and helped me surmount it.

When people say the medicine will speak to you a lot of people expect it to actually speak to you. It didn't happen that way for me. Each Iboga experience is very different and personal. For me, what would happen is it would guide my thoughts and it would bring me so deep inside myself. It let me explore areas of my psyche that I had completely blocked off, mostly due to traumas. Traumas are painful and your mind doesn't want to go there.

For me, Iboga lets me access those memories and thoughts. It allows me to do it in a way where I am detached and I can examine it objectively and make sense of it. It gives me clarity and meaning. It has taken me back into my past and pinpointed specific instances or events that were completely life changing. Those events changed the direction of my life, but I had never made the connection with those events and the trajectory of my life until I started working with Iboga.

Sometimes, it is not so subtle. In my first flood, the trauma I was processing was my father's death. My father died when I was in my mid 20s. I was his caregiver and he died of cancer. It was incredibly traumatizing and difficult for me. I didn't realize how deeply this loss had affected me. During my first Ibogaine experience while in the visual portion of my flood, it was as though I was watching a movie on a loop of my father's death. I experienced his death, over and over again. As soon as it would end and he would die, it would start all over again. This went on for hours upon hours. At the beginning, it was so painful to go through and I would think "Thank god that is over." Then it would start again. It was non-stop and I was getting so exhausted. Then, all of a sudden, although it still kept replaying it became less and less painful. The way I was responding to it was changing. The way I remembered and imagined it was changing. Instead of feeling massive grief and loss it was changing to love and acceptance. It took hours. I don't remember any other visions or messages from that first flood. It felt like it went on for the entire session. When I came out of that, I released a huge amount of grief I didn't even know I was still carrying. I had gone through years of counseling already with little benefit. They had diagnosed me with CPTSD but I refused medications and found little relief in talk therapy. My Ibogaine experience changed everything for me, in regards to that event. It was a massive weight lifted off me and allowed me to accept living in a world without my father. I am able to look back on it and not get the same trauma response that I did before. That changed for me immediately after my treatment.

Sometimes, it takes time or working with the medicine a little longer to decipher the message. During the time period, where I was working intensely with the PTA booster doses, I would often take breaks and work on integrating the teachings from the medicine. I would do this when I would get stuck on something and I couldn't move past it. I would take the medicine with the intention of working through that one specific problem. It never disappointed me. I always got the answer that I needed, which was often not the answer I wanted. If you work with the medicine and use it as a tool, it is incredibly powerful.

I also worked with an integration counselor for about 6 months. This was a really great experience, I found it very helpful. I had a very skilled therapist who didn't try to "fix" me. She merely guided me and gave me the courage and strength to rely on my intuition. She helped nurture the healing that Iboga was extending to me.

**How did you prepare? Would you prepare differently for subsequent times?**
I didn't prepare for that first time, at all. I just hopped on a plane and went to Mexico. I didn't think I needed any preparation or any aftercare. I thought that the only physical prep that needs to happen prior to a flood is medical testing and I did this the first and second time that I flooded. EKG and blood work as well as ensuring that I was not on any medications that were contraindicated with Ibogaine. Some providers suggest restrictive diets, fasting or coffee enemas prior to a flood. These are dangerous practices as they can throw off your electrolyte imbalance and result in cardiac issues during a flood.

I waited 7 years before flooding again. During those 7 years, 2 of them were spent studying and training to work with the medicine. I also did a lot of work on myself during that time. It was another traumatic and life changing event that was the catalyst for my second flood. I set up supports for myself pre and post flood this time around knowing that it was not something that I could do on my own. This included involving my partner, family and friends as well as securing professional counseling.

**What medical precautions did you take to make sure it was a safe experience?**

Both times that I did it, I went to a clinic that had a medical doctor on site, who did all the testing prior to the session. I did all my own testing at home too before the second flood.

The first one was a medical type environment. I didn't like the environment, it wasn't conducive to a comfortable session. It was one of the first Ibogaine clinics established and the doctor was very involved in the clinical Ibogaine trials that were done at that time. The second clinic had a less clinical type feeling, but there was still a doctor and nurse on site. I made sure I asked all the safety precaution questions. I vetted them both very carefully before I went making sure they were safe and that they followed best practices.

**What was your intention?**

The intention the first time was to detox and anything else it could give me.

The second time was just to explore the healing I had previously been given a glimpse of. I hadn't fully experienced the healing before, but I knew I needed to work with it again.

The micro-doses/booster doses were taken after my second flood to continue to work on that healing.

**How did you consume Iboga? What did you take and where? What was the form? Total dose?**

The first time was Ibogaine HCL. That was in Mexico. I was underdosed the first time. I believe I was given around 10mg/kg. It was not enough to get rid of the withdrawals. They did give me a booster dose the next day because they could see I was still in withdrawal. I was only there for three days and at that time there was no chance of me getting more medicine.

The second time I ended up getting dosed over two nights with PTA which is purified total alkaloids. PTA contains about 96% Ibogaine and the two alkaloids Ibogamine and Ibogaline. I received the equivalent of a 15mg/kg flood dose the first night and two nights later I received a second lower flood dose of approximately 10mg/kg. I also had my CYP2D6 metabolizer test done, because I was curious to know if I was a rapid or moderate or slow metabolizer. I fall into the moderate category, certain medications and drugs don't have the same effect on me. I have an incredibly high tolerance for alcohol and opiates and narcotics in general. I'm also someone who if I'm given certain medications, I get all the side effects and none of the benefits, because of how I metabolize them. We are still learning how this impacts an Ibogaine treatment and knowing this information helps us understand how individuals may respond to the medicine.

For me, PTA resonates. I don't like TA, I don't mind root bark for micro-dosing. Ibogaine HCL is fine too but I resonate well with PTA.

**Why did you decide to do it this way? Why did you pick this center or facilitator?**

I did a lot of research, I had already been involved with the community for some time. The second time it was because I wanted to go to South Africa as well, I figured why not? I could go there for treatment and it's less expensive. They were reputable and had a good safety record.

The first clinic I went to I spoke to Deborah Mash, who holds the patents for Ibogaine, and she gave me the details of the doctor I went to see in Mexico. She gave me two different places. One of them couldn't take me in the timeframe that worked for me and the other one had availability. I went to the one that could take me! When I was doing my research, her name (Deborah Mash) came up and I figured she would know where it was safe to go. I didn't trust the limited information I could find online.

Googling "Ibogaine center" is the worst way to find a place to go. I knew that already, in 2007. I thought "How am I going to find somewhere safe to go? Read the medical journals, find names and track people down. This is the only way you are going to find a reputable place to go to." That's how I approached it.

**What would be your advice to people considering Iboga?**
My first question to people who are enquiring about treatment is trying to understand what their motivation is. Whether they are doing it for detox or psycho-spiritual growth. Right now, I spend a lot of time educating people about the dangers of Ibogaine and the importance of going to a center and not doing it themselves. The majority of people that come onto online forums are desperate and are willing to take huge risks with their life. I have to give people tough love, I tell them “This is not something you should just jump into out of desperation. You HAVE to prepare yourself for this experience. It is not something that you can do yourself. You must work with an experienced provider.” It’s challenging trying to convince someone in the throes of addiction that they cannot do this “their own way."

It's such a challenge with individuals suffering from addiction because they are so desperate to get out of this loop, that they are in. They are so conditioned to chase instant gratification and instant relief that they get from their drug of choice. When they find out about Ibogaine they think "This is amazing! This is exactly what I've been looking for, it's the answer to all my problems."

It's painful to have those conversations with them because I have to explain, it's not a magic pill and it’s not something you can do on your own. This isn't going to fix everything for you. You need to mentally prepare yourself to work as hard on your recovery post Ibogaine that you did to previously fuel your addiction. If you don’t do this (the work), you're going to end up exactly where you were but $7,000+ poorer, feeling terrible because you will feel like you have failed. It's so challenging to get someone in active addiction to approach this medicine responsibly and do it in the right way.

When I was doing treatments, I would often take months to get to know and prepare clients for treatment. I would encourage them to make changes in their life BEFORE they started working with Ibogaine. People often think "As long as I'm using, I'm a bad person, I'm in a bad place and I'm not getting better." When I explain to them, you can start making positive changes in your life right now, you don't have to wait until you've taken the Ibogaine, until you're off the drugs. You can start making healthy changes, NOW. Do the simple things: get yourself into a routine, go to bed at the same time, get up at the same time, do something for yourself every day, do some meditation, deep breathing, start volunteering, find something that engages you and gives you purpose. I focus on getting them to start changing the way they think about themselves. This helps them be more receptive to the medicine when they get it.

There are a lot of people who can't get there. It breaks my heart when I communicate with someone and they say "I've decided, I'm going next week for my flood." I plead with them that they need to have “after care” and start preparing themselves before they go. Maybe a month later I will get another message that says "I screwed up, I relapsed, I ruined everything." It's heartbreaking.

Then you have to have the discussion, a relapse doesn't mean you've undone everything you've learned and everything you've gained. This is part of your journey, this is something that you needed to go through and it doesn't mean that you have to go back to where you were before. You are not the same person, you have learned, and now you have to decide what it is you want. Who's to say and who am I to judge if someone chooses to continue using even after they have taken Ibogaine, who am I to say that they shouldn't be doing that and that they have failed? It's not my decision to make. I am still going to support that person, regardless of what their choices are. If they want to continue using drugs, as long as they are content, happy, safe and doing the best that they can, what more can I ask of somebody?

Also, I always told my clients, don't go by the accounts you read online. People embellish things, they can be selective with how they remember things. They like to fill in the blanks. I would say to my clients "Please don't go by any of that because if you do, you will be disappointed and upset if you have a different experience. The medicine will show you and give you what you need. Don't expect anything. There is no way for you to know what will happen and how you will respond to the medicine. Just let go and let the medicine do its work."

Often people will come out and think "I totally didn't get what I should have gotten, from that experience. It didn't work for me." It puts them in a negative mindset. That makes it more challenging to work through the integration period, because they feel they don't have anything to integrate. But they are going exactly through the process that they need to. It's hard to explain that to someone, if you haven't explained that to them ahead of time. We need to be accepting of the experience we are given.

**What are your thoughts on micro-dosing?**

The popularity of micro-dosing has encouraged a lot of people to explore Iboga. Unfortunately, many individuals do not do their due diligence before ordering and taking a substance. This is a huge concern with Iboga as even small doses can have severe interactions with medications or pre-existing conditions. It is possible to have a serious cardiac event with very low doses of Iboga. For this reason, I insist that anyone who is interested in micro-dosing Iboga undergo all of the same medical screening and testing that is done prior to a flood.

I do encourage people to micro-dose or booster dose after a flood, especially for people that have taken Ibogaine for addiction interruption. It makes all the difference to maintain that store of NorIbogaine in your system. It's a huge help. You have to be doing "the work" along with it. Most people who are disciplined enough to continue with micro-dosing and booster doses, do want to continue to grow and that's the reason why they do that.

**Is there anything you wish you knew about Iboga beforehand?**

I had the same preconceived notions, because I read the online testimonials, I had my expectations and I didn't feel like I had an experience like I was supposed to have. I was somewhat disappointed. My experience was incredibly challenging and I was left in terrible withdrawals.

The second time I took it, I was so familiar with the medicine already, that I understood how it worked. I understood that it would give me what I needed. I had all the information that I could have possibly gathered before that second treatment.

**Do you plan to do Iboga again?**

Absolutely. I would like to go to Gabon, to experience a Bwiti initiation. Every time I have worked with Iboga, it was in a medical setting, I really want to experience the spirit of the medicine and the country and culture from where it comes. Knowing how Iboga root bark works, and how it works on my body, I know it is going to be the most brutal experience of my life but I also know it will be worth it. It is something that I am definitely going to explore.

**Was there a memorable moment or particularly profound vision? Has this vision come true?**

This is related to Iboga, but it is not directly related to an Iboga vision. It's a curious turn of events...

When I was very young, 6-7 years old, I used to lie in bed at night and I would imagine two traumatic events in my mind. The first was watching my parents getting ill and wasting away until they were just skin and bones. I imagined caring for them, cleaning, feeding, washing, dressing them. I would cry myself to sleep. That was one "vision" that I constantly played in my head.

The second was that I would imagine what it would be like to have a still born child. I would imagine how horrific it was for a mother to carry a dead baby in her womb and have to wait to give birth. I had never been exposed to either circumstances, at that young age and I have no idea why these thoughts consumed me.

In 2001, my father was diagnosed with cancer. He wasted away in front of my eyes. I washed him, I cared for him, I fed him and I changed him and I lifted him up in bed. I was there when he took his last breath. My father had never been sick for a day in my life and within a matter of months he went from a strong and fit man to someone completely dependent on my care. It was devastating and traumatic.

At a very young age I was told that I would likely never become pregnant. In 2013, my husband and I were delighted with a surprise pregnancy. I did not announce my pregnancy until I was 6 months pregnant due to the fear of a potential miscarriage. A week after my announcement, on the anniversary of my father's death, I went for an ultrasound and the baby had no heartbeat. They sent me home to "let nature take its course." After spending the entire night sobbing and hysterical I got on the phone and advocated for myself insisting on being induced. I could not bear the thought of holding on to the pregnancy any longer. Twenty-four hours later I gave birth to and held our beautiful daughter in my arms. I hemorrhaged after the delivery and they did not have a surgical suite available for me immediately. Due to the delay, I nearly died from the blood loss. I remember becoming so tired and feeling strangely OK with the feeling that I was slipping away. I was not relieved when I woke up from surgery. I slipped into a very deep depression which only lifted after my second Iboga flood.

Both things that I obsessed over as a child, and I can't explain why, both of those things came true. Iboga did not give me answers but it helped heal me from those two traumas. Dealing with those two losses was the hardest work that I have had to do in my life, much harder than quitting opiates. A loss of a parent is somewhat expected but when the loss comes too soon it can be difficult to contend with. The loss of your child is different and much harder. It is losing your future, you are not only mourning the loss of an individual but a piece of your identity as a parent. Your hopes and dreams for a future with that child. I don't think I will ever fully heal from this loss.

**Has Iboga affected your spirituality at all?**

That's a tough one for me. I really struggle with the word spirituality. It means so many different things to each individual. I never know what somebody means when they say it. I know what Iboga does for me, it gives me clarity. It has also given me an ability to connect to others in a way that I couldn't before.

To me, that has an air of spirituality to it. There is something 'special' about the medicine. I feel that the medicine is so powerful, it unlocks things within me that I couldn't access previously. I do feel more connected to the people in my life and the people I care about. I feel more of a connection with strangers too, all humans in general. It has made me a kinder, more patient, more loving person. All of those things are "attributes" that people who try to incorporate spirituality into their life aim to have. In that way, I would say yes...

It also connects me with the natural world. I am less inclined to spend time on a screen, I would much rather be outside, walking in the woods, being in nature. Iboga brings that out in me and makes me want to connect. When I was in active addiction, I would do everything to disconnect. It promotes connection and not separation. There is an air of spirituality to that, to connectedness.

**Is there anything else you'd like to add that we haven't covered today?**
No experience is the same. Even if you've done it more than once you're not going to get the same experience twice from this medicine.

**Author's Note:**

Agnes's interview shares an often overlooked perspective on opiates and their role as medicine. Her story taught me to cultivate compassion towards the poppy (opiates), as it can save people's lives. Opiates may keep someone alive through a harrowing ordeal by soothing and numbing the pain, which would otherwise crush them. Throughout the interview, I felt a kindness and deep compassion for others' safety and well-being radiating from within Agnes. She is genuinely concerned about others' health and positive outcomes working with Iboga.

Also, Agnes's story highlights the power of small doses of Iboga coupled with earnestly examining oneself, over a long period of time. Small doses and deliberate work go a very long way and can be just as transformative, if not more so than a large flood dose.

Agnes was recommended to me by an Ibogaine provider who stressed Agnes didn't get the wide recognition and respect she deserves from the broader community for her constant work in educating and helping people make safe decisions in Iboga and Ibogaine treatments. Her attention to detail, and unique method of tracking researchers and experts down, at a time when little information was available publicly about Iboga, illustrates her safe and respectful approach to working with the medicine.

**Britta...... Ketamine Addiction and Psycho-spiritual Growth.**
***Bio:*** *Britta Love. 24 when first working with Iboga 34 now. Total Alkaloid (TA). Agender. USA. Britta weaves between the worlds of conscious sexuality and psychedelic ritual as a writer and facilitator. Britta was initially motivated to work with Iboga to heal a Ketamine addiction and subsequently for psycho-spiritual growth.*

**Author's Introduction:** Before working with Iboga Britta shares that they "never smiled" in photos and were addicted to ketamine, a dissociative that takes people out of their body. Talking to Britta on the phone now, I realized that this is a person deeply connected to nature, their body, spirit and laughter. Before Iboga and doing the work, Britta's life could be seen as gray. Now, I felt that Britta's life was technicolor. A rich life filled with emotion, laughter, childlike silliness and exploration.

**Where did you first hear about Iboga?**
I first read about Iboga in Daniel Pinchbeck's "Breaking Open the Head" in 2009 or 2010. Despite later realizations about the author's problematic behavior in his communities, that book was formative in my early phase of exploring psychedelics. It was the first time I had heard about Iboga as opposed to the more commonly known psychedelics. It stuck out to me as quite a remarkable experience that Daniel Pinchbeck had in that book, although also really fraught with the challenges he encountered in Gabon. I read that and put it aside in my brain somewhere, as at the time I had no idea of going to Gabon and didn't know anywhere else to work with it.

**How were you called to Iboga? Did you feel spiritually called to Iboga?**
At the time when I first decided to work with Iboga, I had actually been looking for another place to work with Ayahuasca, because I had relapsed into Ketamine addiction. In my search, I stumbled across a place in Costa Rica that was a retreat for Iboga. At that moment, I remembered, "Oh, addiction - Iboga!" and from there it fell into place that that's where it made more sense for me to be working instead.

It was a sort of long term calling since I was so excited when I first read about it, but then put that aside for several years before I stumbled onto a path forward.

**What was your life like before Iboga?**
There is a clear demarcation in my life between "before Iboga" and "after Iboga."

Before Iboga I was incredibly anxious. I had no connection to spirit or trust in the flow of the universe around me. I felt no sense of my mission or purpose in the world. I was coping with all of that through dysregulated relationships: with food, alcohol and substances, at different points in my life. As well as overworking as another form of addiction.

To be honest, I hardly recognize the person I was before Iboga. I think I was quite lost. I now see that through my risk taking and drug use I was definitely seeking. I guess I was a good candidate for someone to have a life changing experience.

**What is your life like after Iboga?**
It's been a long time since I first worked with Iboga in January 2012. Nine years later, I've done many sessions with Iboga since then, with different dosages - as well as many other forms of medicine and many different forms of healing work and integration work. I don't want to misrepresent the vast change that has occurred as the result of a single ceremony as opposed to years of emotional and spiritual work.

But it is a vast change. I still have anxiety, I still have struggles, but I have a core belief and connection and trust in the forces around me. I feel woven into a web of interconnectedness with all life. That fuels me and allows me to stay grounded overall. I have a much deeper sense of purpose and place in this world. I feel such a debt of gratitude to Iboga that really drives my mission and what I am about now.

Before Iboga I was never smiling in pictures, I couldn't smile naturally. After my first ceremony I immediately had a totally different smile - I call it my "Iboga smile" - and a really free laugh. It can be quite loud and intense at times, like a liberated force within me. So, there is a lot more joy. In some ways there is also more pain. I am more connected to all of my feelings and all of what is happening in the world. After experiencing a lot of trauma I had developed a strong dissociative response. I was anxious certainly, but I didn't really feel grief, sadness, or depression very often, I was wired and intense almost all the time.

In a way, Iboga brought me out of dissociation and more firmly rooted in my body, more connected to my core self. With that, I am more in tune with the harder emotions as well. I consider that part of healing because I feel it's important for us to experience the full range of emotions in life, especially grief which American culture has a deep avoidance of.

Iboga has given me a very strong sense of what it means to be in integrity. That's integrity with myself, with the people around me and with the ecosystem that I belong to. I am nowhere near claiming that I am fully in integrity, I think it's a very hard world to be in integrity with because there are so many powerful forces - capitalism, systemic racism, patriarchy, colonization and more. We're all impacted by and complicit in these forces to some degree, regardless of how "good" we try to be. But I'm more conscious now and something that really guides me and my approach to life is learning how to stay in integrity with myself and my relations.

It helps that Iboga has gifted me a lot of self-awareness. I have my share of issues and neuroses like anyone, but I have a good map of the territory thanks to my work with Iboga. I have a good sense of what my traumas have been, how I am likely to hurt myself and others as a result of my own hurt, what to watch out for and what parts of myself I need to continue to build relationships with. I very much believe that there are "no bad parts" as Richard Schwarz teaches in Internal Family Systems, which is one of several therapeutic lenses that have been very helpful in integrating my work with Iboga (alongside EMDR and somatic experiencing.)

So in those ways I am wiser, but also wise enough to know that I'm not at all wise!

I know many people have photos of themselves both before and after Iboga and they see a physical difference! Maybe it's about the soul being a bit more in the eyes and in the smile too.

**How did you prepare? Would you prepare differently a second time?**
When I first worked with Iboga in January 2012, I did not really prepare at all. This was a very different era of psychedelic taking. There wasn't a big culture around psychedelics discussing the preparation, intentions and integration work. I thought I was going to go, have this intense experience and hey presto, it would change my life.

I would say that I basically did very little preparation other than mentally preparing to come back from Costa Rica and not use ketamine anymore. I remember leaving the apartment arranged differently and cleaning up the area I used to use ketamine in. I did a spiritual cleansing of the space, to change the energy of what I was going to come back to. This helped my brain move on from old habits.

Today, when I consult with people who are about to have a ceremony or want to have one, I strongly advise people to prepare well. I believe a lot of what you get out is what you put in. Taking the time to set intentions, to plan for what your integration practices are going to be, and mapping out your support network is so important. I suggest really creating rituals around the week or weeks approaching the ceremony.

At the center in Costa Rica the only preparation we were asked to do was make a list of questions to ask our soul. I wrote a really long list of questions that helped to focus my intentions, although the pressure to then answer them during the trip was very anxiety inducing and not supportive for me. I won't share who I worked with in Costa Rica, because I wouldn't recommend them to others.

Overall, I would really recommend seeking out someone to help guide you through the process.

**What precautions did you take to make sure it was a safe experience?**
At the time, none and the retreat I went to didn't ask me to do an EKG. I don't remember if they did any medical screening, they might have just asked what prescription medications I was on. It is nothing like I would expect from a safe and skilled practitioner today.

Ideally you want someone involved who has a medical background, especially for detoxes, who is coordinating the intake. They should be looking over your medical history and following up on anything that stands out as a risk or red flag. At a minimum, you must have an EKG that shows a normal QT interval as Iboga can lead to Torsades de Pointes (an irregular heart rhythm) that can be fatal. Ideally someone should be medically monitoring you during the experience but at least screening your EKG before is a good harm reduction step. Another must is guidance on transitioning from any medications or substances that you're using on a regular basis in the lead up to ceremony.

**What was your intention?**

My main intention was to heal the root of my addiction. I didn't know what that was, but I knew I had hit a rock bottom in terms of harming my body and my relationships. With those two things falling apart simultaneously I really knew that I needed to find a way out from where I was. I don't have a clear memory of everything (it was nearly a decade ago) but I had a list of 25 questions that I wanted to ask my soul: about my purpose in life, how to heal my family, how I should approach things moving forward. I had more questions than one could ever hope to find answers to in a single evening, even a single evening on Iboga - but I think the core of it was to transform my life and experience a rebirth.

**How did you consume Iboga? What did you take and where? What form? Total dose?**

We were given a little bit of root bark at the beginning and then we had capsules of total alkaloids (TA) extract. We were not told how much we were taking, how much was in each capsule, or how strong the extract was. So I have no clue how much I consumed on that journey.

I've worked with Iboga many times. I've had 6 or 7 floods. That's more than I recommend! Hahaha! For sure!

As a tangent, I would say that I really only did it that many times because I thought I was never "breaking through" to what a lot of traditional trip tales about Iboga portrayed. So, I always thought I had to go "further" which is a very sort of macho, consumerist and linear mindset. I have since learned that for myself and many others, especially those who have complex PTSD (which I later realized I did have), less really is more, a lot of the time. For a nervous system that is really overwhelmed and stuck in hypervigilance, going into a peak, intense experience and white knuckling through it (as we trauma survivors had to do through so many other intense experiences in the past) can sometimes be less valuable than building real trust and safety and working with smaller and medium sized doses. There is so much rich insight to be gained staying within our nervous system's "window of tolerance." Not to mention the fact that for trauma survivors, the act of choosing to respect and honor our capacity and limits is healing in itself. As Janina Fisher writes, for healing trauma, "slow is fast" - because we don't risk retraumatizing ourselves by flooding the nervous system.

I think this applies to all psychedelics. In my twenties I spent a lot of time having really intense Ayahuasca and Iboga trips. Yet in some ways, I didn't actually touch on my historical trauma until I started working with low dose Iboga in the past couple of years. So, I just want to put a word in here against that "machismo" that can appear in psychedelic spaces, of having the big trip, the heroic doses, the breakthrough. I really chased that for a long time. And shamed myself for failing in comparison to others as well! Which reinforced old trauma patterns of shame and low self-worth. I actually don't feel I benefited that much, beyond my initial first flood, in pursuing that. I actually went much deeper in subsequent smaller trips.

**Why did you decide to do it this way? Why did you pick this center?**
At the time, it was the only space I could find that was facilitating with Iboga outside of a medical detox framework. I knew that even though I was struggling with ketamine addiction, I wanted someone who would hold space for a psycho-spiritual journey. I didn't have a physiological dependency on ketamine. I also didn't have much trust in modern allopathic medicine, I have a lot of medical trauma. I wanted a space that was held more "shamanisticly." When I found the center, which was run by a supposed 10th generation Nganga, I thought that would be the right place for me. I didn't really have much nuance or maturity in how I screened providers at that time. There were so many red flags that I ignored because I assumed just because they were a Nganga they were safe and good to work with. I was lucky I went to the center with a partner who was able

to hold space for me afterwards and provide good support that was missing there.

A year after that I traveled to Gabon with this same Nganga. My partner was making a film for him in his village, about a group of Westerners coming to be initiated into Bwiti. I was initially coming along to help him make the film. At the last minute, one of the women on the trip dropped out. I was asked if I wanted to be initiated into Bwiti in her place. I was so excited! It felt meant to be, I knew I couldn't be going all that way just to film rather than participate.

On that trip, spending a month with this provider I found so many breaches of basic ethics and safe space holding that my partner and I ended our relationship with him and never finished editing the film. My initiation into Bwiti was actually an initiation into understanding how harm takes place in psychedelic spaces. This was its own gift and spiritual teaching. It gave me a new lens and put me on a whole different path in my psychedelic work. It was not the initiation I was anticipating.

**How does harm happen in psychedelic spaces?**

Harm happens in so many ways. It happens in all the ways it happens in other healing spaces, but it is even more intensified because psychedelic states leave participants in such a vulnerable place.

There are a whole range of kinds of harm. The traditional roles of healer, Nganga, shaman etc. are roles of power. Both traditional and nontraditional psychedelic facilitators can be attracted to that power, in the same way that people are attracted to becoming politicians or CEOs. These aren't necessarily the most empathic and trustworthy people to hold space because their intentions are not in integrity with the work. Those people tend to cause the most egregious forms of harm, preying sexually on clients, creating cult-like environments of narcissistic worship, and being on power trips. In my initiation, my Nganga was more concerned with having an impressive documentary rather than the participants' experiences.

There's also a lot of very well-meaning people who cause harm. I think that happens through not having peer supervision, not having people that you check in with. It happens when there is no foundational work done around empowering participants' choice and voice, around consent. It happens when facilitators are not trauma informed. A lot of people don't have easy access to their "no" even when they are sober, never mind when they are in an altered state. I think it's safe to assume that any of us are capable of causing harm at any time, but especially in an unequal power dynamic where people are coming to heal their deepest wounds.

I think that a lot of us are not aware of our shadow. That is the most important work a healer can do, our shadow is going to show up in all of our relationships, especially if we are holding space for other people. If one (healer or facilitator) doesn't have a healthy relationship to their shadow, a safe place to allow those parts to exist so that they don't show up inappropriately and do harm, an awareness of when they are showing up where they shouldn't, it can be really dangerous and harmful.

**What would be your advice to people considering Iboga?**
If you are hearing this call, then you are hearing a call to be in a relationship (with Iboga). What you enjoy, or how you benefit from that relationship will be determined by how you develop it. For me, starting out with speaking to the plants and finding ways to be in reciprocity with the plants, the lands the plants grow on, and the people who have traditionally stewarded them is very important. The lasting power of the work you do with Iboga will be a reflection of the integrity (or lack thereof) of how you approached it. It is so important to know: where the medicine is coming from, who you are working with, how they work, who they are accountable to. And it is so important to resource yourself before and after the experience, whether that's through therapy or community or art or dance or other creative expression.

Move at your own pace. And if in doubt, ask the plants.

**What are your thoughts on micro-dosing? Did you micro-dose after a flood dose for integration?**
I have done a lot of micro-dosing. I did not micro-dose after my initial floods. I later got into micro-dosing, as a way to stay connected to the plant without going back to a flood. I have also done low doses of Iboga on a regular basis.

There was a year where I was taking a trip of about 300mg of TA every month and took the time to really integrate in between. That is the time I went deepest into unpacking and discovering my childhood trauma. My initial flood really helped me reconnect to a sense of trust in the universe. It took years of developing that trust and integrating it for me to be ready to trust the memories that would come up around my childhood experiences. So, I could treat them as valid and take them seriously, rather than underplaying their importance.

Those memories were accessed when I was working with low dose Iboga, but not at all in my flood doses. Now I will work and talk with Iboga in a micro-dose format when I feel like I want to invite that energy and spirit back into my life on a sporadic basis. I make sure to create ritual and intention even for those tiny doses.

**Is there anything you wish you knew before doing Iboga about the process?**
There are a lot of things I wish I knew then, information that is much more easily available now. I do feel it would have been wonderful to not shame myself for years for not having visions. Most of the time I don't experience the intelligence of Iboga in a visual format. I experience it through feelings and sensations in my body, through emotions that arise, words and thoughts that come into my head. But because all the popular narratives were about visions, I always felt that I was “making it up” somehow. I was waiting for the movie screen to appear and show me everything so that I could *really* trust the information I was receiving, but I seldom had visions and they were usually very brief. I really wish I hadn't spent 7 floods trying to find that out! Hahaha!

I'm very lucky I didn't have any medical issues, but I wish I knew a little bit more about the seriousness of working with Iboga, especially in a flood dose. I also think it would have been wonderful to have a supportive community and stories from other people about approaching Iboga from a conscious psychospiritual, relational and sustainable perspective, because there wasn't much around my first experiences.

**Has Iboga affected your spirituality?**
Deeply, yes. I would go as far to say it helped to form my spirituality. I think I was opening to spirit through my other psychedelic experiences, with Ketamine

and LSD particularly. I started seeing the western materialistic perspective as quite arrogant. But I wasn't really able to access my own trust and belief in spirit on a deep level until my work with Iboga. It really awakened that for me. The experiences I had, even the little glimpses of visuals I had were a teaching in trust in forces bigger than me. That really formed the basis of my emerging spirituality.

**Was there a memorable moment or particularly profound vision you had? Has it come true?**

There were three little moments I can pick out briefly. One was a series of visions where I saw a little girl standing on top of a mountain pointing at the sky, trying to get up through this hole in the clouds - then the vision would quickly fade, my mind overthinking it. The same vision appeared again and she was holding onto the edge of the clouds, afraid to let go through this hole in the sky. Then I started getting anxious and the vision went away again. Finally, it came back and I/she was able to let go through that hole in the sky. I opened my eyes and there was this invisible screen lifting over my field of vision. It was like I was now seeing the spirit world. It felt like Iboga was training me to "let go."

In the second vision a little later on, this solid silvery woman appeared next to me with my eyes opened, which had never happened to me before or since. She was a bit like an angelic being without wings. She was kneeling over me, taking care of me, stroking my forehead and then she would get up and gesture at the stars, casting spells. At the time I mocked myself for having this vision "Oh wow, you saw an angel." I thought it was irrelevant, trivial, silly. I don't believe in "Angels" per say and I didn't think it was a very deep or meaningful experience. That dismissiveness and cynicism was a reflection of the place I was in at the time. What I realized afterwards is it gave me an embodied memory of being able to trust in being cared for by unseen forces. That has really guided me ever since. That vision has continued to unfold for me and has allowed me to flow a lot more with the universe around me and let go.

The last one I had was a flash of an image of my 5 year old self locked in a cage, being whipped. I completely forgot I even had that vision until last year. That's when I started to unpack the deep self-hate and self-criticism I carried within me, a result of my own childhood trauma. It's amazing that that image was there ready for me to better understand almost a decade later. I am still learning from that trip in 2012!

**What did Iboga Teach or give you?**

Iboga gave me a new lease on life. It gave me the gift of my first real relationship with a plant.

When I first went to Costa Rica I had two floods in one week, which is definitely not what I would recommend. The first trip I didn't get far, I was really struggling with the medicine. I was so nauseous, I couldn't surrender to it at all. The second journey I was so desperate, we had spent our entire savings to go down there. It was my last chance to save my marriage and my body. I was really in such a place of determination. I was really trying to focus on letting go and just breathing and being. Finally, I felt these shivers coming up my body. I realized "Iboga is here." I thought "Wow, thank you Iboga for coming!" I heard in my head the reply "Thank you for finally letting me in!" Hahaha! It was really this experience of being in a relationship, having that dialogue that was really part of the healing. I really felt I had found an ally in the world, who I could speak to, check in with and who would strongly and lovingly correct me when I was on the wrong course, or out of integrity, or when I was blindsided by shadow or my trauma.

Iboga has given me so much clarity and connection.

**Anything else you'd like to add?**

I want to mention that I'm comfortable giving this interview because this book has a focus on sustainability and the larger environmental and socio-political issues around Iboga. In recent years, since my initial evangelical "Iboga saved my life, everyone should do Iboga!" phase after my first healing experiences, I've come to get a little bit quieter about it. There are so many disturbing things happening in the "psychedelic renaissance." Psychedelics going mainstream means they're being scaled up in such an unsustainable way and reproducing some of our most tragic and unsustainable practices in terms of inaccessibility, exploitation and appropriation, all of it.

It has made me very wary about screaming about Iboga from the rooftops in a time where we still don't have sustainable Iboga. People are not concentrating on that for the most part, when they are focusing on miracle cures. Capitalism doesn't have a great history when it comes to "borrowing" Indigenous medicines. I'm comfortable expressing my joy and continued devotion to Iboga in this context because I know that it is being held in a container where we are making sure we are in a reciprocal relationship with this incredible plant and the people who have been its stewards for centuries.

**Author's note.**

I too, noticed that a lot of people become much better looking after working with Iboga. It seems to be that some of the deep pain, angst and general feeling of being "adrift at sea" is obliterated or at least handled by Iboga. There can be a sense of peace found afterwards. This is often reflected in the "Iboga smile" that emerges in the months following working with it. For me, it took 6 months after working with Iboga for my Iboga smile to emerge, I truly felt it hard to feel anything, as I processed my own experience until then. Like Britta, I still continue to process it 5+ years later, but now with a smile.

Also, I resonated with "letting Iboga in," in Britta's words. A lot of the psychedelic experience can be spent fighting and keeping our defenses up, while often in a very foreign and challenging ceremonial or treatment space. For me, the true magic and transformation happened when I fully surrendered. Put frankly, I became so tired that I could no longer fight or "play defense" with Iboga any longer. I think there is a lot of wisdom in building trust, and a genuine friendship with the provider and community you are working with, before consuming Iboga. This may make it easier to "let Iboga in" and let it walk you to the places you need to go for your own healing.

Finally, Britta mentioned that there was some regret about not having visions during the 6-7(!) flood doses that they undertook. Many people may feel shame, that they are broken or that they are "not doing it right" if they don't have profound visions through working with Iboga. However, this is perfectly normal, many people don't have visions and it's part of the tailored process that Iboga facilitates for each person.

**Asha...... Depression, Obesity, and Healing a Lifelong Eating Disorder.**
***Bio:*** *Asha Caravelli. 39 at time of first treatment, Now 54 years. Female. Originally from the USA. Treated in San Pancho, Nayarit, Mexico. Ibogaine HCL, 5'3" 74 kilos at tx. Dosage 8.6mg/kg 640mg total in TX 1. Asha went onto become an Ibogaine Facilitator for the Awakening in the Dreamhouse, End of Life Doula with EKR Mexico Centro, and Psilocybin provider & sitter to this day. Asha was initially motivated to work with Ibogaine for "Depression, obesity and lifelong eating disorder."*

**Author's Introduction:** Asha was truly a delight to talk to and so warm and funny on the phone. My conversation with her widened my perspective on the range of conditions that Iboga can tackle. Food addictions, presenting as obesity are not often thought of as an addiction or ailment of the mind. Asha's journey highlights the comprehensive transformation of life, body and mind Iboga can facilitate.

**Where did you first hear about Iboga?**
My ex-husband Rocky first told me about Ibogaine in early 2002. At that time, he had a life threatening poly-substance addiction. He came to me and said that a friend of his had told him that he wanted to take him to Amsterdam, to have him eat this root that was going to cure him of his addiction. He also told me that he saw an article in National Geographic magazine about this plant from Africa which could "cure" heroin addiction. I had never heard of Ibogaine, not even once.

In the end, he didn't go to Amsterdam to eat Ibogaine. He found a clinic in Tijuana Mexico. He saved for 10 months for him and his girlfriend to get treatment.

I would say, it's absolutely noteworthy, that in my first interaction with the medicine I completely rejected it. I didn't want to hear another word. I thought he was crazy. I thought he was out of his mind. He was going where?! To do what!? I had never heard of anything like this before. I turned my back on Iboga and put my hand up to Iboga. I said "You cannot cure addiction with drugs. You can't cure drug use with drugs."

**How were you called to Iboga?**

I didn't give it (Iboga) much thought early on, I thought it was nuts. Until Rocky went to Tijuana and was treated with Ibogaine. I spoke with him on the 3rd day after he had received the medicine... I would say Iboga is very clever and much smarter than I am. What I heard in Rocky's voice in that first conversation after he took the medicine was Iboga. I heard the medicine in his voice. Iboga spoke to me, through Rocky's voice, just saying what it was. I was deeply affected by that. Not only was it a return of the man that I knew back into his body, after a very long and perilous addiction. But, there was also something in his voice that I didn't understand but I was responding to.

I was then much more open to hearing about Ibogaine and Iboga. I was very curious what this thing was that had happened to him. It was very clear there was a transformation. So, when I speak of my own calling, it was rooted in a mix of curiosity, fear and willingness. I had my own deep need for healing and I thought perhaps, this medicine could help me.

**What was your life like before Ibogaine?**

Not like it is today! Hahaha. I was 39 years old when I took medicine for the first time. I'm 52 now. When I was 36 that is when it first came into my greater awareness, through rocky. It permeated our family unit beginning with him.

At that point in my life, I had just tipped over into the obese category. I was really overweight. And had struggled with weight since puberty. I was very depressed. I was a single mother of two beautiful children. I worked full time, even though I was depressed. I had a lifetime of athletics behind me, I'm a soccer player. I had some joy from my children and being involved with them. I could show up and be present and be their mother. But me inside, as a woman... What I say is that "fire in your belly?" Well mine was smoldering. It was going out. I was in Portland Oregon, with no sunshine. The conditions for my growth were deteriorating and I, with them. The force of my life was like a smoldering ember.

My depression was like being tarred & feathered with depression. I was really trying to help myself. In my mind I was trying to be different, than what I was. That revealed itself to be a lifelong lesson. Up until I was 39 I was trying to be something other than what I was. I never felt right. In the 54 years of my life, I don't know if I've spent a quarter of it in the Goldilocks Zone, where I have been happy with myself as a person, the conditions in my life, my relations and how my career is going. Most of it has been awful, really self-critical and not nice to myself.

There was a big in-congruence between my internal life and my external life. Neither one felt correct. My body didn't look right, it wasn't healthy, I didn't feel right. I wasn't healthy. I couldn't get these conditions off of me!

**What is your life like after Iboga?**

In 2006, Rocky left Portland Oregon where we were living. We always lived in the same city, even though we were divorced, because we had kids to share. Rocky moved to Mexico and opened up the Dreamhouse. He worked, facilitating treatments for the first two years with staff that came with him from Oregon. I was still in Oregon with the kids. Halfway through our second child's senior (final) year of High school Rocky asked me to come to Mexico and help. I did. It was my first opportunity, where both of our children were grown-ups. I became a parent at 21 years old. I had been dreaming of this journey of self-discovery, finding out who I am now. I became a grown up and a parent at the same time. This would be my first adventure just as me, as an adult. This was in 2009. In the fall of 2009, I left Portland, Oregeon, left our kids there and went to Mexico. I've been in Mexico ever since.

I came to begin working at the Dreamhouse (working with Ibogaine) 11 years ago. That began my training. My life has been transformed. It's not the same life in any other sense than, I'm in the same body. But the body is very different and my mind functions differently. My career is vastly different. I was a career waitress, soccer player, mom. My skill sets have been melded into a very hands-on training. I walked into a very busy clinic that was facilitating 8-12 Ibogaine Detoxes a month. I hit the ground running.

All of my training has been on the job training. Rocky is my mentor and trainer. I have also spent time working with Christopher Laurence and Clare Wilkins, who are also long time facilitators. What Rocky had always said to me was "You need to learn something from everyone who knows about this medicine. Bring it into you and present who you are as a provider."

It's not a change, I am a transformed person. That sounds woo-woo and hippy, I'm not really like that. It was a series of breakdowns, teardowns and rebuilds. I've worked with the medicine, primarily in those first 7 years. Not abusively, not a lot. I was being trained at different dose levels. I was relating to people who were being treated at all different doses. My training was dependent on my relationship with the medicine.

I've been able to work through this, because I'm not "tarred and feathered" anymore. I can take action, things can happen. I don't say the medicine transformed me. I say the medicine created conditions for transformation to be possible.

**How did you prepare? Would you prepare differently a second time?**
I did ask Rocky, what can I do to get ready? He replied "Just be open." I had no idea what that meant so I created this mental imagery for myself, a personal guided meditation where I would imagine anything opening. Anything in the world! Boxes, doors, refrigerators, windows, safes, packages, presents. I kept imagining these openings until I couldn't do it anymore. I would just imagine things that opened.

Physically, there wasn't a lot of preparation. Besides fasting the day of the medicine, going in relatively blind and full of trust in the facilitator. I went in believing that I was being given the medicine because it would help me.

For subsequent times, ceremonies have developed. Oftentimes, I do writing in advance of taking medicine. I would advise myself and people to prepare differently depending on where they are. We should meet people where they are and help them prepare from there. I try to do that same thing for myself.

**What precautions did you take to make sure it was a safe experience?**
I didn't do much that first time. The dose range I received was just under what we call "pre-initiatory" work. I went just to the threshold, because I had never had an experience with a drug like this before. There was no pre-screening for me. As a facilitator, I wouldn't give Ibogaine to anyone without an EKG, a blood test and lots of conversation, so we can start sussing out where that person's vulnerabilities are. Where their strengths are, what this experience means for

them, individually going in. That would be the start. Then I would begin to prepare them physically, emotionally, mentally.

We also have a Jungian psychoanalyst who meets with our clients before they take medicine. This helps to refine their intentions.

It also helps to coordinate foods, medications, stabilization medications or supplements they might need. Everything gets more specific to that person.

**What was your intention?**
My intention specifically was to address my eating disorder. That was the first one, to try to figure out what it was. Why was I stuffing food in my mouth? What was I hungry for?

After that, there have been many different intentions. Sometimes the intention is just to experience the medicine for the sake of understanding the experience of the people I'm giving it to. Sometimes it is to try to move myself out and see what Iboga has for me.

I haven't had a big saturating dose (flood dose) since intentions became all the rage, haha. I'm not blasée about it, I'm not thoughtless as I go in. But I also know most of my intentions are not important when I'm there. Once the medicine is in my body, it's Iboga. For me, intentions and agendas feel a little intertwined.

I like the idea of putting your intention down at the ceremonial door and picking it up again afterwards. Because your reason for working with this medicine is valuable. But I think in there, you need to be the receiver of what Iboga has. My intentions have never been answered specifically or in a straight way by Iboga, ever! Not a lot of people say, we went through my intention list together... It's always his (Iboga's) territory. That's the territory of the spirit.

**How did you consume Iboga? What did you take and where? What form? Total dose?**
I have worked with Ibogaine and Iboga in all the forms that I know it is available in. Total Alkaloid, Purified total alkaloid, Hydrochloride from Iboga,

Hydrochloride from Voacanga Africana. Primarily, all the purified Ibogaine that I have ingested personally has been made by a gentleman in Italy who is sadly no longer making Medicine.

My first dose was 8.6mg per Kilogram, somewhere in the range of 500mg of Ibogaine. It may have been a little more than 500mg because my body weight was more at that time. Essentially, that's the dose I started at. The highest dose I've ever taken is 14.1mg per Kilogram of purified Ibogaine. My favorite dose is around 500mg of Hydrochloride (Ibogaine HCL), with a little TA to widen it. I don't want to sound like I take that lightly, this medicine is a big deal to me, it is a big deal.

**Why did you decide to do it this way? Why did you pick this center?**
It all had to do with my training at the Dreamhouse. Also, I was in constant treatment of depression. For a couple of years, even though the very first treatment yielded a great loosening of my depression, it took a couple of years to really get my internal chemistry and internal & external beings aligned enough, not to keep slipping back in.

I don't work with Hydrochloride (HCL) unless there is a situation where I would personally need it. It requires a big amount of Iboga to make a small amount of Ibogaine HCL. That in itself is always a calculation I do when treating people, making sure they understand that this might be a little capsule but this capsule represents a tree that was in the ground for years! Maybe it was tended to by a person, or by nature. But what you have has passed through a long lineage to get here. The person consuming the Iboga has to go through a long journey to meet the medicine. Because it's valuable in that way and I have no need of it (HCL) I don't take that medicine. With total alkaloid (TA), certainly you can get a higher yield out of the same amount of plant. A little goes a long way for me now. I don't need much medicine to enter into the stream of consciousness of the plant.

The only reason I took the HCL then was to treat my depression, eating disorder and as part of my training.

**What would be your advice to people considering Iboga?**
Take your time to learn about what this is, before you make a decision. Don't rush to Ibogaine or Iboga. Take a moment to learn what it is. Most people think the process is going to be all up in their head and about punishment, retribution and pain for their wrong doings. That they're going to get their noses rubbed in it. That's an anxiety that creates a whole matrix of how you move.

In general, I would tell people to clean up their diet, start to increase their hydration (with water and electrolytes), and start to move their bodies. Start to get some education about Ibogaine, the treatment, Iboga, initiations. Start to speak to people and try to get references and recommendations from one person to the next. So that you're not blindly out there. I will offer to someone who wants to work with us to speak to someone who has worked with us before. That takes me out of selling, I don't like the "selling" of Ibogaine (healing). I don't like to sell treatments. My job is to screen people and find out who we are safely and competently able to provide medicine for.

You can give general advice to anyone: clean up your diet, hydrate more, start to move your body, take your time to learn what the medicine is and ask questions.

**What are your thoughts on micro-dosing? Did you micro-dose after a flood dose for integration?**
I think that there are a few reasons for someone to micro-dose after they have been saturated (flooded). What that would look like, is really individual for each person. Do I bring it up to everyone? No. Do I bring it up to people who ask about it? Yes. If people don't ask and I don't have a sense that they need or want more - maybe they had a particularly difficult treatment - I won't offer micro-doses. Some people don't want to see Iboga for a while after a treatment.

Most people will ask about micro-dosing. There is a gentleman in Germany, all I know is he is on an Ibogaine Facebook page I belong to. He put up a protocol that I think is really lovely for micro-dosing. I refer people to his protocol. I try to get people to understand that 200mg is not a micro-dose. What a micro-dose actually is, how much, how often. Then what I say, is the way to start this. The next step is you need to put the medicine in your body and listen to Iboga. If you wake up in the morning, regardless of your schedule, and you don't want it, don't take it. If you get up and the answer is a natural yes, then (respectfully) put a little medicine in your body. That's the relationship that you're following, what is happening with your internal guidance system? The way you are relating to the medicine is more important than what I say about micro-dosing. I keep it fluid and dynamic and empower them to be fluid and dynamic. micro-dose intuitively and with breaks every few days.

**Is there anything you wish you knew before doing Iboga about the process?**
No.

As I look back, I see the blessing and the way in which the medicine has moved through our lives. I could not have come up with a better plan or wish for the way it has all happened for us. I have trust in the way it unfolds. At least today I feel that way. I trust the medicine. It's way smarter than I am. In the meantime, chop wood and carry water. Hahaha.

**Would you do Iboga again?**
I sort of feel like I should.. I have felt like I should for a couple of years.

**Was there memorable moment or particularly profound vision you had? Has it come true?**
The one that changed my direction and really knocked the course of my life in a new direction is this…

In the experience, what's in front of my field of vision is all black. Out of that comes a city alleyway. It's dark, filled with grays, blacks, and sepia colors. Iboga is always pretty monotone for me. Occasional splashes of color but not colorful. I'm looking down this long city alleyway. It's wet, there's wind blowing. There's all these papers around. Papers occasionally are blowing up in-front of my face. I'm getting this sense over my shoulder of, do you want to look at this? Because Rocky had told me "Say yes to everything." I said "Yeah, I'll look at that" and I would go into a little dream scenario. I would come back out of the dream and the papers would swirl, the wind would blow and another one would come up. At one point, in this dream-like way, it is all being folded in thirds, like a newspaper. Then the newspaper is thrown down to the end of the alley, there's a puff of dirt as it hits the back wall. Over my shoulder I hear "You're reading yesterday's newspaper." This is all yesterday's newspaper. I realized that I get up in the morning and read yesterday's newspaper, I head out into the world as if that's today's news. It all needed to change. I don't often have 'aha!' moments in the experience but that was like "Fuck!" I knew that, it just won't do anymore.

**What did Iboga Teach or give you?**
I think what he gave me was like spiritual turpentine. It got the tar and feathers off of me. It gave me the ability to get out of the condition I was stuck in. That feels like a gift, because I was really stuck.

There are so many teachings from Iboga but it's not just to me personally. So, I have taken medicine, Rocky has more time with the medicine than anyone in our family. We have two children, who are both grown up now, but they both had their first medicine at 17. It was their rite of passage into adulthood. Also he gave medicine to his mother. For all these years, this has been a conversation that has been going on in our family. The clinic, what's happening with us individually, what's happening with clients, with the collective of staff. This conversation around the teaching of Iboga, perhaps our situation is unique in that the teachings come ALL the time. They present themselves as a living thing. It's a big question to answer, because I can't list it all. The list could look like: self-esteem, presence of mind, discernment, equanimity, it melted the wax in my ears and took the sharpness out of my tongue. Iboga has been so very generous to me.

Another thing that comes to mind is Iboga really says "See this with your own eyes, not somebody else's. You have to live your life through your own eyes, according to what you see and what is true for you. Not what is true for somebody else, or what somebody else says is the truth. What's true based on what you see with your own eyes."

**Has Iboga affected your spirituality?**
Absolutely. Partly the way in which it has affected my spirituality is to help me understand and reconnect what happens in my internal world, my consciousness and mind, and back into my body. It has helped me create a place

where consciousness is okay inside my body. There's a level of comfort and acceptance there.

Previously, spirituality wasn't something I had in a mature form. I've always believed in something greater. There's always been a presence of something else in my life. Now, I think in terms of spirituality I understand that the thing that exists inside of my skin can permeate a membrane into another place. It can go away and it can come back (from this physical world). My spirit is a thing that is tethered to this form, at this time, but it is also separate from that. It can transcend time, space and the regular boundaries.

**Is there anything else you'd like to add?**
I imagine spending the rest of my life talking about and working with this medicine in some way shape or form. I have an education in wine knowledge from years of being a server, this (Iboga) education is alive. Similar to wine, what's happening this year, in this terrain, in these conditions. You learn about wine and then you learn about regions, and then you learn about houses, then soils. Specific to all these different things. You can extrapolate the education, I find that to be true with Iboga as well.

This thing that we talk about (Iboga) here and now, is BIG. It is really BIG. It's not a drug that you take one time, for some people it might be. When you can allow the medicine to come in, and receive what it has and be an ambassador for understanding your truth and your vulnerabilities as a human being. Living though how this has affected you in your internal compass. Be guided by something other than your mind, I think that you can find a place with Iboga. Iboga finds a place with everybody. It leaves a little piece of itself with everyone. Some people get tasked with bigger jobs, like writing books or facilitating treatments. Some of us get jobs from this medicine. But Iboga stays there, there is something for you.

Rocky says, "Iboga stamps his name on your cells, every one of them. Boom, Boom, Boom. I live here."

## EXTRA QUESTIONS.

**What do you recommend for integration?**
If we say we are going to talk about integration, we need to be specific about what things are covered, that we have decided together, constitute or define what the integration is. From there, the conversation is potentially a lot easier because there is less chance to misunderstand each other, we can assume we are talking about the same thing. You have to agree upon what precisely you are integrating. You can't integrate your psycho-spiritual experience in a kindergarten classroom, that's not an appropriate place.

I think of integration as a way of living. When you graduate from high school, you've gone through 12 years of school. Then there is some type of ceremony that marks the end of that period. Then you move into a period of integration, where you are beginning to see where the education you have received is usable in your world.

It's also useful to think of integration as something structural. Where all of the parts and pieces are put in place. Everything has to be working in unison, so there's harmony and a smooth flow.

Martha Beck speaks about integration and integrity as something structural. She uses an analogy of an airplane, with all of the many small parts being where they should and functioning as they should, so the whole can fly and reach a higher potential.

It's useful to take the whole system and break it down into smaller pieces. We can return this to the plane... You have the totality of you, moving into the smallest parts of you, to check where their functionality is, maybe you have to tighten some part, or give some type of attention to another aspect, as you reassemble yourself. Something like Ibogaine can bring you apart quite a bit.

With a plane (your integration), you wouldn't rush to have it fixed. You wouldn't put it back in the sky until you were sure that the wings weren't wobbly and the engine wouldn't fall apart. You would take your time to be sure, go slowly, and listen to the experts. Only when everything checks out and you pass all the pre-flight safety tests, then would you consider going back on the runway.

There seems to be some rush to integrate. I think because people want to have their next experience. I understand the rush, we are behind in our consciousness. We have a lot of catching up to do! But if we move forward with loose bolts, what's going to happen?

**How did Iboga change your relationship to food?**

This is a big subject. Because I don't know exactly when my relationship with food became abhorrent. I don't know. There's no single moment. Even with drugs, there's no single moment where things turn. Maybe sometimes there is. Often it is a long series of events. With food, it is always there. What are you putting in your mouth? Why are you putting it in your mouth? These are enormous questions to be asking yourself at every meal.

I know food is such a huge issue for a lot of women. I want to bring it back to how unnatural it was, that I was not preparing my own food. I want to highlight how unnatural it is, that we don't grow our own food. I have come to be much closer to the source of where my food is grown. I happen to be very lucky. I now live in a city where people grow their own food. People will often say "I grew some lettuce, do you want some?" "I baked some bread, can I bring it around?" That's part of the relationship, it's not just what I eat, but what is the consumer path that I am on? Where does the food come from? How much of what enters my body through my mouth is made by a machine? Because that kind of food disconnects me. The more machine-made food, or the more unknown-source of food, the further I feel away from myself. I really have to get my hands in my food, I have to do it every day now, by washing and preparing produce that is not sterilized when I buy it. I have to be willing to make the extra effort in my home kitchen every day as a way to soothe myself.

Before working with Ibogaine, my life seemed to go so fast. I was working all the time, raising kids, it felt like my time was moving very fast or I had none. I was always seeking to slow down and comfort this frenetic pace. Food was what all that got attached to. It goes back to "What did or didn't protect me? What did or didn't nurture me?" Ibogaine, over time, helped me come back and mourn for the little girl who didn't receive the kind of nurturing she wished she had. I wanted to be loved and nurtured. When it didn't come from people, I went and found a way (with food). That is just natural, we all do that.

We have given away our ability to nurture ourselves on the most basic, daily level. It might be a little boring, but if you were to follow me around for a week and do the things that I do, and eat the things I eat, there would be a difference. If someone lets me help them get a few cycles of food through their bowels, I really think that it is just like gasoline. If you change the gasoline, the engine runs differently. But when it happens to you, and I can say this as someone who is highly triggered and sensitive to highly processed food and sugar, I can see what happens when the trigger is activated. When salt, fat and sugar hit the receptors, something intense happens. It requires emotional detachment for me to notice it. Not everything you eat has to taste good. That is something really difficult for people who have no weight issues to grasp. Just because you can eat whatever you want, and you won't get fat, the consequences of your eating choices aren't necessarily worn on the outside of you.

For me, my food choices were written all over my body. I wore them on my sleeves. I made bad food choices and you could tell because I carried a lot of extra weight on my body. I was going around and doing all the things that regular-weighted people did, but I was fat. People can hide their alcohol from others for years. You can hide your other addictions. Food addiction was not hide-able for me. For me it was so shameful. I couldn't even hide it. Everyone could see my lack of will power and my lack of self-control, that's what I felt like. That made me feel even more ashamed which drove me to eating more.

I learned how to be less ashamed of myself by listening to others. Especially those who came to the Dreamhouse for Ibogaine detox treatment. The things they were ashamed about, I thought "I am a lightweight!" All the shame I carried around was nothing. I had something else that was "I think I am so bad, but this person has been through so much worse, and they are able to talk about it!" They were able to speak and bring it out into the open. They had courage and bravery. Where with me, because I was so ashamed I didn't talk, it all went inside. It wasn't coming out. It was too much going in and not enough coming out.

The shame loop was fueled partly by the constituents of the food. That's the way any human body would respond if it was repeatedly fed this way. The food is made to perpetuate the shame loop. It's made to keep you trapped in it.

**So Iboga helped you break out of the food and shame loop?**
Yep. It helped quite a bit to really study and contemplate what happens when food goes past your neck. It still has almost your whole body left! What you choose to put into your mouth, passes through 30 feet of me before it leaves! It's 6 inches above the neck (the mouth and brain) and 30 feet below. I wasn't taking into consideration what would happen after I swallowed the food. There was 30 feet more to go! A lot more would happen after I swallowed my food. I needed to learn what that was, the more I learnt the less I wanted to put things that were going to tear, acidify or gum my body up.

**Author's note.**

Asha's interview highlights the similarities in how Iboga operates when treating many different addictions and issues. It appears to highlight a blindspot, shining light for us to confront some of our greatest fears, issues and challenges. It can also provide a circuit breaker, disarming any loops or repetitive behavior we are stuck in, so we can see clearly and break habits. From a liberated state, we can then either see our issues in either crystal clear detail, or repeatedly face it until it is no longer terrifying and immobilizing (as Agnes did in her experience). Then, after we have made peace with it, it shows us a new way to be. Often through expanding and heightening consciousness, to a new vantage point where we can choose how we want to interact with an old program, belief or event. By removing or disarming the fear, and inviting us to engage with ourselves in a new way, we can create a new world for ourself and others.

For many people, that seed of darkness or initial event, might not have yet grown into an addiction or life-threatening condition, but Iboga can still take us there and help extinguish it before it becomes a full-blown forest fire. With that said, every experience is wildly different and Iboga appears to give the perfect, custom-made 'treatment program' for each brave soul working with it.

**Rocky...... Healing Heroin, Methamphetamine and Methadone Addiction.**
***Bio:*** *Rocky Caravelli. 39 years old when first working with Iboga, 57 now. Male. From the USA currently living in Mexico. Ibogaine HCL. Rocky is an Ibogaine provider, training for 1 year at a clinic and 6 months with a Gabonese Nganga. Today, he feels good about himself, living a life free from street drugs. Iboga gave him a new life and has helped him grow into a good man and father. Rocky has continued to work with other chemical dependent people for 18 years and is beginning to train new providers called to the medicine. Rocky was initially called to Ibogaine to heal "Heroin, Methamphetamine and methadone addiction."*

**Author's Introduction:** Rocky is a warrior and relentless worker for Iboga and Ibogaine. His interview provides a rough roadmap for people dealing with both heroin and methamphetamine addiction. It explores some of the trials, tribulations, and setbacks that can come up. On top of this, Rocky was very funny and extremely knowledgeable about Ibogaine during our interview, there was a real energy and passion for Iboga and Ibogaine that burned through the line.

**Where did you first hear about Iboga?**
The circumstances surrounding my need to meet Iboga were based on and linked to heroin. I had only been doing heroin for a year, but I had a long history of methamphetamine dependency up to then. I met a woman, we were sober for four years. She relapsed and I followed her 6 weeks later. After bi-lateral carpal tunnel surgery on both hands, I got these bottles of pain pills and I was going to try and switch from Heroin to pain pills. I made it 4 days.

When my hands were tied up in little mittens (following carpal tunnel surgery), I was reading Discovery Magazine. There was an article in it titled "End of cravings." I still don't know what issue and what article that was. I've never seen it again. It was like it blew in and blew out of the house. It was talking about 'MC18' the synthetic compound that would interest big pharma because it had no psychotropic effects and could be mass marketed. In the last paragraph, it said Ibogaine is being used currently in various countries around the world and you can go to these clinics and get off of Opiates.

The next day a friend of mine knocked on my door and said "Look, I'm going to take you to Amsterdam and you're going to eat this root and we're going to get you off this shit (heroin)." It was a friend of mine from AA. I thought "Woah, that is so strange, I just read this article yesterday about how this plant does this. He wanted to take me to Amsterdam, Sarra Glatt's house. I asked if my girlfriend could come. He said "Absolutely not. I hate your girlfriend. So, I went online and searched for "Ibogaine." I found a place called Ibeginagain, it was Eric Taub's who is Richie ******. He started giving me his pitch. His pitch was, you come to Florida, and you have to get a hotel, bring a caregiver, organize plane rides in and out, it was getting very expensive, very quickly. Or he said I could go to these new guys that just opened up down south of San Diego. He said "Since you're on the west coast, why don't you give those guys a call?"

It took me 10 months to save up for that treatment for me and my girlfriend. The treatment cost $6000. We had 2 drug habits, were trying to hold a house with kids together and whilst keeping my job. I also did furniture reconditioning from stuff I found around town and sold it on the weekends as a garage sale. I did side jobs every weekend and sent the money down before I spent it on drugs, to the Ibogaine Association. It was a lot of work.

It was like a lightning bolt. It was weird. At the time, I was in the first 2500 people in the Western world to take Ibogaine for addiction interruption. That was 18 years ago. We're maybe at 45,000-50,000 people today.

**What was your life like before Iboga?**

I had quite a good life considering my handicap of chemical dependency coming and going, I struggled with addiction, I could not get free. I could get times of freedom, in 12 step programs and when I was put on medication for mental health conditions. They didn't know what I had "You're Bi-polar, a rapid cycler" they called it. I've been through the whole mental health system. I've been through rehab systems, I'd been through the jail system, I'd been through medical systems. Nothing had really worked.

I was a good carpet layer, I was good at it. It gave me a good living. I had a nice house, but I didn't own it. I never owned anything. I had a nice truck. My girlfriend had a Volvo. We had a little house that we rented, near a forest. Across the street was our 12 step home group in Fairfax California. That was our existence. We worked and at the end of the year there was nothing left. We made good money, but there would never be a penny leftover. I had two children, she had a child. That was our primary focus, to show up for our kids. That was my life before we relapsed.

**What is your life like after Iboga?**

It's another life. When I took Iboga, the best way to describe it is like this... Do you know what a wrist rocket is? A slingshot? I felt like a marble in a wrist rocket. Somebody pulled back that sucker and let me go. It shot me forward. My life was at such a perfect moment for change. Me and my girlfriend were done, my body was done with carpet laying. My back was gone. They told me, if you don't stop (working as a carpet layer) now, you're going to be in a wheelchair at 50. I was tired of living in Marin county. I was tired of the dope.

Iboga came in like a catalyst. Even my step father said "You were ready to change!" It just happened to be the catalyst. Iboga came in and emptied out the old life and filled me with a new life, which was the spirit of Iboga.

I'd always tried to somehow connect to spirit, even when I was younger. I didn't like God or any manifest religion. I was violently anti-religious. I used to terrorize Jehovah's witnesses out of their house and make them leave the neighborhood. Bad shit. Just rebellion towards any kind of organization or organized religion.

When I went to go into something like AA, which was the only form of recovery modality that was available in the western world, it felt like it was hopeless. This idea of "higher power" and all these kinds of things.

From the beginning, I had been working with spirit guides, in other words they had revealed themselves to me through the music that I wrote. When I first went into recovery in 1992, I realized that the songs I had written were actually prayers. I started using my music as a way of connecting. That started to develop an awareness and understanding that there are spirits on the other side and that I can have access to them. Iboga on the other hand, I touched it. It lives. I followed its guidance and direction down to Mexico and opened up an above ground rehabilitation center for detoxification, which was licensed. That was kind of impossible to do!

It was remarkable. I knew I couldn't die. I was on a mission and it wasn't until my 3rd flood dose that I received permission to begin facilitating treatments. I took Ibogaine 3 times, 8 months apart each time. The first time was a physical detox, the second time was a mental and emotional detox. I got the inner help and progress, I started to move forward. On the third one, I was introduced to Bwiti by a woman who had worked with Bernadette Ripoine under the Disumba tradition.

I had met Iboga in my first session at 5 mg/kg. I went unconscious during the second ceremony, at 10 mg/kg. The combination of residual methamphetamine and Ibogaine caused me to blow a fuse in my mind. I just went unconscious. They woke me up four hours later. I don't have any memory. 2 and ½ years later I received my 3rd third ceremony/session. I guess I had earned my wings, I was ready for it. You can't receive something you're not ready to receive. It took 2 and a half years of doing my own inner work.

I stayed off drugs (except for a 5 day meth run) for 8 months after my 1st session. By the time I was introduced to Bwiti in the 3rd session/ceremony, I could receive it. I was rewarded by Iboga with the introduction to Bwiti. It was an incredibly remarkable night.

I'm not normally a fan of psychedelics, honestly. I was prepared to go through anything to get off that dope. I was relieved when it wasn't so bad.

The initial introduction was really powerful, because I did meet a tree spirit. I could see in detail up close the pattern of the trunk and it was like blood flowing inside, it was a living tree. It tried to intimidate me. I remember saying out loud, "I know you, I'm not afraid of you, I have met you before!" I still don't know where that came from. It roared at me. It screamed through me, and it blew all of the other spirits out of me, that were attached to me, located at my back. There was a popping sensation, Iboga would roar, like a wind blowing. Except it was like a wind of sound that blew through me and pushed all the bad spirits out.

The second session I didn't have any visions whatsoever. It was done during the day time. I got the medicine in my body. The Nor-Ibogaine took me on a good ride. Basically, that second time was a period of inner work. I went back to the US, moved to Portland, got into therapy and found the "Awaken in the Dream" group by Paul Levy. A lot of remapping my existence and reforming my character for what was to come.

The third session/initiation, which was my smallest dose (10mg/kg) which would have been the equivalent of 5-7 spoons of root bark. It lit me up. I was ready. Iboga was these 3 little cussing gremlin type beings saying "What do you want to know Rocky?" It showed me how worlds are created, it showed me how molecules are held together with creator gods and architect beings. I saw an alien world. I just relished in the awareness that we and anything in and around our world is made of stardust. All the information is in us at all times. Iboga can act like a key and can unlock this information, but you must be able to receive it.

Iboga allows, in some cases, for that information to be opened up to our consciousness. It'll stream for a while and then it closes. I don't think I'll have an experience like that one again. That was my favorite night of my life. Iboga said "What do you want to know?!" It taught me to come from my heart when asking questions. The spirit of Iboga would cuss at me and say "You come from your heart, you punk ass! You come from your fucking heart you mother fucker!" I would respond "Okay, okay... Well how do you make a blade of grass?" Iboga responded "Okay, that's a good question, let's go." This went on all throughout the night. It was awesome.

At the end, Iboga gave me specific instructions with a specific list of essentials that had to take place and had to be available to receive people and to allow people to come down to Mexico.

Right before I left for Mexico, I initiated my 17 year old daughter. She had written a letter to Iboga asking if she could be introduced. She had come of age sexually and it was time. She and Iboga are real buds. He passed on a message, he said "I approve of what you're doing" I cried through the whole thing. She had Iboga speak through her and passed on a message, Iboga adored her.

Something happened in my first experience, whenever somebody would start talking about their visions, I could actually see what was going on in their heads. I could see the dreams. Eventually I realized I was trespassing. I stopped going into the dreams with people unless I was invited. If somebody talks about their dreams, I can vividly see them in my mind's eye.

5 years ago I quit alcohol. I had to let go of everything in order to get rid of that spirit (alcohol). In that, I had to let go of everything I'd done with Iboga. I did realize I had a lot tied up in that. The identity of being a provider. The work that we had done. I had to let everything go, or else I wasn't going to live. I really wondered if I would ever come back to it again. What is happening now is a whole new wave of service work that we're being called to. There's a real need for it.

**Do you feel smarter or wiser now?**
I actually realized how much less I know, now. It's like that Bob Dylan song "I was so much older then, I am younger then than now." I feel like I am going back in time as my body gets older. I feel like I know less and less, the more I live.

**How did you prepare? Would you prepare differently a second time?**
I didn't prepare (for the first time.) I took some supplements. I took magnesium, potassium, and calcium electrolytes. There was no Bwiti. There was no music. There was a Japanese Oboe playing on a CD for the first 45 mins. There was no preparation. There was no information other than "take these vitamins."

When we got there, we were so crashed out. We were 4 days out from any methadone. 5 days no Meth, 3 days no heroin, I was so sick. I was out of my body. I was like a robot being moved from one place to another. I couldn't put things together in my head. I was really, really sick when I took the medicine.

That first time for me was kind of like a joke, with how they were providing the medicine. I had done pre-treatment physical reports, EKG, blood work, but I don't know if they even looked at it. They thought "If we keep the body alive, then the treatment will work." It was the (absolute) baseline type of preparation.

Since then, that's all changed. When we work with clients, we always have 3-4 days prior to treatment, with people to modify their diet, get their bowels moving, stabilize them on short acting opiates, help them to sleep, share as much information as we can about the experience. Prepare them for the worst and hope for the best. We do medical screening too. Sometimes we need to get repeat reports: For blood work or EKG. If there's any question of stability, especially with stimulants because they affect the heart's rhythm. Methamphetamine supplements energy that the body normally produces, when you take it away you see a change in heart rhythm, and you have to wait till the body begins to provide a stable heart rate without stimulant help.

For me personally, each time I've worked with the medicine it takes weeks or months to get myself ready to take a good dose. I don't know if I'll be able to do another full dose. My body has gone through some really bad infections, I never really fully recovered. The alcohol binging didn't help either. I don't know If I'll ever be up for another full dose. I do work with low and medium doses often, every couple of months.

**What precautions did you take to make sure it was a safe experience?**
Screening is the biggest part of it. There are so many ways to work with Iboga. I work in the Missoka tradition, where Iboga is used in many different dose ranges, for therapies. There are different doses for parasites, depression, grief, possession of bad spirits, to break spells or beliefs, and aid in chronic pain management. There is so much to learn for each person's case and needs.

The first thing in screening is to determine what this person's needs are. This helps build a profile, an outline of a type of diagnosis. It's super, super important. Other than detox, which I did for many years, what we've learned now is that there are all these different levels of therapy that are available. You have to really listen to know if people are ready. Where they are in the chapter of addiction is it time for Iboga. There's a lot of people I could give Ibogaine to, that really don't want to quit. The whole point of the screening process is to determine what this person's needs are and how to best prepare them for that.

We don't talk about it anymore in the sense of "detox," if we're going to do that type of treatment we use the description of initiation. In preparing someone for an initiation level experience, as a result of that experience, as a side effect, it will take care of your addiction problem. We've moved the attention away from detox and towards having a life, death and rebirth experience.

The preparation is more and more going through hoops in order to come and work with us. Those hoops are going to be different for each person. There is a bite. There has to be a sacrifice. There has to be some level of humility present in an individual for Iboga to get in. Otherwise Iboga will just do the physical effect of stopping withdrawals, but not what they wanted to some degree but they are never getting what they want.

It's our responsibility as providers to determine "Are we talking to their ego or are we talking to their heart?" If I'm speaking to someone's heart and they are called to medicine, I have a responsibility to provide it for them. My job is to listen to the ones that have the call. A lot of times that might be, they've heard about it and then they have a dream about it. The whole process is a pilgrimage. For people like me, it started 10 months before I took it. It was a whole process of creating the ideal conditions for me to be able to receive freedom. I had to do Garage sales on the weekend, I would send the cheque off, instead of buying dope.

There were all the little moments it took to put the treatment together. It was 10 months of work and sacrifice on top of a regular life. There was all this energy built into the treatment that made it successful. People build into their pilgrimage what they want. That will have a reflection on what their experience is when they take the medicine.

**How did you consume Iboga? What did you take and where? What form? Total dose?**

The original dose was 5mg per kilogram. Which was the "test" dose. That's way more than a test dose, you start dreaming at 5mg per kg. It was in powder form, hydrochloride Ibogaine 98% which means that it was 92% Ibogaine and 4% Iboganamine, which is 10x stronger than Ibogaine. They were synergistic. It's better than pure 100% Ibogaine. That comes from Italy. It's the lab that we used for many years. 45 minutes later you take a dose equivalent to 10mg per kilogram, taking your total to 15mg per kilogram. That will knock a habit out.

I took two more booster doses, somewhere between 3-4 mg per kilogram. I probably tapped out at 20-21 mg per kilogram in total. That's a big dose, in a short time period, over 4 days total. I took a gram and a half total.

I didn't touch it (Iboga) or even want to look at it for myself. I didn't want anything to do with it for 8-9 months after that treatment.

**Why did you decide to do it this way? Why did you pick this center?**
It was the only place that was available at the time, except for going to see Richie in Florida. The idea of doing it in a motel room, and trying to find a nurse to watch over didn't sound very smart. Not that the place I went to did an amazing job, they put EKG machines on us and did some basic screening but it was kind of a joke. I didn't realize it at the time, it took me a while to actually realize. I don't want to share the name of the individual, because he's responsible for deaths. His attitude was "Addicts die. And they die a lot. They die a lot during detox." When I realized that, I thought "I have to get out of here, these guys are not who I want to continue working with." My whole family was going to move down there. Right before they did, Asha (my ex-wife) quit her job and gave up the house lease, packed up their stuff, and took the kids out of school. Then I said, NO we can't move here!

I had a 5 day methamphetamine relapse on fathers day, after I watched a guy die. Two weeks later I watched another guy have a psychotic break. I realized that the facilitator was not in it for the right reasons. When I got permission to leave, I left. It was a good experience to work for 9 months under supervision just watching the cycle of how the medicine works in people. 75 people came down in that 9 month period.

**What would be your advice to people considering Iboga?**
I think people should be sponsored, or have an initiated person guiding them, preparing them, giving information, modifying their diet, helping with breathing exercise, and building a support group before you take it.

Also, people should try to get out of unhealthy relationships, create a space post treatment to integrate, and to allow for the medicine to reach in and start creating new patterns and habits. Research and educate yourself before the treatment about people who have worked with the medicine or organizations that do this professionally. It's important to prepare and help integrate people. You have a sponsor that takes you through the process of preparation, may or may not be there at your session, probably not. You're most likely to go somewhere your sponsor knows of, someplace they would recommend and have sent people before. When they come back, they have a whole aftercare program.

More and more, I think in order to take Iboga there should be a sponsor initiated guide, throughout the process. They do this in Gabon, you have a Papa, Nganga, musicians. It's an entire community preparation. There's somebody that provides food for you. In an ideal situation, you'd come into a house or facility, live there for a week or 3.

Also, 12-24 days after the treatment are so vital. 12-24 days after the treatment are the key to the foundation to your new life. You would be in a container with other people who have just taken Iboga. You'd be creatively building and imagining your new life together. This is where you start to set the foundation, as you enter out after those two weeks, then the NorIbogaine is active. The body and mind are recovering on the physical plane, now you are integrating it into life.

That would be my advice, you come into a facility, you don't want to take Iboga in the same place you live. You go to take Iboga. After that process is done, you have to leave. You're basically coming out of the old self's life, and entering a new life. Separation from the scene of the crime, so to speak. After the detox, you have to switch environments, this will take an additional week or 2 for integration. We call it the "crystallization." The nor-Ibogaine is beginning to absorb through the fat cells, as the body is recovering from the heavy draw of life energy that going through the process requires, and now you're beginning to have the experience of a presence within. In detox your drawing double amounts of energy, the Ibogaine experience draws tremendous energy, and the detox is still going on internally the changes within are taxing the system.

We focus on ways to conserve energy building up for treatment, especially emotional energy, fear is a big burner of energy, we try to accommodate people where they are at, not to make changes in tolerance or change things just keep people stable and build trust that we won't take anything away without replacing it with something. Ibogaine is the trade for drugs they are dependent on.

There's a whole process of a part of you dying. Then you need to take them out of there, it can pull them down. A lot of people struggle with sleep, and are tired, but as soon as they go to the integration house, everything flips. In other words, it closes the ceremony. The change of environment symbolizes the rebirth, it starts day one of recovery. It's the completion of the ceremony, they say life, death, rebirth. It's really death, rebirth, life. This is the description of an initiation.

When I first took it, there was no mention or conversation about 'sacred medicine'. I didn't know what the term meant. At that time Ibogaine was a drug for detox. There was no mention of the history or the traditions, initiation, Bwiti or music. Nothing. It was just a flat detox: take the Ibogaine, go home. No reverence towards any of these plants. I had a little bit of awareness, but nobody had ever taken me through a journey before. Everything was done alone. I used alone. It was a very isolated, separate world that I came from. Iboga is like any kind of medicine, you never do it alone, ever! It's always done with others who are personally experienced. They have to have gone through the experience.

There's a lot that goes into how a dose affects someone. We've had sessions where we've done a yoga retreat group, there were 7 people. The oldest gentleman, who had the most powerful visual experience, had the smallest dose of 5.5mg per kilogram. He had 400mg of Ibogaine. I gave a woman 21mg per kilogram and she had nothing! She was a psilocybin facilitator and kept saying she had a high tolerance to medicine , after taking 21 mg/klg she couldn't move for two days but she didn't have the stream of consciousness given to her. There's something about being able to receive the information.

Iboga is just a key. More and more, we don't do it based on dose, what we're doing is trying to create an experience. Where you're in the stream of its consciousness, this dose is different for everyone. There is no real consistency. We start people off at a spot that can open up that experience. Either it is going to open, or it's not. If it doesn't there's no reason to push forward at all. We just let the medicine do its work. You can tell, at 300-400mg for someone like you or me, If there's going to be an open dream, but a lot of people for different reasons don't get into this stream, people who have been on psych meds, or benzos like Valium, they don't dream a lot of times, same with heavy cannabis smokers, it dulls the dreaming frequency in the brain's activity.

Also, with dosing root bark is very different, it depends on where it's grown, how it's grown, how old it is, has it made fruit? There were plants that I ate wood from, that were 30 years old! There was one plant that was an 80 year old bush. One spoon of that and you were up all night! At one spoon of this root bark you can see and hear EVERYTHING. It was far more than a hunter's dose.

**Was there a memorable moment or particularly profound vision you had? Has it come true?**
Yeh, that was the one where I saw the living tree. It was a fire and brimstone sort of vision, with haze and a burnt sky. No trees, all rocks. Even the tree had no leaves on it. It looked like an oak tree. I got really close to it, and I said to myself "Oh, it's a living tree!" I looked up at a branch and this branch grew kind of like a turd coming out. On the end of it was a light, when the light got in my face, it had a hat on and these big gnarly teeth roared at me. It did this over and over again. That was the spirit cleansing me and blowing through me. That was my first initial vision. I said "I know you, I'm not afraid of you. I've met you before" I said this out loud. I tripped on that for two years, thinking "Where the hell did that come from?!" I guess I had. I guess I did. This happened as my very first experience with my very first dose.

**What about that second dose when you passed out or went unconscious?**
When the 2nd dose kicked in it started in my feet, it always starts in your feet (for me). It was like there were green roots that were following the pathways of my arteries and veins and were following their way up my left side all the way up, through my body, through my heart. Up my neck. It felt like a hand was inside my head. I could see all the green roots spreading out on the inside of my brain. It was a hand of roots. I remember saying "I'm going to let the medicine heal me." Before my cheek hit the pillow, I was out. I was gone. I was unconscious and woken up four hours later. If somebody passed out in the

middle of a session, it would make me really nervous. People don't normally sleep on Ibogaine. I am lucky. I am lucky I didn't get hurt.

Like I said, I tried really hard to find methamphetamine on Friday, we were leaving on Saturday morning. I mean, I hunted and hunted and hunted. And I couldn't find any meth. I thought back much later, after working with medicine for a few years and realized that I couldn't find meth because it would have killed me. What good would I have done then? Iboga was protecting me before I even ate it. I know that for a fact. I know how to find drugs. I am good at it. I was scared. As soon as the meth wears off, you stop moving. You can't move, you can't walk. You're out. I was thinking, how are we going to get down there and make it until Monday if we don't have any meth? We had one little shot of heroin on Sunday. I was really sick.

I think that confrontation is a major part of healing. You have to get called out. You have to be exposed. I've worked with a lot of people, I won't take them to that place unless they ask for it. Sometimes I can feel like I know that I didn't get all of the bad spirits out, but they didn't ask me to do that. They asked me to do something else. I'm not the master of this medicine, I'm just the ambassador. I have to follow the rules, I can't do things that I'm not given permission to. I think that's part of being a good provider or good Nganga.

Good and old Nganas have their egos in balance. Younger Nganas can get quite egotistical. It can get kind of weird.

**What did Iboga Teach or give you?**

One of the main gifts was realizing that life wasn't about paying rent. Life is about serving. If you play the position of someone in service, all your needs will always be met. You will have a quality of life, that you will get to live as a result of that commitment to service, that is modest but never wanting for more.

Also, that it's the journey where life happens, not the accomplishment or the completion. I wish I would have been more aware of being on the journey. I wanted us to be a success in the sense that we created a place I wish I could have gone to.

**Has Iboga affected your spirituality?**
Of course! It created the awareness of how close the spirits really are. I could feel them, I could hear them, I could understand them. Their words would come through me.

Hahaha, I can't share this. I guess I have to now, I was making love to a woman, and Iboga loves sex. You have to be very careful because he makes women very fertile and increases men's sperm count to a really high level. It's really, really easy to make babies when you take Iboga. Iboga told me "Go down on her!" I could hear it in my head a couple times, so I did, I thought I was going to choke. She came so much that I was choking on it! I was like wow! That was really fun.

As far as spirituality, I've never had the experience of walking a path that was already written. It was like a story that I hadn't read but was playing a major role in. As I kept on, other people came and joined the path. It reminded me of the "Field of Dreams" movie, with the quote "If you build it, they will come." There was a prophecy. We were told that a man would come from Africa, that would bring Iboga. That was Moughenda, before he turned into whatever. When he first came, he was a really cool dude. Then the cameras came and he changed. He became the Ngana/shaman/front man. For the first 6 months, he was a good guy. We were told something would happen on the 8/8/08. At midnight on 8/8/08 I got an email from this guy (Moughenda), saying he had come to America, that he was sent by Bwiti to find someone. He wanted to introduce Bwiti to the western world. We made contact that night. Three weeks later, he was down in Mexico. He had never heard of Ibogaine. I taught him it was the extraction from the root bark. He loved it. He used to have to eat handfuls of wood every time we did ceremony. He used to say "Let me pop one! Give me another one, I want to pop one!" He loved it. That the medicine was concentrated and not having to deal with the difficulty in consuming dry wood

He was really cool when he first got there, but then he got really weird with girls. I had to ship him out of there. It was kind of a crisis. But that's the young Nganga thing!

**Anything else you'd like to add?**
Iboga is so bizarre. You have to really take into consideration how Iboga made it to the west. In the Western world it did it through the interruption of chemical dependency, through drug addiction. Why did it choose that channel? And it came as a masculine spirit. The Ibogaine we use is masculine, in its context it's always been the same masculine spirit. My daughter has met 12 different spirits, all of different nationalities that all came and did work on her. They were from Russia, Cambodia, other parts of southeast Asia, Siberia, North and South America. They came from all around the world. These different healers came and did work on her, they came through Iboga. There is a representative of Iboga in a form or character, we knew him as Darney, very masculine, but through Iboga were many different spirits, male and female.

It chose several of us. It chose Howard Lotsoft, I knew howard. I asked him, how much medicine did you take? He said 500mg. He took half a gram and kicked a habit. It was a 33 hour experience, he was walking the streets of New York in the first hours, he went to a therapy session for an hour, he talked to his therapist. Went home, went through the whole night dreaming, got up exhausted and BOOM, it hit him "I'm not dope sick and I don't have any fear in me." That's the key. The desire, which is craving and fear, was neutralized. It told him what was happening inside. It said "It's neutralizing fear and taking away desire." Both of those things are directly connected to being chemically dependent. That's when he gave it to seven other people and most of them quit drugs after that experience. 500mg is small. It's basically the 5mg/kg test dose that I took. Even in my experience 5mg per kilogram can break a habit. I know it wouldn't have gotten me through it. But that 1st 5mg did go through every cell and the tips of my hair, I even realized that the withdrawals had stopped. But it wasn't enough to complete a methadone detox.

I met a guy at the methadone clinic, the director, who had worked with Ibogaine sulfate back in the 1970s. Somehow a bit came through and a very small handful of people got to take that medicine. One of them was Howard, another one was this guy. He pulled me back into his office because I went back to the methadone clinic and I ripped up my methadone card. It really made the desk guy mad that I had done that. He sent me to the director's office. The director said "You took Ibogaine?" I said "Yeah, that's how I got off the methadone." He said "I took Ibogaine! What did it do for you?" I said "It took away the withdrawals, everything. He had no idea. And he ran a methadone clinic and had done Ibogaine! He took Ibogaine Sulphate. These are all elements of how Ibogaine bends nature. It shouldn't do that. That dose of 500mg for Howard shouldn't have done what it did.

Also, after my second ceremony, the mental and emotional detox, there were downloads every night about the manifest and the un-manifest. What's on the other side, where all the souls are, how it all works. There's doorways and keys to get between the dimensions, it goes on and on. There's so much going on, that if we could see it all, we wouldn't be able to move. There's layers of stuff going on that we can't see. There are moments where you can understand and comprehend. It's a far stretch for western conditioned mindset, these things just aren't discussed with any real value or importance. Our western world is very shallow in a lot of ways. It's all remarkable. We're not evolved enough yet to communicate at that speed and be able to comprehend and understand. We are where we are.

**Author's Note:**

I felt zero judgment or shame on or for Rocky's behalf regarding his mentioned relapse. His story highlights that even people who have made great progress in healing and managing addiction can slip back. Challenging seasons happen for everyone, and that might be the medicine or experience that is needed for them at the time. It again shows that Iboga is not a "miracle" but rather a technology and gift that can be cultivated and approached when someone "needs to be saved." Even though some experience miraculous results, that doesn't necessarily mean that state will last for a lifetime.

I learnt similar lessons to rocky on my own journey. Iboga shifted my time frame and perspective on life, from being a short-term renter, chasing shiny objects and achievements to really asking myself, "How can I invest in both myself and the world? What can I truly do to help people long term?" Although this might not be explicitly said by many interviewees, I noticed that many interviewees were focused on service and helping others and not just themselves. It seems that Iboga can take us out of focusing on our own short term lives, into a life based on long term service and joyful, meaningful work. Our own healing is aided through assisting the healing of others, through helping them we help and continue to heal ourselves.

**Ryan...... Healing Alcoholism.**

***Bio:*** *Ryan Graves. 36 when first working with Iboga, 39 now ("no booze in between!"). Approximately 10 grams (1 spoon) of Iboga root bark. Male. USA. Ryan is an author, explorer, husband and a proud dad. Ryan was motivated to work with Iboga to stop drinking alcohol.*

**Author's Introduction:** Ryan did a huge amount of work with only a small amount of Iboga (approx 10 grams, or one spoon!) Abstaining from alcohol for many years, after one treatment is truly impressive. His journey demonstrates the healing that can be experienced with preparation, professional integration assistance and a clear intention.

**Where did you first hear about Iboga?**

In 2018, after two years of sobriety, I was a mess and I drank again. Alcohol was my thing. I had done Ayahuasca in the fall of 2018. I then had another relapse in March of 2019. When I was coming back to my senses and trying to figure out what to do, my options were rehab or Ayahuasca again. I did some serious research and I stumbled upon a blog article that Amber from "Awaken your Soul" had written. Her post spoke about the differences between Ayahuasca and Iboga. That spoke to me. I knew immediately that my work was with Iboga. Iboga was already working on me before I went to Costa Rica. I knew it was what I had to do.

**Did you feel called to Iboga?**

Yes. I felt called to Iboga. After I read Amber's blog post, I began to understand the call. There was always fear, well really terror, but there was a knowing in my heart that this is what I had to do, to better my life. That trust carried me all the way to Costa Rica.

**What was your life like before working with Iboga?**

I'm an alcoholic and I've struggled with that for most of my adult life. Sobriety was lonely, I was depressed, I was sad. I was stuck and looking for answers. I was on the verge of giving up, until I found Iboga.

**What is your life like after Iboga?**

I like to call it "living in flow." I don't necessarily wait for things to come to me, I just go. I try to be the best version of me. It has opened up my world to my authentic self and what I really want to do. Instead of trying to find jobs and panicking, I became at peace with who I am.

I'm a writer and that has been a gift given to me by Iboga. I have already written a story and I'm talking to an editor this week. I'm very excited about it. I feel called to give back and share my story, in the hope it will help other people.

My wife has also been doing plant medicines (not Iboga) and we have three children. Our focus has always been on them, because I had a very traumatic childhood. Together, with my wife, we are just doing the very best we can to raise our children as awesome as we can.

I always knew I wanted to write, but I never knew what I wanted to write about. After doing Iboga it was this realization of "Oh, I have all kinds of stuff to write about!" It has opened up my world. I feel like I have a literary imagination in my brain. It has cleared so many negative thoughts, that I had been punishing myself with for years. To be free of that, is life changing.

I lost my little brother to drug addiction in 2016. I did Iboga in April, 2019. That summer (2019) I was able to understand that I had never grieved his death. I can tell you right now, if it wasn't for Iboga, that never would have happened. I was angry, I didn't understand why. But since Iboga made me a lot more aware of what is going on, I connected the anger with sadness. Once I did that I was able to release so many tears. I could grieve my brother's death. That has changed my life in itself. I've been able to move on and follow his spirit, which I've been able to get in touch with. It has been incredible. I have a better relationship with him now than when he was alive. That is a gift.

**How did you prepare and would you prepare differently subsequent times?**

I prepared very similarly to how I prepared for Ayahuasca. That was the only similar experience I had. I ate clean, I stopped smoking cannabis. I wasn't drinking. I was spending a lot of time with Ryan, "me." I was doing what I had to do, talking to coaches. I had a coach who really helped me get prepared. It is really hard to prepare for these things. I didn't know what I was getting myself into. I kept following my heart.

In my book I talk about two strings. There was one that was pulling me to Costa Rica and one that was telling me to stay away; fear and knowing. I knew I had to go. I followed my heart, I am so glad that I did.

I don't think I would prepare differently in subsequent times. It is heavy stuff, I would probably do a lot of the same. I would have a different intention for a subsequent time, so I would have to see. I have a good relationship with Iboga, so I think I did it right the first time.

**What medical precautions did you take to make sure it was a safe experience?**
I had to get an EKG, which I took care of. I think they had to take a scan of my liver. This is a protocol at “Awaken Your Soul” healing center. I did all that without issues and I was good to go.

**What was your intention?**
My intention was to stop drinking. It was the intention of eliminating the cycle of addiction that runs deep in our family. I come from a long line of addicts and drunks. On both sides of my family. I wanted to put an end to it. I haven't drunk since. I can tell you with 100% certainty that I never will again. It's like I was reborn. I don't have those same thoughts, it's just something I don't do anymore.

My intention, to make it simpler, was to find the source of my pain. The people I had been working with had all told me, "If you want to stop drinking, ultimately you need to get to the beginning of this problem, to the bottom of this pain." When talking about something as intense as alcohol you have to go back to the beginning. I always assumed my childhood was a fairy-tale. I had a traumatic event happen when I was a freshman in high school, I lost a six year old cousin to cancer. I assumed that was the reason why I was the way I was. But these people (coaches and mentors) I had been working with made me curious. So, I was determined to go to the beginning. Find the source.

Nobody had told me to go further back, but I really wanted to know what the source of my pain was.

I will tell you what it was, I'm not afraid to admit this. It was a vision of me, when I was in a crib, when I was an infant, left alone in the dark for hours and hours. No one came to get me. I was terrified, I was afraid, I felt unlovable. Understanding all of that, I put a blanket over it.

It's been a process. I didn't integrate this in a week, it has taken a long time. Understanding that vision was all I really needed to see.

**How did you consume Iboga? What did you take and wear what was the form? And do you know the total dose?**
I was at "Awaken your Soul" with Amber and Anthony. I didn't take any TA. I just took the Iboga and it was in powdered form (powdered root bark). I had a spoonful, I believe it was 10 grams. I never took anymore and I didn't do a second journey. That was all I needed. I was ready for it.

Amber was the one who wrote the blog post, so I reached out and talked to Anthony (co-founder of Awaken your soul). I was a mess. I was just coming off a bender. It was all kinds of unconscious. That was the place I was supposed to be. I believe that now. I was supposed to work with those people. I followed my heart. I did some research on other places, but I liked their jive the most! I'm so glad that is where I went.

**What would be your advice to people considering Iboga?**
Take it seriously. This isn't something to be taken lightly. That's what a lot of my story is about, you know. I've been doing it the traditional way, going to ceremonies. Prepare! Talk to people.

I'll share what my coach told me. It was the best advice and I needed it before my experience. I asked "What do I do while I'm on Iboga?" He said "Imagine a black canvas. Imagine you are trying to locate an animal. Instead of peering, try gazing. You are kind of looking everywhere." It might sound silly, but that was monumental to my experience. There was a black canvas. There were so many things happening. I couldn't focus on anything. I just had to gaze.

**What are your thoughts on micro-dosing? Did you micro-dose after your flood dose for integration?**
Like any other medicine, I believe if someone feels called to micro-dose, then, yeah, go for it. I've micro-dosed a number of medicines and have had really good results. As far as Iboga, I chose to micro-dose instead of the second flood dose during my time at Awaken Your Soul. So, this was three days after my first experience. I wasn't quite ready for it then. (Laugh) But, I guess, looking back, it did teach me a valuable lesson. One that I just learned! You see, that's the beauty of this medicine.

**Is there anything you wish you knew before doing Iboga about the process?**
No. I think not knowing was the best thing for me. People can watch YouTube clips, read blog columns and all this other stuff. That might just get them stir crazy and bring in more fear. I think it's trusting your heart and going with your intuition. Leave that other stuff out (extra research), that is what worked for me.

**Would you work with Iboga again?**
Absolutely. I will be doing it again. But when it's meant to happen, I'm not in a rush.

I have a wife that's very supportive and I know she would like to work with Iboga too. I know I want to go to Gabon too, I feel called to that. I'm 37 with 3 small kids, so it's not any time soon, but it is something I am going to pursue. Absolutely.

**Was there a memorable moment or particularly profound Vision that you have and has this Vision come true?**
The best part for me was Discovery Day. That's what the day after an Iboga journey was called at "Awaken your Soul". A lot of things made sense that day. It was extremely profound.

I can tell you a different thing that happened to me because of Iboga and other medicines. I told you already that I have always wanted to write a book. I've been looking to do this for a long time. This vision happened 7-8 months after I did Iboga. I had a spiritual awakening of some sort. It was right in everyday life, on a Tuesday in January. I had everything come together. My whole life made sense, I was exactly where I was supposed to be.

All that came to me was the first line in my story, and that ended up changing my life. Once I had that first line, that one line turned into 140,000 words. That's what's important for other people to understand, is that you can't just expect to go and do Iboga then come back and be this new person. You have to do a lot of work. You HAVE to do work. You have to put what you learned into your daily life and act on it. When you do that, you are going to see results. That's why I believed that happened to me. It's because I was doing the work. I was following my heart and my intuition. That was a gift from not only Iboga but God or whatever you want to call it. It was profound and it has changed my entire life.

"I ate mushrooms once" is the first line to my book. It goes back to eating mushrooms in high school and how it relates to everything I have experienced with Iboga and other medicines. It is insane, it is all connected. That's what I was saying, it all fell into place. It was amazing.

**What did Iboga teach or give you?**
It taught me how to follow my intuition and how to follow my heart. It taught me how to grieve my brother's death. It taught me how to let go of alcohol completely. It taught me how to love myself, I never even knew what that was. I really understood what it means to love yourself unconditionally. It's still a work in process for me, to be honest with you. That was what I needed then and I'll never forget that. It taught me how to connect with spirit in everyday life. It taught me how to cry and how powerful crying is for healing.

It has taught me, when I get certain feelings or 'tingles' that is Iboga talking to me. That still happens now. I don't know if I'm unique but I had an experience where I figured out that I had done this before. Iboga has always been a part of me. I know that, for sure. I really felt connected to the music. It has taught me more than anything else in my entire life.

**Author: I feel the 'tingles' as well. I don't know if it is Iboga, some other spirit guide or my higher self, but something is communicating. I like the phrase you used before about "pulling on the string." It feels like something is pulling on the string of your soul, and it is resonating. It's beautiful. There is this great, resonating tingle. Often it coincides with a thought or some information: Go there, read this book, remember this line, talk to that person, work on this etc.**

Ryan: I'm tingling right now, all over. Boom. I've got goosebumps. I wish I could show you.

**Author: I don't have the right word for it. It's a mixture of goosebumps, tingles, energy running up your spine. I wish I had a word for it, but I don't!**

**Has Iboga affected your spirituality?**

I'll share this with you, during my ceremony I asked questions and I asked if my deceased brother was okay. What I saw was a white light, it started hovering, shining and going up into the black canvas. When it got to the top, it just kind of sat there. It disappeared very quickly into this other world. I understood it immediately, his light is still shining. I just don't know where the fuck he is!

That changed my whole perception because it was so important for me to know my brother is okay. There is so much more to this, in this life, that was something that I desperately needed. I'm starting to cry. I desperately needed that. I was in search of something, anything that could get me to believe in something greater than myself. That's what happened. It changed everything.

**Is there anything else you'd like to add?**

All I can say is that I was a 35 year old end stage alcoholic, and this worked for me. It's that simple. I hope other desperate drunks and addicts understand and know that there are other options available. This option is much cheaper than rehab facilities. I believe in this work so much, I believe it can really help our world.

**Author's Note:**

Ryan's story highlights that a little Iboga can go a long way, when coupled with a precise intention and adequate preparation. Ryan had clear questions beforehand, and had already begun to unpack them and get upstream of "I want to stop drinking." Preparation, integration, the perfect timing, coupled with a little Iboga can foster miracles.

Additionally, the power of Iboga to heal intergenerational trauma is demonstrated here. Intergenerational trauma is commonly defined as the behaviors, beliefs, epigenetics, and conditions we inherit from our parents and ancestors. Ryan stated that he "came from a long line of addicts and drunks," indicating that his trauma was likely intergenerational and passed down from his ancestors. Iboga helped him to re-tell the conditions of his formative baby years and change his unexamined, engrained, and subconscious beliefs about loneliness and the cruelness of the world. This healing is made apparent by his continued sobriety and his love for his children.

I was blown away by Ryan's openness, vulnerability and willingness to share his difficult stories.

He is a great example of someone who is happy, grateful and living well. That is the ultimate way to thank those beings (people, plants and spirits) who have helped us. Any clown can say thank you, it's best to share that gratitude by being happy and of service.

**Jennifer...... Depression, Substance Misuse, Developmental and Adulthood Trauma.**

***Bio:*** *Jennifer Patterson, 32 when first working with Iboga, 41 now. 2.3 grams TA (did three separate flood dose ceremonies around this dose). Queer, nonbinary person. USA. Jennifer is a sliding scale healing arts practitioner and published author working with herbal medicine, breathwork, and creative writing to support trauma healing and community care. Jennifer was initially motivated to work with Iboga for "Depression, substance misuse, developmental and adulthood trauma."*

**Author's Introduction:** Jennifer is a truly interesting soul who has worked hard for a long time to heal and manage alcohol use, controlling tendencies and mental health. The combination of 5 powerful tools: Iboga, breathwork, herbalism, taking a long term approach and courage to consistently do the work shine through in this interview.

**Where did you first hear about Iboga?**

In 2013 I was in a graduate program and I met somebody who was sharing about their work with Iboga among other medicines. I had never really heard of Iboga before. I grew up during the 80s where the conversations were about staying away from drugs, not working with drugs for healing.

I started reading up about it, reading things online and listening to podcast episodes, trying to find information about it. Something clicked when I first heard about it but I wasn't sure if it was what I needed to do, or if it would be helpful to do. Actually, I was very sure that other people I knew needed to do it. As I started sitting with the information, I realized "Oh, I'm the one who needs to do it!" It was a long and winding process for me to realize it was me who needed Iboga!

From there, I committed to doing a ceremony. For about a decade before I worked with Iboga I was on a lot of antidepressants, anti-anxiety pills and mood stabilizer pills. Because they were contraindicated for working with Iboga, I had to taper off all of those in preparation for the ceremony.

**How were you called to Iboga? Did you feel spiritually called to Iboga?**
I did and do. I am a herbalist; I am in deep relationship with plants and plant spirits. Once I learned there was a very, very strong psychedelic plant I could work with, it felt like a powerful way to do some of the healing I'd not been able to do through medications and traditional talk therapy.

**What was your life like before Iboga?**
I am 41 now. For the bulk of my life, from childhood up to adulthood I experienced different kinds of violence. I experienced abuse in my childhood, then sexual assault in my late teens and a couple of physical assaults in my 20s as well as some harmful/ complicated longerterm partnerships. For a very long time, I believed that my resting state was massive depression. I was on medications. I was in therapy. I think in my 20s I was very aware of how much I had been impacted, but I wasn't quite aware that my life could feel a bit different. In some ways, I had given up on "feeling better" but a deeper part of me knew there was still potential. The possibility of going outside of more traditional, at least here in the US, ways of healing trauma brought me some hope.

It felt like those things - medication and talk therapy - helped keep me alive but it didn't offer me much of a quality of life. Alongside all of that I spent a long time in my 20s and early 30 drinking pretty heavily. I was getting into trouble in my relationships, had sustained a broken nose and deviated septum while drinking, and I also got a DUI and had to go through the court system which included mandatory AA.

Learning that Iboga is often used as an addiction-interrupter, I felt even more drawn. Though much of the research is centered on interrupting opiate addiction, from my research and in talking with my friend, it was clear that Iboga could potentially support me in changing my relationship to alcohol as well as some other adaptive, and harmful, behaviors I had developed in response to an overwhelming amount of trauma.

It's also important to say here that no, Iboga is not a cure for addiction. Rather, I see it as an entryway into a deeper and embodied understanding of the why – like why am I choosing to drink to excess? Why am I choosing these relationships? What's at the root? Though I knew the "why" intellectually, Iboga offered me an opportunity to really feel the "why" in a more embodied, somatic way. And while a ton came through in the ceremony each time, integration, or even disintegration, and a deep commitment to doing the work outside and after the ceremony is also necessary to see sustained change.

Another big part of what brought me into wanting to work with Iboga back in 2014 was being in a new relationship. I was really feeling the impact of the childhood trauma I had experienced. It was affecting my attachment to others; in my teens and young adult years I had a lot of unhealthy relationships. I just did not feel very grounded in myself or connected to my sense of self. I felt really scared of being alone then, my attachment wounds were all encompassing. I really struggled to feel "Ok" outside of a relationship. I had hoped that maybe some of that could shift as I came into a deeper understanding of how the violence and abuse I'd experienced had shaped me.

**What is your life like after Iboga?**

Between 2014 and 2017, I did a full flood dose of Iboga three separate times. Each time I felt a substantial shift in the heaviness I was holding in my body. In each ceremony, I dove even deeper into the abuse I'd experienced, the lineage of abuse and violence in my family and the generations before, and came face to face with a true embodied understanding of how much I resisted being alive.

In the first flood dose ceremony that I did I really got to feel a lot of the impact of the abuse in my life, in my body, in my child body and in my older adult body. Knowing more somatically, what I felt like as a child in an abusive home helped me develop understanding and compassion for both my child self and my adult self that quite frankly, didn't want to be alive anymore. The harm I was holding in my body was so foundational, so all-encompassing and in some ways, it became clear I needed to rescue the child, offer love, safety, and understanding. I became known to myself, it was a very "Oh, wow, of course you feel the way you do now – I felt what it felt like at just 8 years old, feeling the lack of safety and stability in that home."

After the first time, I felt good. The facilitators and I took a photo before and after the ceremony and even just in that photo after, it was clear a huge dark cloud had been dispersed. Because it was my first experience with a psychedelic, I had no idea what to anticipate. In the days and months after, it was hard to pin down what exactly had shifted but it was also clear there was a substantial shift internally. I never went into the ceremonies with the intention to stop drinking entirely but I was very interested in changing my relationship and lessening the charge and dependence. Each time I worked with Iboga, my dependent relationship on alcohol lessened to the point where I drink casually and in a way that doesn't harm me or others now. With each Iboga ceremony drinking alcohol felt less and less necessary as a way of adapting to the world. I also changed my relationship to coffee for a number of years and even now, drink much less of it.

Before Iboga I was drinking to escape myself and escape how I felt, to dull everything out. After Iboga, my desire to work with substances became focused on their healing capacity, as a way of connecting back to myself, as a way of coming back into my aliveness.

**Do you feel smarter or less depressed day to day?**

It's hard to say after these last couple years navigating a global pandemic. I do feel less depressed in the day to day but I certainly still experience states of depression, anxiety and still feel the presence of complex PTSD. But I stopped taking all the medications to work with Iboga the first time and I never started those back up– it's been almost a decade since I was on them.. Through my work with Iboga and working with other herbal medicine and breathwork, I feel more solid and anchored, more able to stabilize myself.

I want to say that medications for mental health certainly save lives; they are tools that are sometimes necessary. I honor whatever people need in their own unique process. Medications kept me alive for sure. But they also kept me dull, far away from actually dealing with the impact of abuse and violence in my life, far away from connection to my own spirit. The fact that I'm no longer on a range of medications for mental health (9 years as of this interview) feels like a huge win, something I didn't believe was possible. For a long time I was told by doctors that I would have to be on medications forever. I internalized that and believed that I was just that fucked up, that I was someone who would need medications for forever to simply stay alive. When I didn't feel the need to start it back up, that was something powerful, a true sign that internally I had broken some of the old narratives.

When I was in my early twenties, as well as high school, I had these thoughts like, "I don't want to feel any better." I was really attached to being depressed largely because it was just such an old and familiar way of being for me. But I was also a curious, empathetic, and creative young person writing deeply emotional poetry and making art. I was and still am a big feeler. I had coupled my depression with my creativity and my ability to feel deeply. For a long time, I didn't care that I was depressed. I didn't want to change. I wanted access to that deep well of pain in order to keep my creative work going.

A part of me was able to notice that when I was in highly depressive or triggered states, even if it was for a long time, that something happens in these states that is useful for personal development. It's useful to be in the hard stuff sometimes. It's useful to feel it. It's useful to find our way back out of it. After my work with Iboga, depression is no longer a thing I'm stuck in for the rest of my life. Iboga helped me remember that there is a little part of me that knows there is value in depression and there is also value in finding my way out of those states too, rich with the lessons and wisdom.

Now, even when I feel depressed it's wildly and noticeably different than what it was. It also just makes sense now. Many of us navigate such terrifying and destabilizing experiences in our lives. Coupled with seeing how much abuse, violence, and destruction there is in the larger world, it makes sense that it's a lot to hold. However now, my depression and complex PTSD is infinitely more manageable, with the support of my other rituals and healing practices.

**How did you prepare? Would you prepare differently a second time?**

The first time I wasn't super nervous because I had read a lot about it and I had heard enough personal experience from others to trust that I would be ok. Early in the first ceremony, some fear did come in, but that was largely because of other people being afraid for me, worried about me, and instilling doubt in the process.

As I've mentioned, Iboga was the first psychedelic I ever worked with! In some respects, I had no idea what I was preparing for. I had smoked weed sometimes in my 20s, but I had never done any other drug apart from alcohol and coffee. I didn't know what the hell I was getting into at all. Part of me thought "You're just not going to know what it's like until it happens."

I was more mindful of what I was eating leading up to the first time. I had to taper off my medications, which was a couple of months of decreasing and slowing down the dosing. I stopped drinking a couple of weeks before the ceremony. I wrote a bunch and crafted intentions to help guide the ceremony.

I was told by the facilitators to have questions coming into it. These questions would be asked of me when I was in the peak of the ceremony. I had about 30+ questions which is hilarious. I had way too many questions, so I had to pare down a little bit and get more focused. I did spend a lot of time thinking about what I wanted to get out of it. I brought some items for the altar that felt personal, to help hold the energetic space as a space of healing.

**What precautions did you take to make sure it was a safe experience?**

I didn't travel or go the medicalized route most utilized in clinics and centers. Instead, I worked with two people in their home. One of them was initiated in Gabon and both had deep relationships to the plant and the community in Gabon. It was a very small operation. It was not a big center. I worked with them early on in their work. They did require EKGs, bloodwork, and put in place some medical standards to create even more safety in the work. I knew these people very well, I trusted them and still do! I shared my medical history with them so they knew that the contraindications were limited beyond my medication use which, as I mentioned, I tapered off of for the ceremony. The main thing to share was a pretty extensive trauma history, which I thought would be prominent in the ceremony. It was!

What was beautiful about these practitioners is that all the ceremonies were done on a sliding scale; they were trying to create access for people that couldn't afford to go to Gabon or Mexico or other places. They also were very aware that there was a lot of abuse of power, mismanagement, and harm being committed in many of larger clinics and centers. They were very focused on offering a space as safe as possible. They didn't have a medical background but they learned, adapted, and had a lot of traditional and spiritual practices that helped to hold the container in a safe way.

Having worked with people as well, I do feel conflicted around what the "safest" way to do it is. I think there's immense value in working outside of a medicalized treatment space and I also can see the value of having skilled medical providers on hand. There are a lot of people out there who do not have enough experience, integrity, or personal work under their belt to be facilitating these ceremonies. Fortunately, I had a very positive and safe experience all of the three times I did a flood dose with these practitioners. Overall, I think the whole process of coming to work with Iboga needs to involve a lot of research, personal and vetted recommendations, and deep inquiry.

**What was your intention?**

My main intentions were trying to be with the violence a bit more. In a way that helped me move through it, instead of it being a weight on me, something I couldn't escape. I felt like I had hit walls over and over in so many areas of my life. I felt pretty disconnected from myself. I had spent years disconnecting from myself, after feeling like I had to out of survival as a young person. I wanted to come back into trusting myself and trusting the ways that I was in my life.

I wanted some help in going into the roots of my coping mechanisms, which were drinking and trichotillomania. Trichotillomania is compulsive or impulsive hair pulling that is often linked to trauma, stress, anxiety, overwhelm and PTSD. I knew intellectually why they were so present for me but I didn't know how to untangle myself from them. I wanted healthier relationships too! With both myself and other people.

**How did you consume Iboga? What did you take and where? What form? Total dose?**

The first and second ceremonies I took TA capsules. My third ceremony I did half Ibogaine and half TA. It was a high dose, a full flood dose each time.

Each time I had an extremely hard time with nausea and keeping it down. We broke the doses down into pretty small amounts and took them every 45 mins over a few hours.

**Why did you decide to do it this way? Why did you pick this center?**
It was not in my consciousness until I met these people. The benefits were that it was close to where I lived. I trusted the people. It was more affordable because of the sliding scale. (There's no way at that time I could have afforded a clinic somewhere.) I was able to stay there for 4 days. I wasn't rushed out of there after the ceremony. It is complicated. Again, I think doing it with a medical team, especially if there are contraindications or things to be aware of, is important. For me it felt more resonant to be in a comfortable place and not be hooked up to machines. It made sense for where I was at and what felt the safest for me.

**It must have been a great connection you had with the facilitators? You had no psychedelic experience before and went straight to a flood dose!**
It was! I think I had tried so many things – all those medications for 10 years. I had been in therapy in and out since I was 7 years old. Read so many books. I think for me, I was just ready to try something else. I also veer towards the extremes so part of my thought "Yes, I will do the most intense psychedelic first! Let's go!" But yeah, I did have a very close relationship with the facilitators. We are still very close.

But timeline-wise, I learned about it in August 2013. I did my first ceremony in June 2014, second in 2015 I believe and then third in the spring of 2017 as well as micro-dosing and smaller ceremonies in between.

My control mechanisms were so strong. I think a part of me knew that I needed to be out of control a bit, in a safe way, that I had to break through and understand why those strong desires to be in control existed. I needed to be out of control, in a way that other people could take care of me. A wiser part of me knew that letting go of control a bit would serve me a lot.

To some degree, I went into it from a place of desperation as well as hope. I was doing the things you were meant to do. I was going the route I was told I should go and I still didn't feel okay. I wasn't getting better. I was ready!

**What would be your advice to people considering Iboga?**
Do a lot of research. Heavily research the clinic, heavily research the people that are facilitating, ask around, and see what other people's experiences have been. Over the years, I've found out a lot of scary stuff that happens at treatment centers. There is a lot of violence and abuse of power. I've heard stories of people being sexually assaulted. The research is really important because we are going to be in a vulnerable state, not fully aware. You need to be in a place that is as safe as possible.

I also recognize that getting first-hand recommendations and experience can be hard because it's not legal here in the US. But still, I think finding someone who has done it and is open to talking about it is helpful. Even though the experiences are so different. Their recommendations are good. There are good guides online about safety, spaces, facilitators, and medical procedures. I think if people want to go a medicalized route they can. If people want to go a less medicalized way, either wherever they are living or going to Gabon, those are valid ways too. Regardless, it's important, and in integrity with the plant and the communities still tending these traditions to really be thorough, to not rush, to honor the sustainability of the plant and the people, to access that medicine with really powerful, long-standing teachers and healers.

I also think getting clear on 'the why' is important, even if it changes. I don't think Iboga is for everyone. It's a hell of a ride and can be very overwhelming. Sometimes it's better to start slow or work with a medicine that has a shorter time commitment. We can prepare all we want to for it and then we get in there, into the work, and there's even more to be done.

Take your time with it. A lot of us are coming to it at a crisis point, depending on what we are navigating: opiates, depression, PTSD, other addictions, etc. Oftentimes, we've "tried everything." While the crisis point could be a catalyst to get us to the ceremony, it's important to give ourselves time to prepare and be ready for it. It is really big work and there is no rush.

All plants are powerful, but these are very powerful plants. Once it is in our awareness and once we are feeling called to it, I do think the right opportunities show up. You don't have to push so hard. If you are pushing really hard and it's not coming together, it might not be the right time.

**What are your thoughts on micro-dosing? Did you micro-dose after a flood dose for integration?**

Yes, I did. I don't remember how much. I did it for a few weeks to a month after the ceremony. It was a very small amount of Iboga. I felt it was helpful. It can be such a powerful and overwhelming experience that working with Iboga in a smaller way, to shift back into our lives is really helpful. Staying in relationship to Iboga over the years has felt nourishing. You actually don't even need to ingest it sometimes – just being with the plant, bringing that plant spirit into a meditative practice can be a way to connect back to the wisdom.

**Is there anything you wish you knew before doing Iboga about the process?**

I researched a lot. While I did make a wild choice to jump into it, I spent a lot of time planning. I could have read a little bit less! Sometimes overpreparing puts us in a place where we have a lot of expectations around what it should be when it is so different from person to person.

**Would you do Iboga again?**

I would. Even though the third time I did it I thought, "I am NEVER doing this again! EVER!" Hahaha! I was confident that I would never do it again. But, I think I would!

**Has Iboga affected your spirituality?**

For sure. Yes. I mentioned I am an herbalist. I started working with herbs in a more professional way in 2012. Working in such a deep way with Iboga connected me to the wisdom of plants a lot more and helped me develop a deep trust in and faith in their wisdom. I think in the back of my mind, even when I am in really rough moments, I am often able to say, "You have already done the hardest thing you're probably going to do in your whole life." I think that has been an anchor. It has helped me stay connected to the spiritual plane. I think it's pretty cool to put our trust in something that's not human, but very much alive, and to be able to feel a resonance. I think that has really helped strengthen my trust in the world, myself, the universe, and the potential to heal and keep healing.

I was finally able to feel that healing is actually possible though It might not end. I imagine I will continue doing work to heal for the rest of my life in different ways. But I no longer feel burdened by that. I feel inspired and hopeful. I'm here in this lifetime to grow, change, heal, become more alive, present, and available to the shifts as I can. What a relief to know so intimately that things can soothe, soften, lift, and change.

**How do we learn to trust something that is not human? How do we learn to have faith in a plant or a spirit?**
As I've mentioned, I'm an herbalist, breathwork facilitator and I work with psychedelics in a lot of ways. It's my luck in this lifetime to be in work that requires trusting what I can't see. Those three areas have all been places where I have been "Wow, I'm not actually in control. What a relief." Because I thought I was, I thought I had to be. But control did not keep me safe – I experienced all kinds of trauma over my 41 years of this lifetime. Getting more controlling after each situation didn't mean they stopped. It didn't stop it. Loosening my grip, after doing this transformative work, has brought endless gifts to my life.

For people coming from other abusive backgrounds, trusting other humans is hard. I went through a wave in the ceremony for the first time: I even became so suspicious of the facilitators though they were my dear friends! It made it so clear how much I struggled to trust people informed, of course, by being abused by people I trusted in my life before the ceremony. But then I realized that was a lie, an old story. They were just people trying to support me! Just people trying to help! People who loved me and would not harm me.

**Was there a memorable moment or particularly profound vision you had? Has it come true?**
Though I've had visions every ceremony, I had the most intense visions with my first flood dose. I know that is not the case for everyone; some people do not have strong imagery or visions. I also think information comes through in lots of different ways, in our bodies or in a precise somatic way. Throughout my three flood doses, I wrote through all three of them, I was taking notes (*Author: this is really unusual!*). This is where my control mechanisms still come in, haha! I kept thinking "gotta get it all down." I have notebooks filled with very profound, to me, thoughts. I'm really grateful I was able to take brief notes.

At one point, I felt called to write one short poem about my dad who was/is abusive. (I am no longer in a relationship with him because of a refusal to take responsibility or change his behavior. We haven't been in touch for 12+ years.) I had this vision of my childhood home. A big sailboat's sail came up in the middle of the living room and a huge sail puffed out. It started spinning around over and over again. It destroyed everything in the house. It all turned to rubble. I wrote something down like, "My childhood home has been destroyed, I am not surprised. It makes sense." It was so matter of fact. Even though trying to tease out what that meant now, I think for me when I was in that moment, I felt the profound impact on me growing up in that home. A home is supposed to be safe and that was not my experience. So, after that vision, as well as some others related to that, the narrative in my mind no longer was, "Oh I am just fucked up. I've got all kinds of problems and I can't figure them out." It started to be extremely clear that things that happened, the abuse I experienced, created these thoughts and feelings. And there was release from the echoes of them.

That was the big message that kept coming through in the first ceremony "Of course! Of course I feel this way!" I have felt this way for so long and there are reasons why. I didn't just wake up and suddenly feel bad. There was a series of ongoing patterns of harm and abuse that created my coping mechanisms, that forced me into survival. It was a relief to realize that I actually made sense. Everything made sense. I realized I had developed very wise ways to survive given my life.

**What did Iboga Teach or give you?**

I started to trust that my life had value and that healing and feeling different was possible, that I can catalyze and transform the things I had experienced into something that is generative and positive for myself and also others. Before my ceremonial work, I had already been supporting people as they navigated the impact of trauma and abuse in my work as a healing arts practitioner and writer. I was in the process of editing an anthology called "Queering Sexual Violence: Radical Voices from Within the Anti-Violence Movement (published in 2017) focused on queer people and sexual violence as well as studying and training as an herbalist and breathwork facilitator. It was already happening, but after this work with Iboga and other psychedelics, I started to trust it more, trust myself in work with others more.

Back to trichotillomania (hair pulling), there was another vision I had where I was feeling a pin prick on the top of my head. It felt like a long fingernail was pricking down into my head over and over relentlessly. I was able, in that moment, to recognize that the hair pulling or the drinking were all things that I had picked up to dissociate and disconnect from harm and what I was experiencing. Through that vision, I got the message, and heard a strong voice that said I didn't have to hurt myself anymore. The hurting had ended, it was other people. I don't always remember that but it was really clear and fresh in the weeks and months after.

**Anything else you'd like to add**

I'm glad to hear you are going to be talking about sustainability. I think when things are touted as miracle "cures," the demand becomes too large for the sustainability of the plants and the rightful tenders of these plants. If we come into doing work with Iboga from an extractive place, that is not an honest place to work with the medicine.

Especially as a white person, I thought (and think) a lot about what it meant to be working with a medicine that was not from my personal culture or lineage. How could I do it in a way that was ethical and wasn't extractive? I wanted to be in the right relationship with the plant and the people tending these traditions still. I think a big part of that is sourcing and sustainability. A large part of that falls on big treatment centers that are buying in large amounts of course. Where are they buying from? Are they buying from people who are benefiting? Are the communities benefiting? Are the land and plants being respected in the process? It's important to be in the right exchange and right reciprocity.

Working with Iboga changed my whole life, brought me into a deeper and healthier relationship to myself, and set me up to be in service to others navigating similar hell realms like I did. I'm so incredibly grateful to have had the opportunity to do this work, to be welcomed into work that allows me to show up with more integrity and alignment in my communities.

**Author's note.**

Through Jennifer/Jennye's journey, we are reminded of the importance of softening, letting go, facing ourselves, and allowing ourselves to transition from a mentality of surviving to thriving. Could it be that by allowing ourselves to soften in a very intense and extreme environment, such as the peak of an Iboga experience, we can retrain our mind or be assisted to let go in more regular, easier environments? If we learn to relax and be at peace during "the most challenging thing we will do in our lives," it may be easier to surrender and reduce our controlling tendencies in quieter times.

Additionally, Iboga can help us explore the questions: "Why am I stuck in a survival mode? What caused me to go into survival mode and take me out of thriving?" Are you ready to explore that? If you find yourself stuck in survival mode it may be a good idea to ask yourself if you really want to find out what made you transition into survival. What disconnected you from joyfully connecting to your body and the world around you? These are big questions that Iboga can open the door to explore. Ultimately, each person has to decide if they are ready to walk through that door.

Jennye reiterated a common message that has arisen throughout the book, about pushing or trying too hard to work with Iboga. If you find yourself pushing too hard, it may not be the time to work with Iboga just yet. It sounds odd, but trust that the medicine will assist you and help you work with it when you are meant to. Finally, Iboga was the first psychedelic medicine Jennye worked with. Although not ideal, it shows that having previous psychedelic experience is not necessary to do profound work with Iboga; although broadly recommended for people interested in working with Iboga.

## CONCLUSION.

Every experience with Iboga is wildly different. With the appropriate preparation, intention, facilitator, integration, sacrifice, and supportive community, miracles can occur. But, miracles are not guaranteed. Omitting any of the above factors greatly increases the risk of a bad or potentially fatal outcome. Iboga's miracles are not the "lottery in a pill" type of outcomes, but rather a temporary respite from the sickness of the mind. This temporary peace of mind that Iboga can give, coupled with spiritual guidance can lead someone to rebuild their nightmare of a life into a dream. A temporary liberation from someone's unique demons enables a new path to be forged, leaving the monsters behind.

In the 'successful' Iboga experiences, true healing of the mind first required a clear intention. Almost all people who had successful outcomes came to Iboga in a state of crystalized desperation; at a minimum they were very clear with their motivation. Humbly asking for help, whether it be direct (to a human, God, a plant or a spirit) or an indirect prayer is the next important step. Finally, when the Iboga ceremony or Ibogaine treatment begins and the cauldron of the experience is fully boiling, a psyche capable of both softness and hardness is essential. Here, Softness means having openness, forgiveness and flexibility to see our stories from a new angle. Hardness is to have courageous determination to keep going deeper, to the root of our issues and to have the strength to rise from the dead.

With the appropriate price paid - this is not necessarily a financial price - Iboga can offer custom-tailored healing. A personalized program to expand consciousness, perfectly made for each person. Iboga meets people at the level of sacrifice and work they have put in beforehand. Profound transformations are possible with a serendipitous, chance meeting of Iboga. However, they are more likely to occur with preparation, a long-term commitment to healing, and integration.

Many interviewees experienced immediate changes; addictive tendencies ceasing, unhealthy relationships dissolving (sometimes abruptly), and behavioral patterns being rewired. Commonly, grand transformations came over a longer time frame. Often this was a one-degree shift that changed the trajectory of someone's life. This could be a realization such as "I am disgusted by cocaine," or "My greatest fear doesn't haunt me anymore." Iboga can help in immediately removing the weeds in our minds, but the glorious seeds of transformation take time to bear fruit.

How would I broadly summarize how Iboga generally works? Iboga typically highlights a blind spot, shining a light for us to confront some of our greatest fears and regrets. It can also provide a circuit breaker, disarming any loops or repetitive behavior we are stuck in. This allows us to see clearly and break habits. From a liberated state, we can then either understand our issues in crystal clear detail, or repeatedly face them until they are no longer terrifying and immobilizing. Several interviewees had the experience of Iboga making them repeatedly face their biggest fear or regret until they were unaffected by it. Once we have made peace with the monster lurking in our blind spot, Iboga can become a teacher who can show us a new way to be. Often this comes through expanding and heightening consciousness to a new vantage point. From here, we can see a new way we want to be and learn how to anchor that into regular reality.

Iboga and the cultural technology around it (Bwiti) can guide a person through this process, but it can't do the gritty work for them. Ultimately, healing is each person's own responsibility, and Iboga is simply there to assist. Iboga is a sacred tool that can help in ripping out the weeds of trauma and letting a new, higher state of consciousness flourish. It requires someone with the equivalent training of an elite surgeon to facilitate and a determined patient. It takes serious work to transform a life and Iboga assists this process.

As someone who loves this plant, it pains me to say that Iboga is not currently the answer to addiction and depression in the west, at least not on a societal scale.

There are many issues regarding the sustainability of Iboga. Iboga is critically endangered in the wild and the rich, traditional cultures that celebrate Iboga face enormous pressures from the modern world. The rapid influx of foreigners consuming the medicine must be managed urgently as well as the pressures placed on local communities from foreign business practices, particularly illegal poaching and logging. Relapsing into substance misuse, although uncommon, is possible following treatment with Iboga and Ibogaine. Integrating back into western culture is not straightforward following treatment, which presents problems for people motivated by both addiction and psycho-spiritual growth. The author, alongside many of the interviewees, can speak from personal experience that it is very hard to adjust back to "normal life," following working with Iboga.

Put frankly, a traditional Iboga initiation can be so brutal that society would rapidly fall apart if many people began working with it. Not everyone can awaken at the same time. If we want to maintain the luxuries of the modern world, mass awakening and liberation should be a gradual and gentle process. The regular, day-to-day activities of those not doing the spiritual, consciousness-expanding work is just as important to all of our collective healing and progress. We require both those courageous enough to take the path less travelled and those dutiful enough to support those hacking into our collective unconscious.

Iboga's most beneficial role for the West is likely to be as a life raft for the desperate and as a turbo charger for the visionaries.

This appears to be the most realistic path forward for two reasons. First, it would help those most crushed by the world to heal and terminate their trauma, especially those stuck in substance misuse cycles. Ibogaine for addiction would help to stop trauma being passed on and projected into the future. Secondly, for leaders coming to Iboga in good health, it can help radically enhance their inner and external worlds. In this way, Iboga would be directly cleaning those most desperately in need to cease their suffering whilst helping the dreamers construct a better world - lifting up the bottom and accelerating the top. Through these conduits, the lessons and spirit of Iboga can reach many people, whilst protecting the physical plant and cultures from extinction.

To be clear, I believe that at this point in time targeted Ibogaine treatments for people suffering from life threatening substance misuse are most appropriate, if they are deeply motivated. If they wish to partake in a traditional initiation into Iboga, it is best to have many years recovering and letting their body heal. For spiritually motivated people, coming to Iboga in great health, a traditional Iboga initiation can be life changing in the best way. With that said, I think it is wise to try many other local spiritual modalities and technologies before working with Iboga. It's good to have done a lot of study before attempting your PhD.

Is there a limit to the conditions and ailments Iboga can treat? For ailments of the mind, behavioral patterns, and general dissatisfaction with life, this book has not begun to scratch the surface of what Iboga's capacity is. It is possible that for any ailment with a seed of trauma or darkness that results in a compensatory addiction or lifestyle emerging, Iboga and Ibogaine can be highly useful. Issues such as unhelpful social media habits, shopping addictions, sex addictions, anxiety, depression, and other coping behaviors can most likely be treated by Iboga. Iboga is an unparalleled "circuit breaker," capable of hard resetting the brain and giving someone the chance to build a new personality and life.

Upon reflection, there is a bias in the interviewee selection. Only people who had a broadly positive experience with Iboga (or Ibogaine), even if it may have been harrowing during their experience, were willing to be involved with this book. There were many stories that have not yet ended in a fairytale. Many interviewees faced profound challenges and relapses following Iboga, even if they were experts and practitioners themselves.

It would have been ideal to be able to include more people who had harrowing, overwhelming experiences with Iboga and find out what went wrong. But these people were reluctant to be interviewed formally. During my own Iboga experience, I labeled it as a "bad trip." Fortunately, it was ultimately the single most healing and positively transformative experience of my life. From conversations with experts and friends, most of the "horrible" experiences occur during home usage, by untrained people, ordering Iboga online. For safety reasons, these experiences weren't included in the book. I did not want to encourage people to think about using Iboga at home by themselves.

What could be the broader role of Iboga in the future? Although many people call it genderless, it is after all a plant and a spirit, I believe Iboga represents an archetype of the Divine Masculine. While Ayahuasca is often described as a "Grandmother" archetype, I imagine Iboga as the loving, but stern "Grandfather or Stepfather." The Divine Masculine is often characterized as being extremely protective, boundary-setting, gentle, nourishing, and a wonderful teacher. The world faces new problems and addictions, stemming from multiple generations of living out of harmony with the Earth. Iboga could be the plant brought into the collective consciousness to help humanity. As the world melts into a boundaryless, high risk juvenile playground set on self destruction, the divine masculine archetype that each human can embody, may be necessitated to avert disaster. Iboga could radically help humanity build better worlds, internally and externally.

An image to end on is a vision that was shared in Tricia Eastman's interview. She reflected that during her studies of traditional Iboga initiations, many of the women looked identical to the Statue of Liberty. The Statue of Liberty was a gift of the French people, who colonized thc home of Iboga, to the American people. Iboga, or more accurately the spirit of liberation, symbolically made its way from Gabon, to France and ultimately to the USA. It stands in the ocean, the representation of the subconscious mind, amid a platform built by the American people. It seems tragically perfect that the USA should be gripped simultaneously by multiple crises: opioid, homelessness, mental health and national identity. It is poised to welcome the spirit of Iboga to its shores fully and anchor in the true spirit of liberation, not just have it as a cultural icon waiting to come ashore. However, there is a lot more work to do before Iboga can help terraform humanity's mind from a grey, robotic existence, to a rich, human consciousness.

Ultimately, the most sustainable medicine is the medicine we carry within ourselves. Consciousness and the many practical tools emphasized throughout this book are always at our disposal to apply to our own lives. Iboga is not a magic cure-all, but one of many keys to unlocking our true selves. Once uncovered, we can access the ultimate medicine of living joyfully. It is up to the individual holding the key to do the work of opening the door and realize their dream life. Iboga makes it easier to find the keys, the doors and the courage to keep walking through them.

**THANKS.**

To Iboga, the plant that saved me from my own mind and gave me a new life, thank you.

This book took two years to write and it was a labor of love; writing it was extremely helpful to my own integration. I feel so fortunate to have met Iboga at twenty five and consider it one of the greatest blessings (and challenges) of my life to have worked with it. May Iboga and I continue a happy, open, spiritual relationship for the rest of this lifetime. Thank you to Tatayo, who introduced me to Iboga and Bwiti. Without Tatayo, this book and my Iboga experience would never have happened!

I would like to thank all the people interviewed in this book for their time, energy, vulnerability, and personal stories they have contributed. I was blown away by their honesty and generosity. I jokingly reflected that the most compelling reason to work with Iboga may just be the maturity, kindness, and sincerity of the interviewees in this book; they have all been truly lovely people. That might plant the best seeds of Iboga in people's minds. How can all of these people be so kind, patient and open?

To my tireless, overworked and talented editors, Kailey Hak and Aion Merila Night, thank you for transforming this book into a readable work. You both infused such magic and emotion into the writing. Despite my best efforts, you transformed the "sterile and impersonal" early drafts, into a book we are all truly proud of. I wish you (and everyone reading) the most incredible journey with Iboga. Thank you.

To my self-proclaimed "long suffering" mother, who has supported me through all my adventures, misadventures, dreams, nightmares, failures, and successes – Thank you. I am so grateful to you and would choose you 100 times over again as my mother. I love you with all my heart.

**CALL TO ACTION.**

Please consider leaving a good review or rating for this book, if you enjoyed it. It is immensely helpful to let other people know what you think of this book, so they too can learn about Iboga. Additionally, your comments and reviews help in improving future versions of this book.

55% of royalties from this book are sent to the Gabon based "Blessings of the Forest" charity. If you're not in a position to help them, leaving a five star review is a simple, ten second way to help and contribute to Iboga's sustainability.

For people looking to work with Iboga, the safest and best way to start your search for a great facilitator is through trusted "real world" friends. Look for people who have worked with Iboga and are in a great place in their life for a sustained amount of time. Ask them who they worked with. The section on how to find a facilitator will be especially useful for you now, if you feel called to working with Iboga.

If you would like to contact the author, I can be best contacted through the website "www.theibogaexperience.com", or through twitter (@Leo_van_v), or Instagram (@leo.vanv). If you take issue with anything discussed, or would like to talk further about Iboga or plant medicines, feel free to reach out.

Finally, and most importantly, if you are interested in Iboga or the broader missions of alleviating trauma and expanding consciousness, please consider donating to Blessings of the Forest. They are a truly remarkable charity, doing wonderful work to conserve and protect Iboga for future generations. I have no financial or professional ties to Blessings of the Forest, apart from an admiration for and friendship with the founders. If you want to support Iboga, and the wider world of plant medicines, Blessings of the Forest is a great organization to donate to or get involved with.

If you have read this far, then hopefully the seed of Iboga has been planted within your psyche. Alternatively, you might have said a polite "No, thanks" or a more forceful "Keep that tree away from me!" Either way, hopefully you now better understand Iboga and its capacity to heal.

# APPENDIX: RESOURCES

Further Interviews with Tatayo

a. https://www.youtube.com/watch?v=REofdD1cWFY
   Iboga And The Bwiti School Of Life | Tatayo ~ ATTMind 130
b. https://www.youtube.com/watch?v=M5xSrf3sL5g
   i. Universe Within Podcast Ep27 - Tatayo - Ebando: Iboga, Bwiti, & Gabon

Retreat centers mentioned in interviews

1. Ebando (Tatayo)
   a. https://ebando.org/en/EN.iboga.htm
2. Awaken Your Soul (Anthony and Amber)
   a. https://awakenyoursoul.co/
3. Iboga Wellness center (Levi)
   a. https://ibogawellness.com/
4. Awakening in the dream (Rocky and Asha)
   a. *https://www.awakeninginthedream.com*

Referenced Articles

1. https://www.Ibogainealliance.org/guidelines/

Dr Barsuglia's mentioned works:

1. https://www.josephbarsuglia.com/work
2. https://www.josephbarsuglia.com/psychedelic-research-gallery

The specific paper Dr Barsuglia mentioned is officially referenced here (but not downloadable from the site):

3. https://www.sciencedirect.com/science/article/pii/S0079612318300931?via%3Dihub

Links to counselors/coaches services mentioned in the book

1. Christina (Chrissy) Sandwen
   a. ChristinaSandwen.com
2. Juliana Mulligan
   a. juliana@innervisionibogaine.com

Further articles on how to find a center or facilitator

1. https://www.plantmedicine.org/podcast/warning-signs-when-selecting-a-psychedelic-facilitator-with-juliana-mulligan
2. https://www.innervisionIbogaine.com/findingaclinic

For more in depth advice on safety from Juliana check out:
https://chacruna.net/Ibogaine-abuses-accountability/

Recommended books mentioned in text:
"*The Root of All Healing*" by Daniel Brett
"Bwiti: An Ethnography of the Religious Imagination in Africa" by J.W Fernande

**BONUS: AN INTERVIEW WITH THE AUTHOR**

***Bio:*** *Leo van Veenendaal, Australian, 25 when working with Iboga, 31 now. Leo consumed Iboga root bark, 14 heaped spoons. Leo began working with plant medicines in 2016 to heal IBS and treatment resistant depression. Leo is an author and engineer, currently based in Peru. He was motivated to work with Iboga for Psycho-spiritual growth, life guidance and depression.*

**Where did you first hear about Iboga?**

I heard about Iboga during my first Ayahuasca ceremony. A clear message came to me "Ayahuasca will heal your IBS but your real work will start with Iboga." I had never heard of Iboga before, it was totally foreign to me. The next morning, I asked all the people staying at my hostel if they had heard about this thing called "Iboga". One person had heard of it and he told me it was the "West African version of Ayahuasca but much stronger." I was immediately curious about Iboga, but terrified.

**How were you called to Iboga?**

I listened to the message that came through during that first Ayahuasca ceremony. In the back of my mind, I noted that I would like to do Iboga someday. Some months later, I began researching places to work with Iboga. It took 2 years of searching and sorting my own life out for the perfect opportunity to come to fruition. I definitely wasn't ready to work with Iboga when I first heard about it. I had wait for that gentle call to become a blaring shout, then I knew it was time. I wanted to wait until I finished my university studies in case I "fried my brain." I had no references, no trusted reviews or friends to talk about Iboga with. I was taking a leap of faith into the dark based on intuition.

**What was your life like before Iboga?**

My life, and especially my mind, was a mess. Every 10-15 minutes my mind would break into some garbage advertising song or crappy cultural conditioning I had seen on TV as a kid. My mind was filled with negative thoughts, depressive emotions, anxious tendencies, sexual images, an extremely short attention span and a crushing desire to be validated by other people. My mental chatter was almost always self-defeating, negative and anxious. My mind churned like a stormy ocean. It wasn't kind to me or anyone around me. I generally looked healthy (from the outside) but on the inside, my mind and spirit were like a ship stuck on the rocks in a storm. Inside I was like a skeletal, drugged out hamster running on a broken wheel. I was miserable, lost in life and drowning in my own drama.

**What is your life like after Iboga?**

Wonderful and totally different. The Iboga process was extremely challenging for me. The best way to describe it is "a thorough and brutal cleaning of my mind." My mind is much healthier and cleaner now. It's no longer a raging ocean, but a peaceful sea. Before I worked with Iboga, about 95/100 thoughts in my head were negative or unhelpful. After working with Iboga, maybe 1/200 are negative. When destructive thoughts arise, I can catch, disarm, and negotiate with them. I can pinpoint their origin and let them go. Iboga helped me to tame my mind. Iboga gave me the brutal mind and ego beating I required, to help rebuild my life, and let go of a lot of the trash I had held onto for so long.

The background chatter of mindless consumption is gone and the inappropriate, conditioned fantasies have died off. I feel like I access a much higher stream of consciousness. I'm genuinely joyful and the monster of depression, that haunted me my whole life is gone. Sure, there are worse days and periods of sadness, but I no longer get depressed. I can sit with darkness and quickly work my way out, rather than letting it drown me. Iboga gave me peace of mind and freedom from own drama. It taught me how to live a happy life and be free from depression.

**How did you prepare? Would you prepare differently a second time?**

I spent almost 2 years preparing to work with Iboga. The whole time I was researching where to do Iboga, I was preparing. During this time, I did a lot of yoga, started running, lifting weights, boxing and tried to meditate every day.

Preparing a second time, I would have done more yoga, more running (improving heart strength) and not done any boxing at all. I don't think it's wise to do Iboga with any recent head trauma. I don't know how much someone can realistically prepare for Iboga. You really just have to decide you're ready and dive in, when the timing works well for you.

I think working with a counselor or psychologist that was familiar with the experience would have been very beneficial as well. A few sessions before the initiation to hone my intentions and 5 or so sessions afterwards, would have been useful to make the most of the experience. I would recommend working with someone professionally, before and after your Iboga experience, to help both with integration and make the most of your experience.

A Vipassana mediation retreat could have been useful as well. It would have helped me clean my mind beforehand and be more accustomed to siting, waiting and being uncomfortable.

**What precautions did you take to make sure it was a safe experience?**
In all honesty, looking back, not enough. I went to my doctor for a comprehensive check up and asked him to do a full profile of my heart health. He found that I had an irregularly low resting heart beat (45bpm), a slightly prolonged QT interval (heart beat) and low blood pressure. I also took a liver panel and it was normal, with no dangerous signs. It would have been beneficial to work with a cardiologist, due to my irregular heart conditions. This would have ensured I had a safer experience and alleviated some worries in the back of my mind.

I had read a few reviews online about the place I was going to, but had no first-hand reviews. No friends recommended it personally. I read a book about Iboga, 'Iboga: The Visionary Root of African Shamanism', but it confused me even more. It might have been a good idea to wait a little longer and have a recommendation from a trusted friend about where to work with Iboga. During the process, I had trouble trusting the community and facilitator. This could have been easily fixed with a first-hand review from a good friend. Alternatively, I could have spent a little more time with the community before starting the work. Looking back, the trust issues were really my own trust issues being brought to the surface.

The Iboga experience, despite it being one of the best of my life, was so challenging and far out, it made me totally re-assess risk and the decisions I was making in my life. I remember thinking, "I don't know if I can ever take a risk so recklessly again!" after the ceremony.

**How did you consume Iboga? What did you take and where?**
I took a full flood dose (for me that was 14 spoons) of shaved root bark with Ebando, under the guidance of Tatayo. This involved an initiation into Bwiti. Ebando is a small community about 1 hour outside of Libreville, Gabon. Ebando is on the coast.

Looking back, that was a lot of Iboga. I had trust in Tatayo and his methods, but that was a huge amount of Iboga for me.

**Why did you decide to do it this way?**
I wanted to have a respectful, authentic and ethical experience with Iboga. I didn't want to consume it without the traditional knowledge or from a dodgy practitioner. Ebando provided a unique opportunity, as the chief, Tatayo, speaks English and French and has been facilitating ceremonies for westerners for 10+ years. He is trained in 'Fang' Bwiti and by all accounts follows the traditions very well.

I was guided towards Tatayo's community Ebando. They were the first and only community I had looked into or researched seriously. Reflecting on it, I think it's important to have a referral from a friend in your regular or normal life. If you don't have a referral, or recommendation from someone you trust, then perhaps you should wait a bit longer to work with Iboga. With that said, it was the perfect experience for me at that time.

**What would be your advice to people considering Iboga?**
Make sure you are 100% ready and really want to do this. If you are 99% sure, stay away. It is likely to be the hardest thing you have done in your life. It's an extremely long process. Budget at least a month afterwards of recovery (preferably not working) if you can. Despite feeling infinitely better for the experience, it took 6 months after the initiation for me to feel that I was back to normal again.

**What are your thoughts on micro-dosing? Did you micro-dose after a flood dose for integration?**
Due to sustainability reasons, I'm against micro-dosing at the moment. It's practically impossible to get high quality, sustainable wood in Australia. I could have micro-dosed following my flood dose to help with integration, but I wasn't game to smuggle it back into my home country.

Longer term, as sustainability improves, I think there are huge health and spiritual benefits to be obtained from micro-dosing Iboga, especially if you have done a flood dose before. I think it is very important to have a relationship with Iboga and ideally be initiated into a lineage before micro-dosing. Iboga and its alkaloids have a very long half-life, so a little micro-dosing everyday can add up to a large ceremonial dose in a short amount of time.

Also, I think it's crucial to know where the Iboga came from and that it was ethically obtained. Sourcing Iboga from Instagram is dangerous.

**Is there anything you wish you knew before doing Iboga about the process?**
It's a very long process and everyone's experience is wildly different. I didn't experience "The movie" of my life. Also, navigating reality was very hard to manage in the weeks immediately following the flood dose. The ceremony goes

for much, much longer than I had imagined. I think that it is typical to feel ungrounded and like you are navigating multiple worlds following an initiation. I wish someone had told me to go slow and be very gentle with myself. Things calmed down for me.... eventually.

**Would you do Iboga again?**

Yes, but not anytime soon. It was easily the hardest thing I have done in my life. Brutal does not even begin to describe it. I will likely be processing this experience for 10 years. I feel I will probably do another flood dose, one more time in my life, and maybe a traditional Bwiti wedding. I am not in a rush! There is a huge amount to integrate and understand first.

With that said, 6 years later, I am beginning to feel the call again. I think I would like to do another initiation, with a specific focus on storytelling, dreaming and visions. I know that the perfect opportunity will present itself, when I am ready. I have a feeling that 8-10 years after my initiation things will align to work with Iboga again.

**Was there memorable moment or particularly profound vision you had? Has it come true?**

Yes, my Iboga experience was extremely visual for me, but also challenging to interpret and understand the visions at the time. It took almost 5 years to understand some of them and my understanding is still unfolding. I'll share two of the visions I received.

One vision was being stuck in a parallel world, in a time loop, for what felt like eternity. In this parallel world, I was separated from my family and all my friends. It was impossible to see them again. I had a clear vision of them sitting around a dinner table making a toast and then drinking a potion, that would protect them and take them to a new universe. My older sister made a toast to me, with some very memorable words. They all drank the potion, were sad and knew they would never see me again. I was stuck in an old universe and couldn't go to the universe they were going to be in.

After this scene, I was taken back to present time in Gabon. I felt totally sober and lucid. I then lived one full regular day, filled with washing dishes, preparing the fire, walking on the beach, talking to the tribe and reading. I was crushed and deeply saddened knowing that I wouldn't see my family again. To be separated from them was my greatest fear. This day then repeated. I lived this same day of being separated and totally removed from my family for an entire lifetime. Each day that repeated was slightly different. I aged. This vision stopped when I was about 60 years old (after 35 years or so). I remember looking down at my hands and seeing old hands. I then had to relive this entire process another 3 times.

At this point, I was at peace with being away from my family. Iboga made me face my greatest fear, until I was at peace with it. During this psychedelic induced eternity, I learnt a lot about the world, I learnt how a fire burns, how an airplane takes off, how plants grow and many other scientific concepts that I knew but never fully understood.

Interesting note, about 4 years later, I had dinner with my older sister and she made the EXACT same toast, with the same memorable words I had seen in the vision. I wrote these words down in my journal after ceremony and she repeated them verbatim, 4 years later!

The second vision was about the foundational forces of Chaos and Order it changed how I saw the world. Chaos was represented as this beautiful "Evil Knievel" spirit that was always causing mayhem and debauchery. The spirit was charming, seductive and extremely attractive. Order was represented as a police officer from Arizona, who was always trying to catch "Chaos." Chaos was hellbent on destroying the world that Order lived in. Order was obsessed with catching Chaos at all costs. But within this, they loved the dance of catching and destroying each other. The basis of their existence was a warped, but genuine love. The visions were truly beautiful, hyper graphic and burned into my brain. From this I have come to be less judgmental. I don't see anything as good or bad, but rather on a spectrum of fostering chaos or facilitating order. We are all free to choose how much order and chaos we want in our life. Our personal perspective of "good and bad" is just perspective based on what we want and our cultural conditioning. At the bed rock of the universe is love, made up of chaos and order constantly f*cking each other.

**How did Iboga effect your spirituality?**

Life after Iboga has been so magical, odd and wonderful that I am not entirely certain if my life now is real. It could be another Iboga vision, from that first ceremony. If I am still in that first ceremony, then I am definitely enjoying this part of it a lot more.

The most tangible difference spiritually from working with Iboga is a connection to myself and a looseness with reality. I try to be the best person I can be, whilst not knowing if anything is real. Waking reality feels much like a dream, albeit a much sweeter one than it was before.

I remember that one of my core intentions was to find guidance in my life. I had just finished university and had no idea what I was going to do career wise. I had narrowed it down to three options: cannabis engineering, recycling engineering or hospitality. I remember being so frustrated because Iboga wouldn't tell me which one of these to do. I had no clear guidance. I had travelled to the other side of the world to search for answers and was very frustrated with myself and Iboga. I felt like I had failed.

Boy, was I wrong…

I didn't receive clear guidance because none of those options were right for me. I wasn't ready to hear that. But I did receive a gentle guidance that has stayed with me ever since. Often a lovely voice will float into my head and say "Go and talk to that person" or "Do this today," and it regularly leads to magic. I also received guidance on how to be open to life. Previously, I would hold onto plans with extreme control. Thinking that I had to make everything happen in a cold and barren universe. Now, I believe that everything is happening FOR each of us, to push us towards greater levels of consciousness and to be the best people we can be.

After Iboga, I feel that I'm gently guided in a much kinder universe. Previously, I felt alone in an indifferent universe.

Iboga liberated me to follow the spiritual path in life, to find what I truly loved. Free of my own capricious monologue and with the judgement of others dimmed, I can pursue a more conscious life. Without Iboga burning the old life and identity I had haphazardly accumulated, I may never have found the path I'm on now. Even better, I get to tap dance along this conscious path, with minimal baggage and being friends with myself.

Made in United States
Troutdale, OR
01/05/2025